# Essentials of Compilation

# Essentials of Compilation
## An Incremental Approach in Racket

Jeremy G. Siek

The MIT Press
Cambridge, Massachusetts
London, England

The MIT Press would like to thank the anonymous peer reviewers who provided comments on drafts of this book. The generous work of academic experts is essential for establishing the authority and quality of our publications. We acknowledge with gratitude the contributions of these otherwise uncredited readers.

This book was set in Times LT Std Roman by the author. Printed and bound in the United States of America.

Library of Congress Cataloging-in-Publication Data

Names: Siek, Jeremy, author.
Title: Essentials of compilation : an incremental approach in Racket / Jeremy G. Siek.
Description: Cambridge, Massachusetts : The MIT Press, [2023] | Includes bibliographical references and index.
Identifiers: LCCN 2022015399 (print) | LCCN 2022015400 (ebook) | ISBN 9780262047760 (hardcover) | ISBN 9780262373272 (epub) | ISBN 9780262373289 (pdf)
Subjects: LCSH: Racket (Computer program language) | Compilers (Computer programs)
Classification: LCC QA76.73.R33 S54 2023 (print) | LCC QA76.73.R33 (ebook) | DDC 005.13/3–dc23/eng/20220705
LC record available at https://lccn.loc.gov/2022015399
LC ebook record available at https://lccn.loc.gov/2022015400

10 9 8 7 6 5 4 3 2 1

This book is dedicated to Katie, my partner in everything, my children, who grew up during the writing of this book, and the programming language students at Indiana University, whose thoughtful questions made this a better book.

# Contents

# Preface

There is a magical moment when a programmer presses the *run* button and the software begins to execute. Somehow a program written in a high-level language is running on a computer that is capable only of shuffling bits. Here we reveal the wizardry that makes that moment possible. Beginning with the groundbreaking work of Backus and colleagues in the 1950s, computer scientists developed techniques for constructing programs called *compilers* that automatically translate high-level programs into machine code.

We take you on a journey through constructing your own compiler for a small but powerful language. Along the way we explain the essential concepts, algorithms, and data structures that underlie compilers. We develop your understanding of how programs are mapped onto computer hardware, which is helpful in reasoning about properties at the junction of hardware and software, such as execution time, software errors, and security vulnerabilities. For those interested in pursuing compiler construction as a career, our goal is to provide a stepping-stone to advanced topics such as just-in-time compilation, program analysis, and program optimization. For those interested in designing and implementing programming languages, we connect language design choices to their impact on the compiler and the generated code.

A compiler is typically organized as a sequence of stages that progressively translate a program to the code that runs on hardware. We take this approach to the extreme by partitioning our compiler into a large number of *nanopasses*, each of which performs a single task. This enables the testing of each pass in isolation and focuses our attention, making the compiler far easier to understand.

The most familiar approach to describing compilers is to dedicate each chapter to one pass. The problem with that approach is that it obfuscates how language features motivate design choices in a compiler. We instead take an *incremental* approach in which we build a complete compiler in each chapter, starting with a small input language that includes only arithmetic and variables. We add new language features in subsequent chapters, extending the compiler as necessary.

Our choice of language features is designed to elicit fundamental concepts and algorithms used in compilers.

- We begin with integer arithmetic and local variables in chapters 1 and 2, where we introduce the fundamental tools of compiler construction: *abstract syntax trees* and *recursive functions*.

- In Chapter 3 we apply *graph coloring* to assign variables to machine registers.
- Chapter 4 adds conditional expressions, which motivates an elegant recursive algorithm for translating them into conditional `goto` statements.
- Chapter 5 adds loops and mutable variables. This elicits the need for *dataflow analysis* in the register allocator.
- Chapter 6 adds heap-allocated tuples, motivating *garbage collection.*
- Chapter 7 adds functions as first-class values without lexical scoping, similar to functions in the C programming language (Kernighan and Ritchie 1988). The reader learns about the procedure call stack and *calling conventions* and how they interact with register allocation and garbage collection. The chapter also describes how to generate efficient tail calls.
- Chapter 8 adds anonymous functions with lexical scoping, that is, *lambda* expressions. The reader learns about *closure conversion*, in which lambdas are translated into a combination of functions and tuples.
- Chapter 9 adds *dynamic typing.* Prior to this point the input languages are statically typed. The reader extends the statically typed language with an **Any** type that serves as a target for compiling the dynamically typed language.
- Chapter 10 uses the **Any** type introduced in chapter 9 to implement a *gradually typed language* in which different regions of a program may be static or dynamically typed. The reader implements runtime support for *proxies* that allow values to safely move between regions.
- Chapter 11 adds *generics* with autoboxing, leveraging the **Any** type and type casts developed in chapters 9 and 10.

There are many language features that we do not include. Our choices balance the incidental complexity of a feature versus the fundamental concepts that it exposes. For example, we include tuples and not records because although they both elicit the study of heap allocation and garbage collection, records come with more incidental complexity.

Since 2009, drafts of this book have served as the textbook for sixteen-week compiler courses for upper-level undergraduates and first-year graduate students at the University of Colorado and Indiana University. Students come into the course having learned the basics of programming, data structures and algorithms, and discrete mathematics. At the beginning of the course, students form groups of two to four people. The groups complete approximately one chapter every two weeks, starting with chapter 2 and including chapters according to the students interests while respecting the dependencies between chapters shown in Figure 0.1. Chapter 7 (functions) depends on chapter 6 (tuples) only in the implementation of efficient tail calls. The last two weeks of the course involve a final project in which students design and implement a compiler extension of their choosing. The last few chapters can be used in support of these projects. Many chapters include a challenge problem that we assign to the graduate students.

For compiler courses at universities on the quarter system (about ten weeks in length), we recommend completing the course through chapter 6 or chapter 7 and providing some scaffolding code to the students for each compiler pass. The course

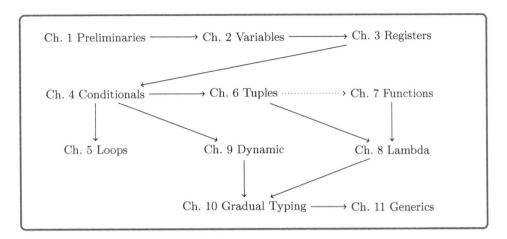

**Figure 0.1**
Diagram of chapter dependencies.

can be adapted to emphasize functional languages by skipping chapter 5 (loops) and including chapter 8 (lambda). The course can be adapted to dynamically typed languages by including chapter 9.

This book has been used in compiler courses at California Polytechnic State University, Portland State University, Rose–Hulman Institute of Technology, University of Freiburg, University of Massachusetts Lowell, and the University of Vermont.

We use the Racket language both for the implementation of the compiler and for the input language, so the reader should be proficient with Racket or Scheme. There are many excellent resources for learning Scheme and Racket (Dybvig 1987a; Abelson and Sussman 1996; Friedman and Felleisen 1996; Felleisen et al. 2001; Felleisen et al. 2013; Flatt, Findler, and PLT 2014). The support code for this book is in the GitHub repository at the following location:

https://github.com/IUCompilerCourse/

The compiler targets x86 assembly language (Intel 2015), so it is helpful but not necessary for the reader to have taken a computer systems course (Bryant and O'Hallaron 2010). We introduce the parts of x86-64 assembly language that are needed in the compiler. We follow the System V calling conventions (Bryant and O'Hallaron 2005; Matz et al. 2013), so the assembly code that we generate works with the runtime system (written in C) when it is compiled using the GNU C compiler (`gcc`) on Linux and MacOS operating systems on Intel hardware. On the Windows operating system, `gcc` uses the Microsoft x64 calling convention (Microsoft 2018, 2020). So the assembly code that we generate does *not* work with the runtime system on Windows. One workaround is to use a virtual machine with Linux as the guest operating system.

**Acknowledgments**

The tradition of compiler construction at Indiana University goes back to research and courses on programming languages by Daniel Friedman in the 1970s and 1980s. One of his students, Kent Dybvig, implemented Chez Scheme (Dybvig 2006), an efficient, production-quality compiler for Scheme. Throughout the 1990s and 2000s, Dybvig taught the compiler course and continued the development of Chez Scheme. The compiler course evolved to incorporate novel pedagogical ideas while also including elements of real-world compilers. One of Friedman's ideas was to split the compiler into many small passes. Another idea, called "the game," was to test the code generated by each pass using interpreters.

Dybvig, with help from his students Dipanwita Sarkar and Andrew Keep, developed infrastructure to support this approach and evolved the course to use even smaller nanopasses (Sarkar, Waddell, and Dybvig 2004; Keep 2012). Many of the compiler design decisions in this book are inspired by the assignment descriptions of Dybvig and Keep (2010). In the mid 2000s, a student of Dybvig named Abdulaziz Ghuloum observed that the front-to-back organization of the course made it difficult for students to understand the rationale for the compiler design. Ghuloum proposed the incremental approach (Ghuloum 2006) on which this book is based.

I thank the many students who served as teaching assistants for the compiler course at IU including Carl Factora, Ryan Scott, Cameron Swords, and Chris Wailes. I thank Andre Kuhlenschmidt for work on the garbage collector and x86 interpreter, Michael Vollmer for work on efficient tail calls, and Michael Vitousek for help with the first offering of the incremental compiler course at IU.

I thank professors Bor-Yuh Chang, John Clements, Jay McCarthy, Joseph Near, Ryan Newton, Nate Nystrom, Peter Thiemann, Andrew Tolmach, and Michael Wollowski for teaching courses based on drafts of this book and for their feedback. I thank the National Science Foundation for the grants that helped to support this work: Grant Numbers 1518844, 1763922, and 1814460.

I thank Ronald Garcia for helping me survive Dybvig's compiler course in the early 2000s and especially for finding the bug that sent our garbage collector on a wild goose chase!

Jeremy G. Siek
Bloomington, Indiana

# 1 Preliminaries

In this chapter we review the basic tools needed to implement a compiler. Programs are typically input by a programmer as text, that is, a sequence of characters. The program-as-text representation is called *concrete syntax*. We use concrete syntax to concisely write down and talk about programs. Inside the compiler, we use *abstract syntax trees* (ASTs) to represent programs in a way that efficiently supports the operations that the compiler needs to perform. The process of translating concrete syntax to abstract syntax is called *parsing*. This book does not cover the theory and implementation of parsing. We refer the readers interested in parsing to the thorough treatment of parsing by Aho et al. (2006).A parser is provided in the support code for translating from concrete to abstract syntax.

ASTs can be represented inside the compiler in many different ways, depending on the programming language used to write the compiler. We use Racket's `struct` feature to represent ASTs (section 1.1). We use grammars to define the abstract syntax of programming languages (section 1.2) and pattern matching to inspect individual nodes in an AST (section 1.3). We use recursive functions to construct and deconstruct ASTs (section 1.4). This chapter provides a brief introduction to these components.

## 1.1 Abstract Syntax Trees

Compilers use abstract syntax trees to represent programs because they often need to ask questions such as, for a given part of a program, what kind of language feature is it? What are its subparts? Consider the program on the left and the diagram of its AST on the right (1.1). This program is an addition operation that has two subparts, a read operation and a negation. The negation has another subpart, the integer constant 8. By using a tree to represent the program, we can easily follow the links to go from one part of a program to its subparts.

(+ (read) (- 8))

(1.1)

We use the standard terminology for trees to describe ASTs: each rectangle above is called a *node*. The arrows connect a node to its *children*, which are also nodes. The top-most node is the *root*. Every node except for the root has a *parent* (the node of which it is the child). If a node has no children, it is a *leaf* node; otherwise it is an *internal* node.

We define a Racket `struct` for each kind of node. For this chapter we require just two kinds of nodes: one for integer constants (aka literals) and one for primitive operations. The following is the `struct` definition for integer constants.[1]

```
(struct Int (value))
```

An integer node contains just one thing: the integer value. We establish the convention that `struct` names, such as `Int`, are capitalized. To create an AST node for the integer 8, we write `(Int 8)`.

```
(define eight (Int 8))
```

We say that the value created by `(Int 8)` is an *instance* of the `Int` structure.

The following is the `struct` definition for primitive operations.

```
(struct Prim (op args))
```

A primitive operation node includes an operator symbol `op` and a list of child arguments called `args`. For example, to create an AST that negates the number 8, we write the following.

```
(define neg-eight (Prim '- (list eight)))
```

Primitive operations may have zero or more children. The `read` operator has zero:

```
(define rd (Prim 'read '()))
```

The addition operator has two children:

```
(define ast1_1 (Prim '+ (list rd neg-eight)))
```

We have made a design choice regarding the `Prim` structure. Instead of using one structure for many different operations (`read`, `+`, and `-`), we could have instead defined a structure for each operation, as follows:

```
(struct Read ())
(struct Add (left right))
(struct Neg (value))
```

The reason that we choose to use just one structure is that many parts of the compiler can use the same code for the different primitive operators, so we might as well just write that code once by using a single structure.

To compile a program such as (1.1), we need to know that the operation associated with the root node is addition and we need to be able to access its two children. Racket provides pattern matching to support these kinds of queries, as we see in section 1.3.

---

1. All the AST structures are defined in the file `utilities.rkt` in the support code.

We often write down the concrete syntax of a program even when we actually have in mind the AST, because the concrete syntax is more concise. We recommend that you always think of programs as abstract syntax trees.

## 1.2  Grammars

A programming language can be thought of as a *set* of programs. The set is infinite (that is, one can always create larger programs), so one cannot simply describe a language by listing all the programs in the language. Instead we write down a set of rules, a *context-free grammar*, for building programs. Grammars are often used to define the concrete syntax of a language, but they can also be used to describe the abstract syntax. We write our rules in a variant of Backus-Naur form (BNF) (Backus et al. 1960; Knuth 1964). As an example, we describe a small language, named $\mathcal{L}_{\mathsf{Int}}$, that consists of integers and arithmetic operations.

The first grammar rule for the abstract syntax of $\mathcal{L}_{\mathsf{Int}}$ says that an instance of the `Int` structure is an expression:

$$exp ::= (\texttt{Int } int) \tag{1.2}$$

Each rule has a left-hand side and a right-hand side. If you have an AST node that matches the right-hand side, then you can categorize it according to the left-hand side. Symbols in typewriter font, such as `Int`, are *terminal* symbols and must literally appear in the program for the rule to be applicable. Our grammars do not mention *white space*, that is, delimiter characters like spaces, tabs, and new lines. White space may be inserted between symbols for disambiguation and to improve readability. A name such as *exp* that is defined by the grammar rules is a *nonterminal*. The name *int* is also a nonterminal, but instead of defining it with a grammar rule, we define it with the following explanation. An *int* is a sequence of decimals (0 to 9), possibly starting with – (for negative integers), such that the sequence of decimals represents an integer in the range $-2^{62}$ to $2^{62}-1$. This enables the representation of integers using 63 bits, which simplifies several aspects of compilation. Thus, these integers correspond to the Racket `fixnum` datatype on a 64-bit machine.

The second grammar rule is the **read** operation, which receives an input integer from the user of the program.

$$exp ::= (\texttt{Prim 'read ()}) \tag{1.3}$$

The third rule categorizes the negation of an *exp* node as an *exp*.

$$exp ::= (\texttt{Prim '- } (exp)) \tag{1.4}$$

We can apply these rules to categorize the ASTs that are in the $\mathcal{L}_{\mathsf{Int}}$ language. For example, by rule (1.2), `(Int 8)` is an *exp*, and then by rule (1.4) the following AST is an *exp*.

(Prim '- ((Int 8)))

$$(1.5)$$

The next two grammar rules are for addition and subtraction expressions:

$$exp ::= (\text{Prim '+ } (exp\ exp)) \tag{1.6}$$

$$exp ::= (\text{Prim '- } (exp\ exp)) \tag{1.7}$$

We can now justify that the AST (1.1) is an *exp* in $\mathcal{L}_{\mathsf{Int}}$. We know that
(Prim 'read ()) is an *exp* by rule (1.3), and we have already categorized
(Prim '- ((Int 8))) as an *exp*, so we apply rule (1.6) to show that

(Prim '+ ((Prim 'read ()) (Prim '- ((Int 8)))))

is an *exp* in the $\mathcal{L}_{\mathsf{Int}}$ language.

If you have an AST for which these rules do not apply, then the AST is not in
$\mathcal{L}_{\mathsf{Int}}$. For example, the program (* (read) 8) is not in $\mathcal{L}_{\mathsf{Int}}$ because there is no rule
for the * operator. Whenever we define a language with a grammar, the language
includes only those programs that are justified by the grammar rules.

The last grammar rule for $\mathcal{L}_{\mathsf{Int}}$ states that there is a Program node to mark the
top of the whole program:

$$\mathcal{L}_{\mathsf{Int}} ::= (\text{Program '() } exp)$$

The Program structure is defined as follows:

(struct Program (info body))

where body is an expression. In further chapters, the info part is used to store
auxiliary information, but for now it is just the empty list.

It is common to have many grammar rules with the same left-hand side but
different right-hand sides, such as the rules for *exp* in the grammar of $\mathcal{L}_{\mathsf{Int}}$. As
shorthand, a vertical bar can be used to combine several right-hand sides into a
single rule.

The concrete syntax for $\mathcal{L}_{\mathsf{Int}}$ is shown in figure 1.1 and the abstract syntax for
$\mathcal{L}_{\mathsf{Int}}$ is shown in figure 1.2.The read-program function provided in utilities.rkt
of the support code reads a program from a file (the sequence of characters in the
concrete syntax of Racket) and parses it into an abstract syntax tree. Refer to the
description of read-program in appendix A.2 for more details.

## 1.3   Pattern Matching

As mentioned in section 1.1, compilers often need to access the parts of an AST
node. Racket provides the match feature to access the parts of a value. Consider
the following example:

$$
\begin{array}{rcl}
\textit{type} & ::= & \texttt{Integer} \\
\textit{exp} & ::= & \textit{int} \mid \texttt{(read)} \mid \texttt{(- } \textit{exp}\texttt{)} \mid \texttt{(+ } \textit{exp exp}\texttt{)} \mid \texttt{(- } \textit{exp exp}\texttt{)} \\
\mathcal{L}_{\mathsf{Int}} & ::= & \textit{exp}
\end{array}
$$

**Figure 1.1**
The concrete syntax of $\mathcal{L}_{\mathsf{Int}}$.

$$
\begin{array}{rcl}
\textit{type} & ::= & \texttt{Integer} \\
\textit{exp} & ::= & \texttt{(Int } \textit{int}\texttt{)} \mid \texttt{(Prim 'read ())} \\
& \mid & \texttt{(Prim '- (}\textit{exp}\texttt{))} \mid \texttt{(Prim '+ (}\textit{exp exp}\texttt{))} \mid \texttt{(Prim '- (}\textit{exp exp}\texttt{))} \\
\mathcal{L}_{\mathsf{Int}} & ::= & \texttt{(Program '() }\textit{exp}\texttt{)}
\end{array}
$$

**Figure 1.2**
The abstract syntax of $\mathcal{L}_{\mathsf{Int}}$.

```
(match ast1_1
  [(Prim op (list child1 child2))
   (print op)])
```

In this example, the `match` form checks whether the AST (1.1) is a binary operator and binds its parts to the three pattern variables `op`, `child1`, and `child2`. In general, a match clause consists of a *pattern* and a *body*. Patterns are recursively defined to be a pattern variable, a structure name followed by a pattern for each of the structure's arguments, or an S-expression (a symbol, list, etc.). (See chapter 12 of The Racket Guide[2] and chapter 9 of The Racket Reference[3] for complete descriptions of `match`.) The body of a match clause may contain arbitrary Racket code. The pattern variables can be used in the scope of the body, such as `op` in `(print op)`.

A `match` form may contain several clauses, as in the following function `leaf` that recognizes when an $\mathcal{L}_{\mathsf{Int}}$ node is a leaf in the AST. The `match` proceeds through the clauses in order, checking whether the pattern can match the input AST. The body of the first clause that matches is executed. The output of `leaf` for several ASTs is shown on the right side of the following:

---

2. See https://docs.racket-lang.org/guide/match.html.
3. See https://docs.racket-lang.org/reference/match.html.

```
(define (leaf arith)
  (match arith
    [(Int n) #t]
    [(Prim 'read '()) #t]
    [(Prim '- (list e1)) #f]
    [(Prim '+ (list e1 e2)) #f]
    [(Prim '- (list e1 e2)) #f]))

(leaf (Prim 'read '()))                              #t
(leaf (Prim '- (list (Int 8))))                      #f
(leaf (Int 8))                                       #t
```

When constructing a `match` expression, we refer to the grammar definition to identify which nonterminal we are expecting to match against, and then we make sure that (1) we have one clause for each alternative of that nonterminal and (2) the pattern in each clause corresponds to the corresponding right-hand side of a grammar rule. For the `match` in the `leaf` function, we refer to the grammar for $\mathcal{L}_{\mathsf{Int}}$ shown in figure 1.2. The *exp* nonterminal has four alternatives, so the `match` has four clauses. The pattern in each clause corresponds to the right-hand side of a grammar rule. For example, the pattern (`Prim '+ (list e1 e2)`) corresponds to the right-hand side (`Prim '+` (*exp exp*)). When translating from grammars to patterns, replace nonterminals such as *exp* with pattern variables of your choice (for example, `e1` and `e2`).

### 1.4  Recursive Functions

Programs are inherently recursive. For example, an expression is often made of smaller expressions. Thus, the natural way to process an entire program is to use a recursive function. As a first example of such a recursive function, we define the function `is_exp` as shown in figure 1.3, to take an arbitrary value and determine whether or not it is an expression in $\mathcal{L}_{\mathsf{Int}}$. We say that a function is defined by *structural recursion* if it is defined using a sequence of match clauses that correspond to a grammar and the body of each clause makes a recursive call on each child node.[4] Figure 1.3 also contains the definition of `is_Lint`, which determines whether an AST is a program in $\mathcal{L}_{\mathsf{Int}}$. In general, we can write one recursive function to handle each nonterminal in a grammar. Of the two examples at the bottom of the figure, the first is in $\mathcal{L}_{\mathsf{Int}}$ and the second is not.

### 1.5  Interpreters

The behavior of a program is defined by the specification of the programming language. For example, the Scheme language is defined in the report by Sperber et al. (2009). The Racket language is defined in its reference manual (Flatt and PLT

---

4. This principle of structuring code according to the data definition is advocated in the book *How to Design Programs* by Felleisen et al. (2001).

```
(define (is_exp ast)
  (match ast
    [(Int n) #t]
    [(Prim 'read '()) #t]
    [(Prim '- (list e)) (is_exp e)]
    [(Prim '+ (list e1 e2))
      (and (is_exp e1) (is_exp e2))]
    [(Prim '- (list e1 e2))
      (and (is_exp e1) (is_exp e2))]
    [else #f]))

(define (is_Lint ast)
  (match ast
    [(Program '() e) (is_exp e)]
    [else #f]))

(is_Lint (Program '() ast1_1)
(is_Lint (Program '()
      (Prim '* (list (Prim 'read '())
                     (Prim '+ (list (Int 8)))))))
```

**Figure 1.3**
Example of recursive functions for $\mathcal{L}_{\mathsf{Int}}$. These functions recognize whether an AST is in $\mathcal{L}_{\mathsf{Int}}$.

2014). In this book we use interpreters to specify each language that we consider. An interpreter that is designated as the definition of a language is called a *definitional interpreter* (Reynolds 1972). We warm up by creating a definitional interpreter for the $\mathcal{L}_{\mathsf{Int}}$ language. This interpreter serves as a second example of structural recursion. The definition of the `interp_Lint` function is shown in figure 1.4. The body of the function is a match on the input program followed by a call to the `interp_exp` auxiliary function, which in turn has one match clause per grammar rule for $\mathcal{L}_{\mathsf{Int}}$ expressions.

Let us consider the result of interpreting a few $\mathcal{L}_{\mathsf{Int}}$ programs. The following program adds two integers:

`(+ 10 32)`

The result is 42, the answer to life, the universe, and everything: 42![5] We wrote this program in concrete syntax, whereas the parsed abstract syntax is

`(Program '() (Prim '+ (list (Int 10) (Int 32))))`

The following program demonstrates that expressions may be nested within each other, in this case nesting several additions and negations.

`(+ 10 (- (+ 12 20)))`

---

5. *The Hitchhiker's Guide to the Galaxy* by Douglas Adams.

```
(define (interp_exp e)
  (match e
    [(Int n) n]
    [(Prim 'read '())
     (define r (read))
     (cond [(fixnum? r) r]
           [else (error 'interp_exp "read expected an integer" r)])]
    [(Prim '- (list e))
     (define v (interp_exp e))
     (fx- 0 v)]
    [(Prim '+ (list e1 e2))
     (define v1 (interp_exp e1))
     (define v2 (interp_exp e2))
     (fx+ v1 v2)]
    [(Prim '- (list e1 e2))
     (define v1 (interp_exp e1))
     (define v2 (interp_exp e2))
     (fx- v1 v2)]))

(define (interp_Lint p)
  (match p
    [(Program '() e) (interp_exp e)]))
```

**Figure 1.4**
Interpreter for the $\mathcal{L}_{\mathsf{Int}}$ language.

What is the result of this program?

As mentioned previously, the $\mathcal{L}_{\mathsf{Int}}$ language does not support arbitrarily large integers but only 63-bit integers, so we interpret the arithmetic operations of $\mathcal{L}_{\mathsf{Int}}$ using fixnum arithmetic in Racket. Suppose that

$$n = 999999999999999999$$

which indeed fits in 63 bits. What happens when we run the following program in our interpreter?

```
(+ (+ (+ n n) (+ n n)) (+ (+ n n) (+ n n)))))
```

It produces the following error:

```
fx+: result is not a fixnum
```

We establish the convention that if running the definitional interpreter on a program produces an error, then the meaning of that program is *unspecified* unless the error is a `trapped-error`. A compiler for the language is under no obligation regarding programs with unspecified behavior; it does not have to produce an executable, and if it does, that executable can do anything. On the other hand, if the error is a `trapped-error`, then the compiler must produce an executable and it is required to report that an error occurred. To signal an error, exit with a return code of 255. The interpreters in chapters 9 and 10 and in section 6.10 use `trapped-error`.

The last feature of the $\mathcal{L}_{\text{Int}}$ language, the `read` operation, prompts the user of the program for an integer. Recall that program (1.1) requests an integer input and then subtracts 8. So, if we run

```
(interp_Lint (Program '() ast1_1))
```

and if the input is 50, the result is 42.

We include the `read` operation in $\mathcal{L}_{\text{Int}}$ so that a clever student cannot implement a compiler for $\mathcal{L}_{\text{Int}}$ that simply runs the interpreter during compilation to obtain the output and then generates the trivial code to produce the output.[6]

The job of a compiler is to translate a program in one language into a program in another language so that the output program behaves the same way as the input program. This idea is depicted in the following diagram. Suppose we have two languages, $\mathcal{L}_1$ and $\mathcal{L}_2$, and a definitional interpreter for each language. Given a compiler that translates from language $\mathcal{L}_1$ to $\mathcal{L}_2$ and given any program $P_1$ in $\mathcal{L}_1$, the compiler must translate it into some program $P_2$ such that interpreting $P_1$ and $P_2$ on their respective interpreters with same input $i$ yields the same output $o$.

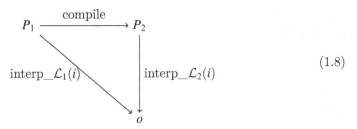

$$(1.8)$$

In the next section we see our first example of a compiler.

## 1.6 Example Compiler: A Partial Evaluator

In this section we consider a compiler that translates $\mathcal{L}_{\text{Int}}$ programs into $\mathcal{L}_{\text{Int}}$ programs that may be more efficient. The compiler eagerly computes the parts of the program that do not depend on any inputs, a process known as *partial evaluation* (Jones, Gomard, and Sestoft 1993). For example, given the following program

```
(+ (read) (- (+ 5 3)))
```

our compiler translates it into the program

```
(+ (read) -8)
```

Figure 1.5 gives the code for a simple partial evaluator for the $\mathcal{L}_{\text{Int}}$ language. The output of the partial evaluator is a program in $\mathcal{L}_{\text{Int}}$. In figure 1.5, the structural recursion over *exp* is captured in the `pe_exp` function, whereas the code for partially

---

6. Yes, a clever student did this in the first instance of this course!

```
(define (pe_neg r)
  (match r
    [(Int n) (Int (fx- 0 n))]
    [else (Prim '- (list r))]))

(define (pe_add r1 r2)
  (match* (r1 r2)
    [((Int n1) (Int n2)) (Int (fx+ n1 n2))]
    [(_ _) (Prim '+ (list r1 r2))]))

(define (pe_sub r1 r2)
  (match* (r1 r2)
    [((Int n1) (Int n2)) (Int (fx- n1 n2))]
    [(_ _) (Prim '- (list r1 r2))]))

(define (pe_exp e)
  (match e
    [(Int n) (Int n)]
    [(Prim 'read '()) (Prim 'read '())]
    [(Prim '- (list e1)) (pe_neg (pe_exp e1))]
    [(Prim '+ (list e1 e2)) (pe_add (pe_exp e1) (pe_exp e2))]
    [(Prim '- (list e1 e2)) (pe_sub (pe_exp e1) (pe_exp e2))]))

(define (pe_Lint p)
  (match p
    [(Program '() e) (Program '() (pe_exp e))]))
```

**Figure 1.5**
A partial evaluator for $\mathcal{L}_{\mathsf{Int}}$.

evaluating the negation and addition operations is factored into three auxiliary functions: `pe_neg`, `pe_add` and `pe_sub`. The input to these functions is the output of partially evaluating the children. The `pe_neg`, `pe_add` and `pe_sub` functions check whether their arguments are integers and if they are, perform the appropriate arithmetic. Otherwise, they create an AST node for the arithmetic operation.

To gain some confidence that the partial evaluator is correct, we can test whether it produces programs that produce the same result as the input programs. That is, we can test whether it satisfies the diagram of (1.8). The following code runs the partial evaluator on several examples and tests the output program. The `parse-program` and `assert` functions are defined in appendix A.2.

```
(define (test_pe p)
  (assert "testing pe_Lint"
    (equal? (interp_Lint p) (interp_Lint (pe_Lint p)))))

(test_pe (parse-program `(program () (+ 10 (- (+ 5 3))))))
(test_pe (parse-program `(program () (+ 1 (+ 3 1)))))
(test_pe (parse-program `(program () (- (+ 3 (- 5))))))
```

**Exercise 1.1** Create three programs in the $\mathcal{L}_{\mathsf{Int}}$ language and test whether partially evaluating them with `pe_Lint` and then interpreting them with `interp_Lint` gives the same result as directly interpreting them with `interp_Lint`.

# 2 Integers and Variables

This chapter covers compiling a subset of Racket to x86-64 assembly code (Intel 2015). The subset, named $\mathcal{L}_{\mathsf{Var}}$, includes integer arithmetic and local variables. We often refer to x86-64 simply as x86. The chapter first describes the $\mathcal{L}_{\mathsf{Var}}$ language (section 2.1) and then introduces x86 assembly (section 2.2). Because x86 assembly language is large, we discuss only the instructions needed for compiling $\mathcal{L}_{\mathsf{Var}}$. We introduce more x86 instructions in subsequent chapters. After introducing $\mathcal{L}_{\mathsf{Var}}$ and x86, we reflect on their differences and create a plan to break down the translation from $\mathcal{L}_{\mathsf{Var}}$ to x86 into a handful of steps (section 2.3). The rest of the chapter gives detailed hints regarding each step. We aim to give enough hints that the well-prepared reader, together with a few friends, can implement a compiler from $\mathcal{L}_{\mathsf{Var}}$ to x86 in a short time. To suggest the scale of this first compiler, we note that the instructor solution for the $\mathcal{L}_{\mathsf{Var}}$ compiler is approximately 500 lines of code.

## 2.1 The $\mathcal{L}_{\mathsf{Var}}$ Language

The $\mathcal{L}_{\mathsf{Var}}$ language extends the $\mathcal{L}_{\mathsf{Int}}$ language with variables. The concrete syntax of the $\mathcal{L}_{\mathsf{Var}}$ language is defined by the grammar presented in figure 2.1 and the abstract syntax is presented in figure 2.2. The nonterminal *var* may be any Racket identifier. As in $\mathcal{L}_{\mathsf{Int}}$, `read` is a nullary operator, - is a unary operator, and + is a binary operator. Similarly to $\mathcal{L}_{\mathsf{Int}}$, the abstract syntax of $\mathcal{L}_{\mathsf{Var}}$ includes the `Program` struct to mark the top of the program. Despite the simplicity of the $\mathcal{L}_{\mathsf{Var}}$ language, it is rich enough to exhibit several compilation techniques.

Let us dive further into the syntax and semantics of the $\mathcal{L}_{\mathsf{Var}}$ language. The `let` feature defines a variable for use within its body and initializes the variable with the value of an expression. The abstract syntax for `let` is shown in figure 2.2. The concrete syntax for `let` is

```
(let ([var exp]) exp)
```

For example, the following program initializes `x` to 32 and then evaluates the body (+ 10 x), producing 42.

```
(let ([x (+ 12 20)]) (+ 10 x))
```

When there are multiple `let`s for the same variable, the closest enclosing `let` is used. That is, variable definitions overshadow prior definitions. Consider the

```
type  ::=  Integer
exp   ::=  int | (read) | (- exp) | (+ exp exp) | (- exp exp)
―――――――――――――――――――――――――――――――――――――――――――――――――――――
exp   ::=  var | (let ([var exp]) exp)
ℒVar  ::=  exp
```

**Figure 2.1**
The concrete syntax of $\mathcal{L}_{Var}$.

```
type  ::=  Integer
exp   ::=  (Int int) | (Prim 'read ())
      |    (Prim '- (exp)) | (Prim '+ (exp exp)) | (Prim '- (exp exp))
―――――――――――――――――――――――――――――――――――――――――――――――――――――――――――――――――――――
exp   ::=  (Var var) | (Let var exp exp)
ℒVar  ::=  (Program '() exp)
```

**Figure 2.2**
The abstract syntax of $\mathcal{L}_{Var}$.

following program with two **lets** that define two variables named **x**. Can you figure out the result?

```
(let ([x 32]) (+ (let ([x 10]) x) x))
```

For the purposes of depicting which variable occurrences correspond to which definitions, the following shows the **x**'s annotated with subscripts to distinguish them. Double-check that your answer for the previous program is the same as your answer for this annotated version of the program.

```
(let ([x₁ 32]) (+ (let ([x₂ 10]) x₂) x₁))
```

The initializing expression is always evaluated before the body of the **let**, so in the following, the **read** for **x** is performed before the **read** for **y**. Given the input 52 then 10, the following produces 42 (not –42).

```
(let ([x (read)]) (let ([y (read)]) (+ x (- y))))
```

### 2.1.1 Extensible Interpreters via Method Overriding

To prepare for discussing the interpreter of $\mathcal{L}_{Var}$, we explain why we implement it in an object-oriented style. Throughout this book we define many interpreters, one for each language that we study. Because each language builds on the prior one, there is a lot of commonality between these interpreters. We want to write down the common parts just once instead of many times. A naive interpreter for $\mathcal{L}_{Var}$ would handle the cases for variables and **let** but dispatch to an interpreter for $\mathcal{L}_{Int}$ in the rest of the cases. The following code sketches this idea. (We explain the **env** parameter in section 2.1.2.)

```
                                        (define ((interp_Lvar env) e)
                                          (match e
   (define ((interp_Lint env) e)           [(Var x)
     (match e                               (dict-ref env x)]
       [(Prim '- (list e1))                 [(Let x e body)
        (fx- 0 ((interp_Lint env) e1))]      (define v ((interp_Lvar env) e))
       ...))                                 (define env^ (dict-set env x v))
                                             ((interp_Lvar env^) body)]
                                           [else ((interp_Lint env) e)]))
```

The problem with this naive approach is that it does not handle situations in which an $\mathcal{L}_{Var}$ feature, such as a variable, is nested inside an $\mathcal{L}_{Int}$ feature, such as the – operator, as in the following program.

```
(Let 'y (Int 10) (Prim '- (list (Var 'y))))
```

If we invoke `interp_Lvar` on this program, it dispatches to `interp_Lint` to handle the – operator, but then it recursively calls `interp_Lint` again on its argument. Because there is no case for `Var` in `interp_Lint`, we get an error!

To make our interpreters extensible we need something called *open recursion*, in which the tying of the recursive knot is delayed until the functions are composed. Object-oriented languages provide open recursion via method overriding. The following code uses method overriding to interpret $\mathcal{L}_{Int}$ and $\mathcal{L}_{Var}$ using the `class` feature of Racket. We define one class for each language and define a method for interpreting expressions inside each class. The class for $\mathcal{L}_{Var}$ inherits from the class for $\mathcal{L}_{Int}$, and the method `interp_exp` in $\mathcal{L}_{Var}$ overrides the `interp_exp` in $\mathcal{L}_{Int}$. Note that the default case of `interp_exp` in $\mathcal{L}_{Var}$ uses `super` to invoke `interp_exp`, and because $\mathcal{L}_{Var}$ inherits from $\mathcal{L}_{Int}$, that dispatches to the `interp_exp` in $\mathcal{L}_{Int}$.

```
                                     (define interp-Lvar-class
                                       (class interp-Lint-class
                                         (define/override ((interp_exp env) e)
   (define interp-Lint-class             (match e
     (class object%                        [(Var x)
       (define/public ((interp_exp env) e)  (dict-ref env x)]
         (match e                           [(Let x e body)
           [(Prim '- (list e))              (define v ((interp_exp env) e))
            (fx- 0 ((interp_exp env) e))]   (define env^ (dict-set env x v))
           ...))                            ((interp_exp env^) body)]
       ...))                                [else
                                             (super (interp_exp env) e)]))
                                         ...
                                         ))
```

Getting back to the troublesome example, repeated here:

```
(Let 'y (Int 10) (Prim '- (Var 'y)))
```

We can invoke the `interp_exp` method for $\mathcal{L}_{Var}$ on this expression, which we call e0, by creating an object of the $\mathcal{L}_{Var}$ class and calling the `interp_exp` method

```
((send (new interp-Lvar-class) interp_exp '()) e0)
```

To process the − operator, the default case of `interp_exp` in $\mathcal{L}_{\mathsf{Var}}$ dispatches to the `interp_exp` method in $\mathcal{L}_{\mathsf{Int}}$. But then for the recursive method call, it dispatches to `interp_exp` in $\mathcal{L}_{\mathsf{Var}}$, where the `Var` node is handled correctly. Thus, method overriding gives us the open recursion that we need to implement our interpreters in an extensible way.

### 2.1.2 Definitional Interpreter for $\mathcal{L}_{\mathsf{Var}}$

Having justified the use of classes and methods to implement interpreters, we revisit the definitional interpreter for $\mathcal{L}_{\mathsf{Int}}$ shown in figure 2.3 and then extend it to create an interpreter for $\mathcal{L}_{\mathsf{Var}}$, shown in figure 2.4. The interpreter for $\mathcal{L}_{\mathsf{Var}}$ adds two new `match` cases for variables and `let`. For `let`, we need a way to communicate the value bound to a variable to all the uses of the variable. To accomplish this, we maintain a mapping from variables to values called an *environment*. We use an association list (alist) to represent the environment. Figure 2.5 gives a brief introduction to alists and the `racket/dict` package. The `interp_exp` function takes the current environment, `env`, as an extra parameter. When the interpreter encounters a variable, it looks up the corresponding value in the dictionary. When the interpreter encounters a `Let`, it evaluates the initializing expression, extends the environment with the result value bound to the variable, using `dict-set`, then evaluates the body of the `Let`.

The goal for this chapter is to implement a compiler that translates any program $P_1$ written in the $\mathcal{L}_{\mathsf{Var}}$ language into an x86 assembly program $P_2$ such that $P_2$ exhibits the same behavior when run on a computer as the $P_1$ program interpreted by `interp_Lvar`. That is, they output the same integer $n$. We depict this correctness criteria in the following diagram:

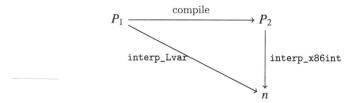

Next we introduce the x86$_{\mathsf{Int}}$ subset of x86 that suffices for compiling $\mathcal{L}_{\mathsf{Var}}$.

### 2.2 The x86$_{\mathsf{Int}}$ Assembly Language

Figure 2.6 defines the concrete syntax for x86$_{\mathsf{Int}}$. We use the AT&T syntax expected by the GNU assembler. A program begins with a `main` label followed by a sequence of instructions. The `globl` directive makes the `main` procedure externally visible so that the operating system can call it. An x86 program is stored in the computer's memory. For our purposes, the computer's memory is a mapping of 64-bit addresses to 64-bit values. The computer has a *program counter* (PC) stored in the `rip` register that points to the address of the next instruction to be executed. For most

```
(define interp-Lint-class
  (class object%
    (super-new)

    (define/public ((interp_exp env) e)
      (match e
        [(Int n) n]
        [(Prim 'read '())
         (define r (read))
         (cond [(fixnum? r) r]
               [else (error 'interp_exp "expected an integer" r)])]
        [(Prim '- (list e)) (fx- 0 ((interp_exp env) e))]
        [(Prim '+ (list e1 e2))
         (fx+ ((interp_exp env) e1) ((interp_exp env) e2))]
        [(Prim '- (list e1 e2))
         (fx- ((interp_exp env) e1) ((interp_exp env) e2))]))

    (define/public (interp_program p)
      (match p
        [(Program '() e) ((interp_exp '()) e)]))
    ))
```

**Figure 2.3**
Interpreter for $\mathcal{L}_{\text{Int}}$ as a class.

```
(define interp-Lvar-class
  (class interp-Lint-class
    (super-new)

    (define/override ((interp_exp env) e)
      (match e
        [(Var x) (dict-ref env x)]
        [(Let x e body)
         (define new-env (dict-set env x ((interp_exp env) e)))
         ((interp_exp new-env) body)]
        [else ((super interp_exp env) e)]))
    ))

(define (interp_Lvar p)
  (send (new interp-Lvar-class) interp_program p))
```

**Figure 2.4**
Interpreter for the $\mathcal{L}_{\text{Var}}$ language.

> **Association Lists as Dictionaries**
>
> An *association list* (called an alist) is a list of key-value pairs. For example, we can map people to their ages with an alist
>
> ```
> (define ages '((jane . 25) (sam . 24) (kate . 45)))
> ```
>
> The *dictionary* interface is for mapping keys to values. Every alist implements this interface. The package `racket/dict` provides many functions for working with dictionaries, such as
>
> (`dict-ref` *dict key*) returns the value associated with the given *key*.
>
> (`dict-set` *dict key val*) returns a new dictionary that maps *key* to *val* and otherwise is the same as *dict*.
>
> (`in-dict` *dict*) returns the sequence of keys and values in *dict*. For example, the following creates a new alist in which the ages are incremented:
> ```
> (for/list ([(k v) (in-dict ages)])
>   (cons k (add1 v)))
> ```

**Figure 2.5**
Association lists implement the dictionary interface.

$$
\begin{aligned}
reg \quad &::= \quad \text{rsp | rbp | rax | rbx | rcx | rdx | rsi | rdi |} \\
&\qquad \text{r8 | r9 | r10 | r11 | r12 | r13 | r14 | r15} \\
arg \quad &::= \quad \$int \text{ | } \%reg \text{ | } int(\%reg) \\
instr \quad &::= \quad \text{addq } arg,arg \text{ | subq } arg,arg \text{ | negq } arg \text{ | movq } arg,arg \text{ |} \\
&\qquad \text{pushq } arg \text{ | popq } arg \text{ | callq } label \text{ | retq | jmp } label \text{ |} \\
&\qquad label: instr \\
\text{x86}_{Int} \quad &::= \quad \text{.globl main} \\
&\qquad \text{main: } instr \dots
\end{aligned}
$$

**Figure 2.6**
The syntax of the x86$_{Int}$ assembly language (AT&T syntax).

instructions, the program counter is incremented after the instruction is executed so that it points to the next instruction in memory. Most x86 instructions take two operands, each of which is an integer constant (called an *immediate value*), a *register*, or a memory location.

A register is a special kind of variable that holds a 64-bit value. There are 16 general-purpose registers in the computer; their names are given in figure 2.6. A register is written with a percent sign, %, followed by the register name, for example %rax.

An immediate value is written using the notation $\$n$ where $n$ is an integer. An access to memory is specified using the syntax $n(\%r)$, which obtains the address stored in register $r$ and then adds $n$ bytes to the address. The resulting address is

```
        .globl main
  main:
        movq    $10, %rax
        addq    $32, %rax
        retq
```

**Figure 2.7**
An x86 program that computes (+ 10 32).

used to load or to store to memory depending on whether it occurs as a source or destination argument of an instruction.

An arithmetic instruction such as addq $s$, $d$ reads from the source $s$ and destination $d$, applies the arithmetic operation, and then writes the result to the destination $d$. The move instruction movq $s$, $d$ reads from $s$ and stores the result in $d$. The callq *label* instruction jumps to the procedure specified by the label, and retq returns from a procedure to its caller. We discuss procedure calls in more detail further in this chapter and in chapter 7. The last letter q indicates that these instructions operate on quadwords, which are 64-bit values. The instruction jmp *label* updates the program counter to the address of the instruction immediately after the specified label.

Appendix A.3 contains a quick reference for all the x86 instructions used in this book.

Figure 2.7 depicts an x86 program that computes (+ 10 32). The instruction movq $10, %rax puts 10 into register rax, and then addq $32, %rax adds 32 to the 10 in rax and puts the result, 42, into rax. The last instruction retq finishes the main function by returning the integer in rax to the operating system. The operating system interprets this integer as the program's exit code. By convention, an exit code of 0 indicates that a program has completed successfully, and all other exit codes indicate various errors. However, in this book we return the result of the program as the exit code.

We exhibit the use of memory for storing intermediate results in the next example. Figure 2.8 lists an x86 program that computes (+ 52 (- 10)). This program uses a region of memory called the *procedure call stack* (*stack* for short). The stack consists of a separate *frame* for each procedure call. The memory layout for an individual frame is shown in figure 2.9. The register rsp is called the *stack pointer* and contains the address of the item at the top of the stack. In general, we use the term *pointer* for something that contains an address. The stack grows downward in memory, so we increase the size of the stack by subtracting from the stack pointer. In the context of a procedure call, the *return address* is the location of the instruction that immediately follows the call instruction on the caller side. The function call instruction, callq, pushes the return address onto the stack prior to jumping to the procedure. The register rbp is the *base pointer* and is used to access variables that are stored in the frame of the current procedure call. The base pointer of the

```
start:
        movq    $10, -8(%rbp)
        negq    -8(%rbp)
        movq    -8(%rbp), %rax
        addq    $52, %rax
        jmp conclusion

        .globl main
main:
        pushq   %rbp
        movq    %rsp, %rbp
        subq    $16, %rsp
        jmp start
conclusion:
        addq    $16, %rsp
        popq    %rbp
        retq
```

**Figure 2.8**
An x86 program that computes (+ 52 (- 10)).

| Position | Contents |
|---|---|
| 8(%rbp) | return address |
| 0(%rbp) | old rbp |
| −8(%rbp) | variable 1 |
| −16(%rbp) | variable 2 |
| ... | ... |
| 0(%rsp) | variable $n$ |

**Figure 2.9**
Memory layout of a frame.

caller is stored immediately after the return address. Figure 2.9 shows the memory layout of a frame with storage for $n$ variables, which are numbered from 1 to $n$. Variable 1 is stored at address −8(%rbp), variable 2 at −16(%rbp), and so on.

In the program shown in figure 2.8, consider how control is transferred from the operating system to the main function. The operating system issues a callq main instruction that pushes its return address on the stack and then jumps to main. In x86-64, the stack pointer rsp must be divisible by 16 bytes prior to the execution of any callq instruction, so that when control arrives at main, the rsp is 8 bytes out of alignment (because the callq pushed the return address). The first three instructions are the typical *prelude* for a procedure. The instruction pushq %rbp first subtracts 8 from the stack pointer rsp and then saves the base pointer of the caller at address rsp on the stack. The next instruction movq %rsp, %rbp sets the

```
reg    ::= rsp | rbp | rax | rbx | rcx | rdx | rsi | rdi |
           r8 | r9 | r10 | r11 | r12 | r13 | r14 | r15
arg    ::= (Imm int) | (Reg reg) | (Deref reg int)
instr  ::= (Instr addq (arg arg)) | (Instr subq (arg arg))
       |   (Instr negq (arg)) | (Instr movq (arg arg))
       |   (Instr pushq (arg)) | (Instr popq (arg))
       |   (Callq label int) | (Retq) | (Jmp label)
block  ::= (Block info (instr ... ))
x86Int ::= (X86Program info ((label . block) ... ))
```

**Figure 2.10**
The abstract syntax of x86$_{Int}$ assembly.

base pointer to the current stack pointer, which is pointing to the location of the old base pointer. The instruction subq $16, %rsp moves the stack pointer down to make enough room for storing variables. This program needs one variable (8 bytes), but we round up to 16 bytes so that rsp is 16-byte-aligned, and then we are ready to make calls to other functions. The last instruction of the prelude is jmp start, which transfers control to the instructions that were generated from the expression (+ 52 (- 10)).

The first instruction under the start label is movq $10, -8(%rbp), which stores 10 in variable 1. The instruction negq -8(%rbp) changes the contents of variable 1 to −10. The next instruction moves the −10 from variable 1 into the rax register. Finally, addq $52, %rax adds 52 to the value in rax, updating its contents to 42.

The three instructions under the label conclusion are the typical *conclusion* of a procedure. The first two restore the rsp and rbp registers to their states at the beginning of the procedure. In particular, addq $16, %rsp moves the stack pointer to point to the old base pointer. Then popq %rbp restores the old base pointer to rbp and adds 8 to the stack pointer. The last instruction, retq, jumps back to the procedure that called this one and adds 8 to the stack pointer.

Our compiler needs a convenient representation for manipulating x86 programs, so we define an abstract syntax for x86, shown in figure 2.10. We refer to this language as x86$_{Int}$. The main difference between this and the concrete syntax of x86$_{Int}$ (figure 2.6) is that labels are not allowed in front of every instruction. Instead instructions are grouped into *basic blocks* with a label associated with every basic block; this is why the X86Program struct includes an alist mapping labels to basic blocks. The reason for this organization becomes apparent in chapter 4 when we introduce conditional branching. The Block structure includes an *info* field that is not needed in this chapter but becomes useful in chapter 3. For now, the *info* field should contain an empty list. Regarding the abstract syntax for callq, the Callq AST node includes an integer for representing the arity of the function, that is, the number of arguments, which is helpful to know during register allocation (chapter 3).

### 2.3  Planning the Trip to x86

To compile one language to another, it helps to focus on the differences between the two languages because the compiler will need to bridge those differences. What are the differences between $\mathcal{L}_{\mathsf{Var}}$ and x86 assembly? Here are some of the most important ones:

1. x86 arithmetic instructions typically have two arguments and update the second argument in place. In contrast, $\mathcal{L}_{\mathsf{Var}}$ arithmetic operations take two arguments and produce a new value. An x86 instruction may have at most one memory-accessing argument. Furthermore, some x86 instructions place special restrictions on their arguments.
2. An argument of an $\mathcal{L}_{\mathsf{Var}}$ operator can be a deeply nested expression, whereas x86 instructions restrict their arguments to be integer constants, registers, and memory locations.
3. The order of execution in x86 is explicit in the syntax, which is a sequence of instructions and jumps to labeled positions, whereas in $\mathcal{L}_{\mathsf{Var}}$ the order of evaluation is a left-to-right depth-first traversal of the abstract syntax tree.
4. A program in $\mathcal{L}_{\mathsf{Var}}$ can have any number of variables, whereas x86 has 16 registers and the procedure call stack.
5. Variables in $\mathcal{L}_{\mathsf{Var}}$ can shadow other variables with the same name. In x86, registers have unique names, and memory locations have unique addresses.

We ease the challenge of compiling from $\mathcal{L}_{\mathsf{Var}}$ to x86 by breaking down the problem into several steps, which deal with these differences one at a time. Each of these steps is called a *pass* of the compiler. This term indicates that each step passes over, or traverses, the AST of the program. Furthermore, we follow the nanopass approach, which means that we strive for each pass to accomplish one clear objective rather than two or three at the same time. We begin by sketching how we might implement each pass and give each pass a name. We then figure out an ordering of the passes and the input/output language for each pass. The very first pass has $\mathcal{L}_{\mathsf{Var}}$ as its input language, and the last pass has x86$_{\mathsf{Int}}$ as its output language. In between these two passes, we can choose whichever language is most convenient for expressing the output of each pass, whether that be $\mathcal{L}_{\mathsf{Var}}$, x86$_{\mathsf{Int}}$, or a new *intermediate language* of our own design. Finally, to implement each pass we write one recursive function per nonterminal in the grammar of the input language of the pass.

Our compiler for $\mathcal{L}_{\mathsf{Var}}$ consists of the following passes:

**uniquify** deals with the shadowing of variables by renaming every variable to a unique name.

**remove_complex_operands** ensures that each subexpression of a primitive operation or function call is a variable or integer, that is, an *atomic* expression. We refer to nonatomic expressions as *complex*. This pass introduces temporary variables to hold the results of complex subexpressions.

`explicate_control` makes the execution order of the program explicit. It converts the abstract syntax tree representation into a graph in which each node is a labeled sequence of statements and the edges are `goto` statements.

`select_instructions` handles the difference between $\mathcal{L}_{\mathsf{Var}}$ operations and x86 instructions. This pass converts each $\mathcal{L}_{\mathsf{Var}}$ operation to a short sequence of instructions that accomplishes the same task.

`assign_homes` replaces variables with registers or stack locations.

Our treatment of `remove_complex_operands` and `explicate_control` as separate passes is an example of the nanopass approach.[1] The traditional approach is to combine them into a single step (Aho et al. 2006).

The next question is, in what order should we apply these passes? This question can be challenging because it is difficult to know ahead of time which orderings will be better (that is, will be easier to implement, produce more efficient code, and so on), and therefore ordering often involves trial and error. Nevertheless, we can plan ahead and make educated choices regarding the ordering.

What should be the ordering of `explicate_control` with respect to `uniquify`? The `uniquify` pass should come first because `explicate_control` changes all the `let`-bound variables to become local variables whose scope is the entire program, which would confuse variables with the same name. We place `remove_complex_operands` before `explicate_control` because the later removes the `let` form, but it is convenient to use `let` in the output of `remove_complex_operands`. The ordering of `uniquify` with respect to `remove_complex_operands` does not matter, so we arbitrarily choose `uniquify` to come first.

The `select_instructions` and `assign_homes` passes are intertwined. In chapter 7 we learn that in x86, registers are used for passing arguments to functions and that it is preferable to assign parameters to their corresponding registers. This suggests that it would be better to start with the `select_instructions` pass, which generates the instructions for argument passing, before performing register allocation. On the other hand, by selecting instructions first we may run into a dead end in `assign_homes`. Recall that only one argument of an x86 instruction may be a memory access, but `assign_homes` might be forced to assign both arguments to memory locations. A sophisticated approach is to repeat the two passes until a solution is found. However, to reduce implementation complexity we recommend placing `select_instructions` first, followed by the `assign_homes`, and then a third pass named `patch_instructions` that uses a reserved register to fix outstanding problems.

Figure 2.11 presents the ordering of the compiler passes and identifies the input and output language of each pass. The output of the `select_instructions` pass is the x86$_{\mathsf{Var}}$ language, which extends x86$_{\mathsf{Int}}$ with an unbounded number of

---

1. For analogous decompositions of the translation into continuation passing style, see the work of Lawall and Danvy (1993) and Hatcliff and Danvy (1994).

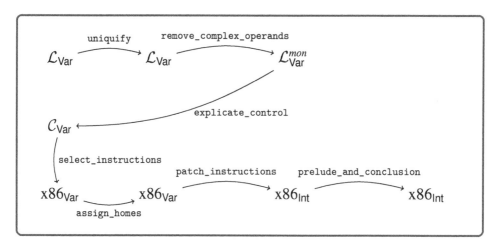

**Figure 2.11**
Diagram of the passes for compiling $\mathcal{L}_{\mathsf{Var}}$.

program-scope variables and removes the restrictions regarding instruction arguments. The last pass, `prelude_and_conclusion`, places the program instructions
inside a `main` function with instructions for the prelude and conclusion. In the
next section we discuss the $\mathcal{C}_{\mathsf{Var}}$ intermediate language that serves as the output
of `explicate_control`. The remainder of this chapter provides guidance on the
implementation of each of the compiler passes represented in figure 2.11.

### 2.3.1 The $\mathcal{C}_{\mathsf{Var}}$ Intermediate Language
The output of `explicate_control` is similar to the C language (Kernighan and
Ritchie 1988) in that it has separate syntactic categories for expressions and statements, so we name it $\mathcal{C}_{\mathsf{Var}}$. This style of intermediate language is also known as
*three-address code*, to emphasize that the typical form of a statement such as
`x = (+ y z);` involves three addresses: `x`, `y`, and `z` (Aho et al. 2006).

The concrete syntax for $\mathcal{C}_{\mathsf{Var}}$ is shown in figure 2.12, and the abstract syntax for
$\mathcal{C}_{\mathsf{Var}}$ is shown in figure 2.13. The $\mathcal{C}_{\mathsf{Var}}$ language supports the same operators as $\mathcal{L}_{\mathsf{Var}}$
but the arguments of operators are restricted to atomic expressions. Instead of `let`
expressions, $\mathcal{C}_{\mathsf{Var}}$ has assignment statements that can be executed in sequence using
the `Seq` form. A sequence of statements always ends with `Return`, a guarantee that
is baked into the grammar rules for *tail*. The naming of this nonterminal comes
from the term *tail position*, which refers to an expression that is the last one to
execute within a function or program.

A $\mathcal{C}_{\mathsf{Var}}$ program consists of an alist mapping labels to tails. This is more general
than necessary for the present chapter, as we do not yet introduce `goto` for jumping
to labels, but it saves us from having to change the syntax in chapter 4. For now
there is just one label, `start`, and the whole program is its tail. The *info* field of the
`CProgram` form, after the `explicate_control` pass, contains an alist that associates
the symbol `locals` with a list of all the variables used in the program. At the start

$$
\begin{array}{lll}
atm & ::= & int \mid var \\
exp & ::= & atm \mid (\texttt{read}) \mid (\texttt{-} \; atm) \mid (\texttt{+} \; atm \; atm) \mid (\texttt{-} \; atm \; atm) \\
stmt & ::= & var \; \texttt{=} \; exp\texttt{;} \\
tail & ::= & \texttt{return} \; exp\texttt{;} \mid stmt \; tail \\
\mathcal{C}_{\mathsf{Var}} & ::= & (label\texttt{:} \; tail) \dots
\end{array}
$$

**Figure 2.12**
The concrete syntax of the $\mathcal{C}_{\mathsf{Var}}$ intermediate language.

$$
\begin{array}{lll}
atm & ::= & (\texttt{Int} \; int) \mid (\texttt{Var} \; var) \\
exp & ::= & atm \mid (\texttt{Prim 'read ()}) \mid (\texttt{Prim '-} \; (atm)) \\
& \mid & (\texttt{Prim '+} \; (atm \; atm)) \mid (\texttt{Prim '-} \; (atm \; atm)) \\
stmt & ::= & (\texttt{Assign} \; (\texttt{Var} \; var) \; exp) \\
tail & ::= & (\texttt{Return} \; exp) \mid (\texttt{Seq} \; stmt \; tail) \\
\mathcal{C}_{\mathsf{Var}} & ::= & (\texttt{CProgram} \; info \; ((label \; . \; tail) \dots))
\end{array}
$$

**Figure 2.13**
The abstract syntax of the $\mathcal{C}_{\mathsf{Var}}$ intermediate language.

of the program, these variables are uninitialized; they become initialized on their first assignment.

The definitional interpreter for $\mathcal{C}_{\mathsf{Var}}$ is in the support code, in the file `interp-Cvar.rkt`.

## 2.4 Uniquify Variables

The `uniquify` pass replaces the variable bound by each `let` with a unique name. Both the input and output of the `uniquify` pass is the $\mathcal{L}_{\mathsf{Var}}$ language. For example, the `uniquify` pass should translate the program on the left into the program on the right.

```
(let ([x 32])                    (let ([x.1 32])
  (+ (let ([x 10]) x) x))    ⇒     (+ (let ([x.2 10]) x.2) x.1))
```

The following is another example translation, this time of a program with a `let` nested inside the initializing expression of another `let`.

```
(let ([x (let ([x 4])            (let ([x.2 (let ([x.1 4])
            (+ x 1))])    ⇒                   (+ x.1 1))])
  (+ x 2))                         (+ x.2 2))
```

We recommend implementing `uniquify` by creating a structurally recursive function named `uniquify_exp` that does little other than copy an expression. However,

```
(define (uniquify_exp env)
  (lambda (e)
    (match e
      [(Var x) ___]
      [(Int n) (Int n)]
      [(Let x e body) ___]
      [(Prim op es)
       (Prim op (for/list ([e es]) ((uniquify_exp env) e)))])))

(define (uniquify p)
  (match p
    [(Program '() e) (Program '() ((uniquify_exp '()) e))]))
```

**Figure 2.14**
Skeleton for the `uniquify` pass.

when encountering a `let`, it should generate a unique name for the variable and associate the old name with the new name in an alist.[2] The `uniquify_exp` function needs to access this alist when it gets to a variable reference, so we add a parameter to `uniquify_exp` for the alist.

The skeleton of the `uniquify_exp` function is shown in figure 2.14. The `for/list` form of Racket is useful for transforming the element of a list to produce a new list.

**Exercise 2.1** Complete the `uniquify` pass by filling in the blanks in figure 2.14; that is, implement the cases for variables and for the `let` form in the file `compiler.rkt` in the support code.

**Exercise 2.2** Create five $\mathcal{L}_{\mathsf{Var}}$ programs that exercise the most interesting parts of the `uniquify` pass; that is, the programs should include `let` forms, variables, and variables that shadow each other. The five programs should be placed in the subdirectory named `tests`, and the file names should start with `var_test_` followed by a unique integer and end with the file extension `.rkt`. The `run-tests.rkt` script in the support code checks whether the output programs produce the same result as the input programs. The script uses the `interp-tests` function (appendix A.2) from `utilities.rkt` to test your `uniquify` pass on the example programs. The `passes` parameter of `interp-tests` is a list that should have one entry for each pass in your compiler. For now, define `passes` to contain just one entry for `uniquify` as follows:

```
(define passes
  (list (list "uniquify" uniquify interp_Lvar type-check-Lvar)))
```

Run the `run-tests.rkt` script in the support code to check whether the output programs produce the same result as the input programs.

---

2. The Racket function `gensym` is handy for generating unique variable names.

$$
\begin{array}{rcl}
\textit{atm} & ::= & (\texttt{Int } \textit{int}) \mid (\texttt{Var } \textit{var}) \\
\textit{exp} & ::= & \textit{atm} \mid (\texttt{Prim 'read ()}) \\
& \mid & (\texttt{Prim '- } (\textit{atm})) \mid (\texttt{Prim '+ } (\textit{atm atm})) \mid (\texttt{Prim '- } (\textit{atm atm})) \\
& \mid & (\texttt{Let } \textit{var exp exp}) \\
\mathcal{L}_{\mathsf{Var}}^{\textit{mon}} & ::= & (\texttt{Program '() } \textit{exp})
\end{array}
$$

**Figure 2.15**
$\mathcal{L}_{\mathsf{Var}}^{\textit{mon}}$ is $\mathcal{L}_{\mathsf{Var}}$ with operands restricted to atomic expressions.

## 2.5  Remove Complex Operands

The `remove_complex_operands` pass compiles $\mathcal{L}_{\mathsf{Var}}$ programs into a restricted form in which the arguments of operations are atomic expressions. Put another way, this pass removes complex operands, such as the expression (- 10) in the following program. This is accomplished by introducing a new temporary variable, assigning the complex operand to the new variable, and then using the new variable in place of the complex operand, as shown in the output of `remove_complex_operands` on the right.

```
(let ([x (+ 42 (- 10))])                    (let ([x (let ([tmp.1 (- 10)])
   (+ x 10))                    ⇒                      (+ 42 tmp.1))])
                                               (+ x 10))
```

Figure 2.15 presents the grammar for the output of this pass, the language $\mathcal{L}_{\mathsf{Var}}^{\textit{mon}}$. The only difference is that operator arguments are restricted to be atomic expressions that are defined by the *atm* nonterminal. In particular, integer constants and variables are atomic.

The atomic expressions are pure (they do not cause or depend on side effects) whereas complex expressions may have side effects, such as (`Prim 'read ()`). A language with this separation between pure expressions versus expressions with side effects is said to be in monadic normal form (Moggi 1991; Danvy 2003), which explains the *mon* in the name $\mathcal{L}_{\mathsf{Var}}^{\textit{mon}}$. An important invariant of the `remove_complex_operands` pass is that the relative ordering among complex expressions is not changed, but the relative ordering between atomic expressions and complex expressions can change and often does. The reason that these changes are behavior preserving is that the atomic expressions are pure.

Another well-known form for intermediate languages is the *administrative normal form* (ANF) (Danvy 1991; Flanagan et al. 1993). The $\mathcal{L}_{\mathsf{Var}}^{\textit{mon}}$ language is not quite in ANF because it allows the right-hand side of a `let` to be a complex expression, such as another `let`. The flattening of nested `let` expressions is instead one of the responsibilities of the `explicate_control` pass.

We recommend implementing this pass with two mutually recursive functions, `rco_atom` and `rco_exp`. The idea is to apply `rco_atom` to subexpressions that need to become atomic and to apply `rco_exp` to subexpressions that do not. Both functions take an $\mathcal{L}_{Var}$ expression as input. The `rco_exp` function returns an expression. The `rco_atom` function returns two things: an atomic expression and an alist mapping temporary variables to complex subexpressions. You can return multiple things from a function using Racket's `values` form, and you can receive multiple things from a function call using the `define-values` form.

Returning to the example program with the expression (+ 42 (- 10)), the subexpression (- 10) should be processed using the `rco_atom` function because it is an argument of the + operator and therefore needs to become atomic. The output of `rco_atom` applied to (- 10) is as follows:

$$
(-\ 10) \qquad\Rightarrow\qquad \begin{array}{l} \texttt{tmp.1} \\ \texttt{((tmp.1 . (- 10)))} \end{array}
$$

Take special care of programs, such as the following, that bind a variable to an atomic expression. You should leave such variable bindings unchanged, as shown in the program on the right:

```
(let ([a 42])                    (let ([a 42])
  (let ([b a])          ⇒          (let ([b a])
    b))                              b))
```

A careless implementation might produce the following output with unnecessary temporary variables.

```
(let ([tmp.1 42])
  (let ([a tmp.1])
    (let ([tmp.2 a])
      (let ([b tmp.2])
        b))))
```

**Exercise 2.3** Implement the `remove_complex_operands` function in `compiler.rkt`. Create three new $\mathcal{L}_{Var}$ programs that exercise the interesting code in the `remove_complex_operands` pass. Follow the guidelines regarding file names described in exercise 2.2. In the `run-tests.rkt` script, add the following entry to the list of `passes`, and then run the script to test your compiler.

```
(list "remove-complex" remove_complex_operands interp_Lvar type-check-Lvar)
```

In debugging your compiler, it is often useful to see the intermediate programs that are output from each pass. To print the intermediate programs, place `(debug-level 1)` before the call to `interp-tests` in `run-tests.rkt`.

## 2.6 Explicate Control

The `explicate_control` pass compiles $\mathcal{L}_{Var}$ programs into $\mathcal{C}_{Var}$ programs that make the order of execution explicit in their syntax. For now this amounts to flattening

```
(define (explicate_tail e)
  (match e
    [(Var x) ___]
    [(Int n) (Return (Int n))]
    [(Let x rhs body) ___]
    [(Prim op es) ___]
    [else (error "explicate_tail unhandled case" e)]))

(define (explicate_assign e x cont)
  (match e
    [(Var x) ___]
    [(Int n) (Seq (Assign (Var x) (Int n)) cont)]
    [(Let y rhs body) ___]
    [(Prim op es) ___]
    [else (error "explicate_assign unhandled case" e)]))

(define (explicate_control p)
  (match p
    [(Program info body) ___]))
```

**Figure 2.16**
Skeleton for the `explicate_control` pass.

`let` constructs into a sequence of assignment statements. For example, consider the following $\mathcal{L}_{Var}$ program:

```
(let ([y (let ([x 20])
           (+ x (let ([x 22]) x)))])
  y)
```

The output of the previous pass is shown next, on the left, and the output of `explicate_control` is on the right. Recall that the right-hand side of a `let` executes before its body, so that the order of evaluation for this program is to assign 20 to `x.1`, 22 to `x.2`, and `(+ x.1 x.2)` to y, and then to return y. Indeed, the output of `explicate_control` makes this ordering explicit.

```
(let ([y (let ([x.1 20])            start:
           (let ([x.2 22])            x.1 = 20;
             (+ x.1 x.2)))])          x.2 = 22;
  y)                        ⇒        y = (+ x.1 x.2);
                                      return y;
```

The organization of this pass depends on the notion of tail position to which we have alluded. Here is the definition.

**Definition 2.1**   The following rules define when an expression is in *tail position* for the language $\mathcal{L}_{Var}$.

1. In (Program () e), expression e is in tail position.

2. If (Let $x$ $e_1$ $e_2$) is in tail position, then so is $e_2$.

We recommend implementing `explicate_control` using two recursive functions, `explicate_tail` and `explicate_assign`, as suggested in the skeleton code shown in figure 2.16. The `explicate_tail` function should be applied to expressions in tail position, whereas the `explicate_assign` should be applied to expressions that occur on the right-hand side of a `let`. The `explicate_tail` function takes an *exp* in $\mathcal{L}_{\mathsf{Var}}$ as input and produces a *tail* in $\mathcal{C}_{\mathsf{Var}}$ (see figure 2.13). The `explicate_assign` function takes an *exp* in $\mathcal{L}_{\mathsf{Var}}$, the variable to which it is to be assigned, and a *tail* in $\mathcal{C}_{\mathsf{Var}}$ for the code that comes after the assignment. The `explicate_assign` function returns a *tail* in $\mathcal{C}_{\mathsf{Var}}$.

The `explicate_assign` function is in accumulator-passing style: the `cont` parameter is used for accumulating the output. This accumulator-passing style plays an important role in the way that we generate high-quality code for conditional expressions in chapter 4. The abbreviation `cont` is for continuation because it contains the generated code that should come after the current assignment. This code organization is also related to continuation-passing style, except that `cont` is not what happens next during compilation but is what happens next in the generated code.

**Exercise 2.4** Implement the `explicate_control` function in `compiler.rkt`. Create three new $\mathcal{L}_{\mathsf{Int}}$ programs that exercise the code in `explicate_control`. In the `run-tests.rkt` script, add the following entry to the list of **passes** and then run the script to test your compiler.

```
(list "explicate control" explicate_control interp_Cvar type-check-Cvar)
```

## 2.7  Select Instructions

In the `select_instructions` pass we begin the work of translating from $\mathcal{C}_{\mathsf{Var}}$ to x86$_{\mathsf{Var}}$. The target language of this pass is a variant of x86 that still uses variables, so we add an AST node of the form (Var *var*) to the *arg* nonterminal of the x86$_{\mathsf{Int}}$ abstract syntax (figure 2.10). We recommend implementing the `select_instructions` with three auxiliary functions, one for each of the nonterminals of $\mathcal{C}_{\mathsf{Var}}$: *atm*, *stmt*, and *tail*.

The cases for *atm* are straightforward; variables stay the same and integer constants change to immediates; that is, (Int $n$) changes to (Imm $n$).

Next consider the cases for the *stmt* nonterminal, starting with arithmetic operations. For example, consider the following addition operation, on the left side. There is an `addq` instruction in x86, but it performs an in-place update. So, we could move $arg_1$ into the left-hand *var* and then add $arg_2$ to *var*, where $arg_1$ and $arg_2$ are the translations of *atm*$_1$ and *atm*$_2$, respectively.

$$var\ \texttt{=}\ (\texttt{+}\ atm_1\ atm_2)\texttt{;} \qquad \Rightarrow \qquad \begin{array}{l} \texttt{movq}\ arg_1\texttt{,}\ var \\ \texttt{addq}\ arg_2\texttt{,}\ var \end{array}$$

There are also cases that require special care to avoid generating needlessly complicated code. For example, if one of the arguments of the addition is the same variable as the left-hand side of the assignment, as shown next, then there is no need for the extra move instruction. The assignment statement can be translated into a single **addq** instruction, as follows.

$$var = (+ \ atm_1 \ var);  \qquad\qquad \Rightarrow \quad \text{addq } arg_1, \ var$$

The **read** operation does not have a direct counterpart in x86 assembly, so we provide this functionality with the function **read_int** in the file **runtime.c**, written in C (Kernighan and Ritchie 1988). In general, we refer to all the functionality in this file as the *runtime system*, or simply the *runtime* for short. When compiling your generated x86 assembly code, you need to compile **runtime.c** to **runtime.o** (an *object file*, using **gcc** with option **-c**) and link it into the executable. For our purposes of code generation, all you need to do is translate an assignment of **read** into a call to the **read_int** function followed by a move from **rax** to the left-hand side variable. (Recall that the return value of a function goes into **rax**.)

$$var = (read);  \qquad\qquad \Rightarrow \quad \begin{array}{l} \text{callq read\_int} \\ \text{movq \%rax, } var \end{array}$$

There are two cases for the *tail* nonterminal: **Return** and **Seq**. Regarding **Return**, we recommend treating it as an assignment to the **rax** register followed by a jump to the conclusion of the program (so the conclusion needs to be labeled). For (**Seq** *s t*), you can translate the statement *s* and tail *t* recursively and then append the resulting instructions.

**Exercise 2.5** Implement the **select_instructions** pass in **compiler.rkt**. Create three new example programs that are designed to exercise all the interesting cases in this pass. In the **run-tests.rkt** script, add the following entry to the list of **passes** and then run the script to test your compiler.

```
(list "instruction selection" select_instructions interp_pseudo-x86-0)
```

## 2.8 Assign Homes

The **assign_homes** pass compiles x86$_{Var}$ programs to x86$_{Var}$ programs that no longer use program variables. Thus, the **assign_homes** pass is responsible for placing all the program variables in registers or on the stack. For runtime efficiency, it is better to place variables in registers, but because there are only sixteen registers, some programs must necessarily resort to placing some variables on the stack. In this chapter we focus on the mechanics of placing variables on the stack. We study an algorithm for placing variables in registers in chapter 3.

Consider again the following $\mathcal{L}_{\text{Var}}$ program from section 2.5:

```
(let ([a 42])
  (let ([b a])
    b))
```

The output of `select_instructions` is shown next, on the left, and the output of `assign_homes` is on the right. In this example, we assign variable a to stack location -8(%rbp) and variable b to location -16(%rbp).

```
    movq $42, a                        movq $42, -8(%rbp)
    movq a, b           ⇒              movq -8(%rbp), -16(%rbp)
    movq b, %rax                       movq -16(%rbp), %rax
```

The `assign_homes` pass should replace all variables with stack locations. The list of variables can be obtained from the `locals-types` entry in the *info* of the `X86Program` node. The `locals-types` entry is an alist mapping all the variables in the program to their types (for now, just `Integer`). As an aside, the `locals-types` entry is computed by `type-check-Cvar` in the support code, which installs it in the *info* field of the `CProgram` node, which you should propagate to the `X86Program` node. In the process of assigning variables to stack locations, it is convenient for you to compute and store the size of the frame (in bytes) in the *info* field of the `X86Program` node, with the key `stack-space`, which is needed later to generate the conclusion of the `main` procedure. The x86-64 standard requires the frame size to be a multiple of 16 bytes.

**Exercise 2.6** Implement the `assign_homes` pass in `compiler.rkt`, defining auxiliary functions for each of the nonterminals in the x86$_{\text{Var}}$ grammar. We recommend that the auxiliary functions take an extra parameter that maps variable names to homes (stack locations for now). In the `run-tests.rkt` script, add the following entry to the list of `passes` and then run the script to test your compiler.

```
(list "assign homes" assign-homes interp_x86-0)
```

## 2.9  Patch Instructions

The `patch_instructions` pass compiles from x86$_{\text{Var}}$ to x86$_{\text{Int}}$ by making sure that each instruction adheres to the restriction that at most one argument of an instruction may be a memory reference.

We return to the following example.

```
(let ([a 42])
  (let ([b a])
    b))
```

The `assign_homes` pass produces the following translation.

```
    movq $42, -8(%rbp)
    movq -8(%rbp), -16(%rbp)
    movq -16(%rbp), %rax
```

The second `movq` instruction is problematic because both arguments are stack locations. We suggest fixing this problem by moving from the source location to the register `rax` and then from `rax` to the destination location, as follows.

```
movq -8(%rbp), %rax
movq %rax, -16(%rbp)
```

**Exercise 2.7** Implement the `patch_instructions` pass in `compiler.rkt`. Create three new example programs that are designed to exercise all the interesting cases in this pass. In the `run-tests.rkt` script, add the following entry to the list of `passes` and then run the script to test your compiler.

```
(list "patch instructions" patch_instructions interp_x86-0)
```

## 2.10 Generate Prelude and Conclusion

The last step of the compiler from $\mathcal{L}_{\mathsf{Var}}$ to x86 is to generate the `main` function with a prelude and conclusion wrapped around the rest of the program, as shown in figure 2.8 and discussed in section 2.2.

When running on Mac OS X, your compiler should prefix an underscore to all labels (for example, changing `main` to `_main`). The Racket call (`system-type 'os`) is useful for determining which operating system the compiler is running on. It returns `'macosx`, `'unix`, or `'windows`.

**Exercise 2.8** Implement the `prelude_and_conclusion` pass in `compiler.rkt`. In the `run-tests.rkt` script, add the following entry to the list of `passes` and then run the script to test your compiler.

```
(list "prelude and conclusion" prelude-and-conclusion interp_x86-0)
```

Uncomment the call to the `compiler-tests` function (appendix A.2), which tests your complete compiler by executing the generated x86 code. It translates the x86 AST that you produce into a string by invoking the `print-x86` method of the `print-x86-class` in `utilities.rkt`. Compile the provided `runtime.c` file to `runtime.o` using gcc. Run the script to test your compiler.

## 2.11 Challenge: Partial Evaluator for $\mathcal{L}_{\mathsf{Var}}$

This section describes two optional challenge exercises that involve adapting and improving the partial evaluator for $\mathcal{L}_{\mathsf{Int}}$ that was introduced in section 1.6.

**Exercise 2.9** Adapt the partial evaluator from section 1.6 (figure 1.5) so that it applies to $\mathcal{L}_{\mathsf{Var}}$ programs instead of $\mathcal{L}_{\mathsf{Int}}$ programs. Recall that $\mathcal{L}_{\mathsf{Var}}$ adds variables and `let` binding to the $\mathcal{L}_{\mathsf{Int}}$ language, so you will need to add cases for them in the `pe_exp` function. Once complete, add the partial evaluation pass to the front of your compiler, and make sure that your compiler still passes all the tests.

**Exercise 2.10**  Improve on the partial evaluator by replacing the `pe_neg` and `pe_add` auxiliary functions with functions that know more about arithmetic. For example, your partial evaluator should translate

$$(+ \ 1 \ (+ \ (\texttt{read}) \ 1)) \qquad \text{into} \qquad (+ \ 2 \ (\texttt{read}))$$

To accomplish this, the `pe_exp` function should produce output in the form of the *residual* nonterminal of the following grammar. The idea is that when processing an addition expression, we can always produce one of the following: (1) an integer constant, (2) an addition expression with an integer constant on the left-hand side but not the right-hand side, or (3) an addition expression in which neither subexpression is a constant.

| | | |
|--|--|--|
| *inert* | ::= | *var* \| (`read`) \| (- *var*) \| (- (`read`)) \| (+ *inert inert*) |
| | \| | (`let` ([*var residual*]) *residual*) |
| *residual* | ::= | *int* \| (+ *int inert*) \| *inert* |

The `pe_add` and `pe_neg` functions may assume that their inputs are *residual* expressions and they should return *residual* expressions. Once the improvements are complete, make sure that your compiler still passes all the tests. After all, fast code is useless if it produces incorrect results!

# 3    Register Allocation

In chapter 2 we learned how to compile $\mathcal{L}_{\mathsf{Var}}$ to x86, storing variables on the procedure call stack. The CPU may require tens to hundreds of cycles to access a location on the stack, whereas accessing a register takes only a single cycle. In this chapter we improve the efficiency of our generated code by storing some variables in registers. The goal of register allocation is to fit as many variables into registers as possible. Some programs have more variables than registers, so we cannot always map each variable to a different register. Fortunately, it is common for different variables to be in use during different periods of time during program execution, and in those cases we can map multiple variables to the same register.

The program shown in figure 3.1 serves as a running example. The source program is on the left and the output of instruction selection is on the right. The program is almost completely in the x86 assembly language, but it still uses variables. Consider variables x and z. After the variable x has been moved to z, it is no longer in use. Variable z, on the other hand, is used only after this point, so x and z could share the same register.

The topic of section 3.2 is how to compute where a variable is in use. Once we have that information, we compute which variables are in use at the same time, that is, which ones *interfere* with each other, and represent this relation as an undirected graph whose vertices are variables and edges indicate when two variables interfere (section 3.3). We then model register allocation as a graph coloring problem (section 3.4).

If we run out of registers despite these efforts, we place the remaining variables on the stack, similarly to how we handled variables in chapter 2. It is common to use the verb *spill* for assigning a variable to a stack location. The decision to spill a variable is handled as part of the graph coloring process.

We make the simplifying assumption that each variable is assigned to one location (a register or stack address). A more sophisticated approach is to assign a variable to one or more locations in different regions of the program. For example, if a variable is used many times in short sequence and then used again only after many other instructions, it could be more efficient to assign the variable to a register during the initial sequence and then move it to the stack for the rest of its lifetime. We refer the interested reader to Cooper and Torczon (2011) (chapter 13) for more information about that approach.

Example $\mathcal{L}_{Var}$ program:

```
(let ([v 1])
  (let ([w 42])
    (let ([x (+ v 7)])
      (let ([y x])
        (let ([z (+ x w)])
          (+ z (- y)))))))
```

After instruction selection:

```
locals-types:
    x : Integer, y : Integer,
    z : Integer, t : Integer,
    v : Integer, w : Integer
start:
    movq $1, v
    movq $42, w
    movq v, x
    addq $7, x
    movq x, y
    movq x, z
    addq w, z
    movq y, t
    negq t
    movq z, %rax
    addq t, %rax
    jmp conclusion
```

**Figure 3.1**
A running example for register allocation.

## 3.1 Registers and Calling Conventions

As we perform register allocation, we must be aware of the *calling conventions* that govern how function calls are performed in x86. Even though $\mathcal{L}_{Var}$ does not include programmer-defined functions, our generated code includes a `main` function that is called by the operating system and our generated code contains calls to the `read_int` function.

Function calls require coordination between two pieces of code that may be written by different programmers or generated by different compilers. Here we follow the System V calling conventions that are used by the GNU C compiler on Linux and MacOS (Bryant and O'Hallaron 2005; Matz et al. 2013). The calling conventions include rules about how functions share the use of registers. In particular, the caller is responsible for freeing some registers prior to the function call for use by the callee. These are called the *caller-saved registers* and they are

`rax rcx rdx rsi rdi r8 r9 r10 r11`

On the other hand, the callee is responsible for preserving the values of the *callee-saved registers*, which are

`rsp rbp rbx r12 r13 r14 r15`

We can think about this caller/callee convention from two points of view, the caller view and the callee view, as follows:

- The caller should assume that all the caller-saved registers get overwritten with arbitrary values by the callee. On the other hand, the caller can safely assume that all the callee-saved registers retain their original values.
- The callee can freely use any of the caller-saved registers. However, if the callee wants to use a callee-saved register, the callee must arrange to put the original value back in the register prior to returning to the caller. This can be accomplished by saving the value to the stack in the prelude of the function and restoring the value in the conclusion of the function.

In x86, registers are also used for passing arguments to a function and for the return value. In particular, the first six arguments of a function are passed in the following six registers, in this order.

`rdi rsi rdx rcx r8 r9`

We refer to these six registers are the argument-passing registers . If there are more than six arguments, the convention is to use space on the frame of the caller for the rest of the arguments. In chapter 7, we instead pass a tuple containing the sixth argument and the rest of the arguments, which simplifies the treatment of efficient tail calls. For now, the only function we care about is `read_int`, which takes zero arguments. The register `rax` is used for the return value of a function.

The next question is how these calling conventions impact register allocation. Consider the $\mathcal{L}_{Var}$ program presented in figure 3.2. We first analyze this example from the caller point of view and then from the callee point of view. We refer to a variable that is in use during a function call as a *call-live variable*.

The program makes two calls to `read`. The variable x is call-live because it is in use during the second call to `read`; we must ensure that the value in x does not get overwritten during the call to `read`. One obvious approach is to save all the values that reside in caller-saved registers to the stack prior to each function call and to restore them after each call. That way, if the register allocator chooses to assign x to a caller-saved register, its value will be preserved across the call to `read`. However, saving and restoring to the stack is relatively slow. If x is not used many times, it may be better to assign x to a stack location in the first place. Or better yet, if we can arrange for x to be placed in a callee-saved register, then it won't need to be saved and restored during function calls.

We recommend an approach that captures these issues in the interference graph, without complicating the graph coloring algorithm. During liveness analysis we know which variables are call-live because we compute which variables are in use at every instruction (section 3.2). When we build the interference graph (section 3.3), we can place an edge in the interference graph between each call-live variable and the caller-saved registers. This will prevent the graph coloring algorithm from assigning call-live variables to caller-saved registers.

On the other hand, for variables that are not call-live, we prefer placing them in caller-saved registers to leave more room for call-live variables in the callee-saved registers. This can also be implemented without complicating the graph coloring algorithm. We recommend that the graph coloring algorithm assign variables to natural numbers, choosing the lowest number for which there is no interference. After the coloring is complete, we map the numbers to registers and stack locations: mapping the lowest numbers to caller-saved registers, the next lowest to callee-saved registers, and the largest numbers to stack locations. This ordering gives preference to registers over stack locations and to caller-saved registers over callee-saved registers.

Returning to the example in figure 3.2, let us analyze the generated x86 code on the right-hand side. Variable x is assigned to rbx, a callee-saved register. Thus, it is already in a safe place during the second call to read_int. Next, variable y is assigned to rcx, a caller-saved register, because y is not a call-live variable.

We have completed the analysis from the caller point of view, so now we switch to the callee point of view, focusing on the prelude and conclusion of the main function. As usual, the prelude begins with saving the rbp register to the stack and setting the rbp to the current stack pointer. We now know why it is necessary to save the rbp: it is a callee-saved register. The prelude then pushes rbx to the stack because (1) rbx is a callee-saved register and (2) rbx is assigned to a variable (x). The other callee-saved registers are not saved in the prelude because they are not used. The prelude subtracts 8 bytes from the rsp to make it 16-byte aligned. Shifting attention to the conclusion, we see that rbx is restored from the stack with a popq instruction.

## 3.2 Liveness Analysis

The uncover_live pass performs *liveness analysis*; that is, it discovers which variables are in use in different regions of a program. A variable or register is *live* at a program point if its current value is used at some later point in the program. We refer to variables, stack locations, and registers collectively as *locations*. Consider the following code fragment in which there are two writes to b. Are variables a and b both live at the same time?

```
1   movq $5, a
2   movq $30, b
3   movq a, c
4   movq $10, b
5   addq b, c
```

The answer is no, because a is live from line 1 to 3 and b is live from line 4 to 5. The integer written to b on line 2 is never used because it is overwritten (line 4) before the next read (line 5).

The live locations for each instruction can be computed by traversing the instruction sequence back to front (i.e., backward in execution order). Let $I_1, \ldots, I_n$ be the instruction sequence. We write $L_{\text{after}}(k)$ for the set of live locations after instruction $I_k$ and write $L_{\text{before}}(k)$ for the set of live locations before instruction $I_k$. We recommend representing these sets with the Racket set data structure described in figure 3.3.

---

Example $\mathcal{L}_{\mathsf{Var}}$ program:

```
(let ([x (read)])
  (let ([y (read)])
    (+ (+ x y) 42)))
```

Generated x86 assembly:

```
start:
        callq   read_int
        movq    %rax, %rbx
        callq   read_int
        movq    %rax, %rcx
        addq    %rcx, %rbx
        movq    %rbx, %rax
        addq    $42, %rax
        jmp _conclusion

        .globl main
main:
        pushq   %rbp
        movq    %rsp, %rbp
        pushq   %rbx
        subq    $8, %rsp
        jmp start
conclusion:
        addq    $8, %rsp
        popq    %rbx
        popq    %rbp
        retq
```

---

**Figure 3.2**
An example with function calls.

---

**The Racket Set Package**

A *set* is an unordered collection of elements without duplicates. Here are some of the operations defined on sets.

(**set** *v* ... ) constructs a set containing the specified elements.

(**set-union** *set₁ set₂*) returns the union of the two sets.

(**set-subtract** *set₁ set₂*) returns the set difference of the two sets.

(**set-member?** *set v*) answers whether element *v* is in *set*.

(**set-count** *set*) returns the number of unique elements in *set*.

(**set->list** *set*) converts *set* to a list.

---

**Figure 3.3**
The set data structure.

---

The locations that are live after an instruction are its *live-after* set, and the locations that are live before an instruction are its *live-before* set. The live-after set of an instruction is always the same as the live-before of the next instruction.

$$L_{\mathsf{after}}(k) = L_{\mathsf{before}}(k+1) \tag{3.1}$$

To start things off, there are no live locations after the last instruction, so

$$L_{\text{after}}(n) = \emptyset \tag{3.2}$$

We then apply the following rule repeatedly, traversing the instruction sequence back to front.

$$L_{\texttt{before}}(k) = (L_{\texttt{after}}(k) - W(k)) \cup R(k), \tag{3.3}$$

where $W(k)$ are the locations written to by instruction $I_k$, and $R(k)$ are the locations read by instruction $I_k$.

There is a special case for `jmp` instructions. The locations that are live before a `jmp` should be the locations in $L_{\text{before}}$ at the target of the jump. So, we recommend maintaining an alist named `label->live` that maps each label to the $L_{\text{before}}$ for the first instruction in its block. For now the only `jmp` in a x86$_{\text{Var}}$ program is the jump to the conclusion. (For example, see figure 3.1.) The conclusion reads from `rax` and `rsp`, so the alist should map `conclusion` to the set $\{\texttt{rax}, \texttt{rsp}\}$.

Let us walk through the previous example, applying these formulas starting with the instruction on line 5 of the code fragment. We collect the answers in figure 3.4. The $L_{\text{after}}$ for the `addq b, c` instruction is $\emptyset$ because it is the last instruction (formula (3.2)). The $L_{\text{before}}$ for this instruction is $\{\texttt{b}, \texttt{c}\}$ because it reads from variables `b` and `c` (formula (3.3)):

$$L_{\text{before}}(5) = (\emptyset - \{\texttt{c}\}) \cup \{\texttt{b}, \texttt{c}\} = \{\texttt{b}, \texttt{c}\}$$

Moving on the the instruction `movq $10, b` at line 4, we copy the live-before set from line 5 to be the live-after set for this instruction (formula (3.1)).

$$L_{\text{after}}(4) = \{\texttt{b}, \texttt{c}\}$$

This move instruction writes to `b` and does not read from any variables, so we have the following live-before set (formula (3.3)).

$$L_{\text{before}}(4) = (\{\texttt{b}, \texttt{c}\} - \{\texttt{b}\}) \cup \emptyset = \{\texttt{c}\}$$

The live-before for instruction `movq a, c` is $\{\texttt{a}\}$ because it writes to $\{\texttt{c}\}$ and reads from $\{\texttt{a}\}$ (formula (3.3)). The live-before for `movq $30, b` is $\{\texttt{a}\}$ because it writes to a variable that is not live and does not read from a variable. Finally, the live-before for `movq $5, a` is $\emptyset$ because it writes to variable `a`.

**Exercise 3.1** Perform liveness analysis by hand on the running example in figure 3.1, computing the live-before and live-after sets for each instruction. Compare your answers to the solution shown in figure 3.5.

**Exercise 3.2** Implement the `uncover_live` pass. Store the sequence of live-after sets in the *info* field of the `Block` structure. We recommend creating an auxiliary function that takes a list of instructions and an initial live-after set (typically empty) and returns the list of live-after sets. We recommend creating auxiliary functions to (1) compute the set of locations that appear in an *arg*, (2) compute the locations read by an instruction (the $R$ function), and (3) the locations written

```
1 movq $5, a
2 movq $30, b
3 movq a, c
4 movq $10, b
5 addq b, c
```

$$L_{\mathsf{before}}(1) = \emptyset, L_{\mathsf{after}}(1) = \{\texttt{a}\}$$

$$L_{\mathsf{before}}(2) = \{\texttt{a}\}, L_{\mathsf{after}}(2) = \{\texttt{a}\}$$

$$L_{\mathsf{before}}(3) = \{\texttt{a}\}, L_{\mathsf{after}}(2) = \{\texttt{c}\}$$

$$L_{\mathsf{before}}(4) = \{\texttt{c}\}, L_{\mathsf{after}}(4) = \{\texttt{b}, \texttt{c}\}$$

$$L_{\mathsf{before}}(5) = \{\texttt{b}, \texttt{c}\}, L_{\mathsf{after}}(5) = \emptyset$$

**Figure 3.4**
Example output of liveness analysis on a short example.

```
                        {rsp}
movq $1, v
                        {v,rsp}
movq $42, w
                        {v,w,rsp}
movq v, x
                        {w,x,rsp}
addq $7, x
                        {w,x,rsp}
movq x, y
                        {w,x,y,rsp}
movq x, z
                        {w,y,z,rsp}
addq w, z
                        {y,z,rsp}
movq y, t
                        {t,z,rsp}
negq t
                        {t,z,rsp}
movq z, %rax
                        {rax,t,rsp}
addq t, %rax
                        {rax,rsp}
jmp conclusion
```

**Figure 3.5**
The running example annotated with live-after sets.

by an instruction (the $W$ function). The `callq` instruction should include all the caller-saved registers in its write set $W$ because the calling convention says that those registers may be written to during the function call. Likewise, the `callq` instruction should include the appropriate argument-passing registers in its read

---

### The Racket Graph Library

A *graph* is a collection of vertices and edges where each edge connects two vertices. A graph is *directed* if each edge points from a source to a target. Otherwise the graph is *undirected*.

(**directed-graph** *edges*) constructs a directed graph from a list of edges. Each edge is a list containing the source and target vertex.

(**undirected-graph** *edges*) constructs a undirected graph from a list of edges. Each edge is represented by a list containing two vertices.

(**add-vertex!** *graph vertex*) inserts a vertex into the graph.

(**add-edge!** *graph source target*) inserts an edge between the two vertices.

(**in-neighbors** *graph vertex*) returns a sequence of vertices adjacent to the vertex.

(**in-vertices** *graph*) returns a sequence of all vertices in the graph.

---

**Figure 3.6**
The Racket `graph` package.

set $R$, depending on the arity of the function being called. (This is why the abstract syntax for `callq` includes the arity.)

### 3.3 Build the Interference Graph

On the basis of the liveness analysis, we know where each location is live. However, during register allocation, we need to answer questions of the specific form: are locations $u$ and $v$ live at the same time? (If so, they cannot be assigned to the same register.) To make this question more efficient to answer, we create an explicit data structure, an *interference graph*. An interference graph is an undirected graph that has a node for every variable and register and has an edge between two nodes if they are live at the same time, that is, if they interfere with each other. We recommend using the Racket `graph` package (figure 3.6) to represent the interference graph.

A straightforward way to compute the interference graph is to look at the set of live locations between each instruction and add an edge to the graph for every pair of variables in the same set. This approach is less than ideal for two reasons. First, it can be expensive because it takes $O(n^2)$ time to consider every pair in a set of $n$ live locations. Second, in the special case in which two locations hold the same value (because one was assigned to the other), they can be live at the same time without interfering with each other.

A better way to compute the interference graph is to focus on writes (Appel and Palsberg 2003). The writes performed by an instruction must not overwrite something in a live location. So for each instruction, we create an edge between the locations being written to and the live locations. (However, a location never interferes with itself.) For the `callq` instruction, we consider all the caller-saved registers to have been written to, so an edge is added between every live variable and every caller-saved register. Also, for `movq` there is the special case of two variables

```
        movq $1, v          v interferes with rsp,
        movq $42, w         w interferes with v and rsp,
        movq v, x           x interferes with w and rsp,
        addq $7, x          x interferes with w and rsp,
        movq x, y           y interferes with w and rsp but not x,
        movq x, z           z interferes with w, y, and rsp,
        addq w, z           z interferes with y and rsp,
        movq y, t           t interferes with z and rsp,
        negq t              t interferes with z and rsp,
        movq z, %rax        rax interferes with t and rsp,
        addq t, %rax        rax interferes with rsp.
        jmp conclusion      no interference.
```

**Figure 3.7**
Interference results for the running example.

holding the same value. If a live variable $v$ is the same as the source of the movq, then there is no need to add an edge between $v$ and the destination, because they both hold the same value. Hence we have the following two rules:

1. If instruction $I_k$ is a move instruction of the form movq $s$, $d$, then for every $v \in L_{\text{after}}(k)$, if $v \neq d$ and $v \neq s$, add the edge $(d, v)$.
2. For any other instruction $I_k$, for every $d \in W(k)$ and every $v \in L_{\text{after}}(k)$, if $v \neq d$, add the edge $(d, v)$.

Working from the top to bottom of figure 3.5, we apply these rules to each instruction. We highlight a few of the instructions. The first instruction is movq $1, v, and the live-after set is $\{v, rsp\}$. Rule 1 applies, so v interferes with rsp. The fourth instruction is addq $7, x, and the live-after set is $\{w, x, rsp\}$. Rule 2 applies so x interferes with w and rsp. The next instruction is movq x, y, and the live-after set is $\{w, x, y, rsp\}$. Rule 1 applies, so y interferes with w and rsp but not x, because x is the source of the move and therefore x and y hold the same value. Figure 3.7 lists the interference results for all the instructions, and the resulting interference graph is shown in figure 3.8. We elide the register nodes from the interference graph in figure 3.8 because there were no interference edges involving registers and we did not wish to clutter the graph, but in general one needs to include all the registers in the interference graph.

**Exercise 3.3** Implement the compiler pass named `build_interference` according to the algorithm suggested here. We recommend using the Racket `graph` package to create and inspect the interference graph. The output graph of this pass should be stored in the *info* field of the program, under the key `conflicts`.

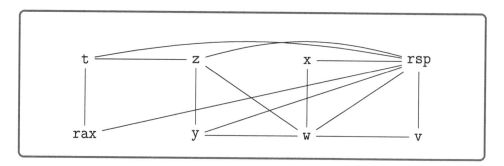

**Figure 3.8**
The interference graph of the example program.

## 3.4 Graph Coloring via Sudoku

We come to the main event discussed in this chapter, mapping variables to registers and stack locations. Variables that interfere with each other must be mapped to different locations. In terms of the interference graph, this means that adjacent vertices must be mapped to different locations. If we think of locations as colors, the register allocation problem becomes the graph coloring problem (Balakrishnan 1996; Rosen 2002).

The reader may be more familiar with the graph coloring problem than he or she realizes; the popular game of sudoku is an instance of the graph coloring problem. The following describes how to build a graph out of an initial sudoku board.

- There is one vertex in the graph for each sudoku square.
- There is an edge between two vertices if the corresponding squares are in the same row, in the same column, or in the same $3 \times 3$ region.
- Choose nine colors to correspond to the numbers 1 to 9.
- On the basis of the initial assignment of numbers to squares on the sudoku board, assign the corresponding colors to the corresponding vertices in the graph.

If you can color the remaining vertices in the graph with the nine colors, then you have also solved the corresponding game of sudoku. Figure 3.9 shows an initial sudoku game board and the corresponding graph with colored vertices. Here we use a monochrome representation of colors, mapping the sudoku number 1 to black, 2 to white, and 3 to gray. We show edges for only a sampling of the vertices (the colored ones) because showing edges for all the vertices would make the graph unreadable.

Some techniques for playing sudoku correspond to heuristics used in graph coloring algorithms. For example, one of the basic techniques for sudoku is called Pencil Marks. The idea is to use a process of elimination to determine what numbers are no longer available for a square and to write those numbers in the square (writing very small). For example, if the number 1 is assigned to a square, then write the pencil mark 1 in all the squares in the same row, column, and region to indicate that 1 is no longer an option for those other squares. The Pencil Marks technique corresponds to the notion of *saturation* due to Brélaz (1979). The saturation of a

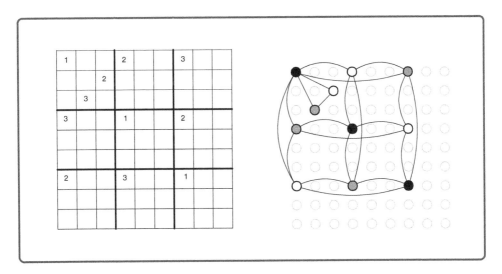

**Figure 3.9**
A sudoku game board and the corresponding colored graph.

vertex, in sudoku terms, is the set of numbers that are no longer available. In graph terminology, we have the following definition:

$$\text{saturation}(u) = \{c \mid \exists v.v \in \text{adjacent}(u) \text{ and color}(v) = c\}$$

where $\text{adjacent}(u)$ is the set of vertices that share an edge with $u$.

The Pencil Marks technique leads to a simple strategy for filling in numbers: if there is a square with only one possible number left, then choose that number! But what if there are no squares with only one possibility left? One brute-force approach is to try them all: choose the first one, and if that ultimately leads to a solution, great. If not, backtrack and choose the next possibility. One good thing about Pencil Marks is that it reduces the degree of branching in the search tree. Nevertheless, backtracking can be terribly time consuming. One way to reduce the amount of backtracking is to use the most-constrained-first heuristic (aka minimum remaining values) (Russell and Norvig 2003). That is, in choosing a square, always choose one with the fewest possibilities left (the vertex with the highest saturation). The idea is that choosing highly constrained squares earlier rather than later is better, because later on there may not be any possibilities left in the highly saturated squares.

However, register allocation is easier than sudoku, because the register allocator can fall back to assigning variables to stack locations when the registers run out. Thus, it makes sense to replace backtracking with greedy search: make the best choice at the time and keep going. We still wish to minimize the number of colors needed, so we use the most-constrained-first heuristic in the greedy search. Figure 3.10 gives the pseudocode for a simple greedy algorithm for register allocation based on saturation and the most-constrained-first heuristic. It is roughly equivalent to the DSATUR graph coloring algorithm (Brélaz 1979). Just as in sudoku, the algorithm represents colors with integers. The integers 0 through $k-1$

Algorithm: DSATUR
Input: A graph $G$
Output: An assignment color[$v$] for each vertex $v \in G$

$W \leftarrow$ vertices($G$)
**while** $W \neq \emptyset$ **do**
    pick a vertex $u$ from $W$ with the highest saturation,
        breaking ties randomly
    find the lowest color $c$ that is not in $\{$color[$v$] $: v \in$ adjacent($u$)$\}$
    color[$u$] $\leftarrow c$
    $W \leftarrow W - \{u\}$

**Figure 3.10**
The saturation-based greedy graph coloring algorithm.

correspond to the $k$ registers that we use for register allocation. In particular, we recommend the following correspondence, with $k = 11$.

   0: rcx, 1: rdx, 2: rsi, 3: rdi, 4: r8, 5: r9,
   6: r10, 7: rbx, 8: r12, 9: r13, 10: r14

The integers $k$ and larger correspond to stack locations. The registers that are not used for register allocation, such as rax, are assigned to negative integers. In particular, we recommend the following correspondence.

   -1: rax, -2: rsp, -3: rbp, -4: r11, -5: r15

With the DSATUR algorithm in hand, let us return to the running example and consider how to color the interference graph shown in figure 3.8. We start by assigning each register node to its own color. For example, rax is assigned the color −1, rsp is assign −2, rcx is assigned 0, and rdx is assigned 1. (To reduce clutter in the interference graph, we elide nodes that do not have interference edges, such as rcx.) The variables are not yet colored, so they are annotated with a dash. We then update the saturation for vertices that are adjacent to a register, obtaining the following annotated graph. For example, the saturation for t is $\{-1, -2\}$ because it interferes with both rax and rsp.

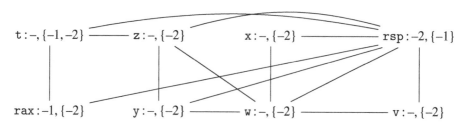

The algorithm says to select a maximally saturated vertex. So, we pick t and color it with the first available integer, which is 0. We mark 0 as no longer available for z, rax, and rsp because they interfere with t.

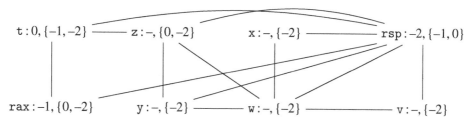

We repeat the process, selecting a maximally saturated vertex, choosing z, and coloring it with the first available number, which is 1. We add 1 to the saturation for the neighboring vertices t, y, w, and rsp.

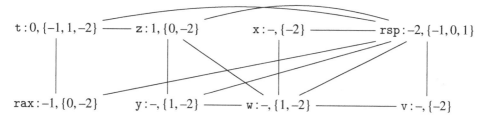

The most saturated vertices are now w and y. We color w with the first available color, which is 0.

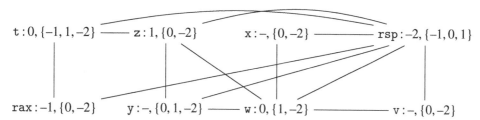

Vertex y is now the most highly saturated, so we color y with 2. We cannot choose 0 or 1 because those numbers are in y's saturation set. Indeed, y interferes with w and z, whose colors are 0 and 1 respectively.

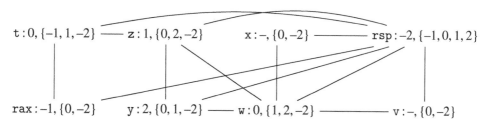

Now x and v are the most saturated, so we color v with 1.

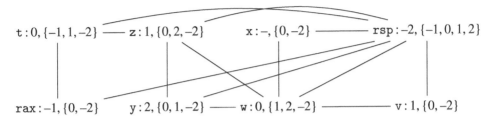

In the last step of the algorithm, we color x with 1.

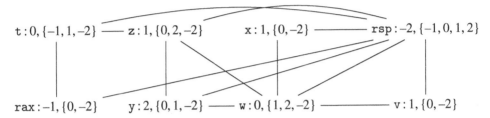

So, we obtain the following coloring:

$$\{\texttt{rax} \mapsto -1, \texttt{rsp} \mapsto -2, \texttt{t} \mapsto 0, \texttt{z} \mapsto 1, \texttt{x} \mapsto 1, \texttt{y} \mapsto 2, \texttt{w} \mapsto 0, \texttt{v} \mapsto 1\}$$

We recommend creating an auxiliary function named `color_graph` that takes an interference graph and a list of all the variables in the program. This function should return a mapping of variables to their colors (represented as natural numbers). By creating this helper function, you will be able to reuse it in chapter 7 when we add support for functions.

To prioritize the processing of highly saturated nodes inside the `color_graph` function, we recommend using the priority queue data structure described in figure 3.11. In addition, you will need to maintain a mapping from variables to their handles in the priority queue so that you can notify the priority queue when their saturation changes.

With the coloring complete, we finalize the assignment of variables to registers and stack locations. We map the first $k$ colors to the $k$ registers and the rest of the colors to stack locations. Suppose for the moment that we have just one register to use for register allocation, `rcx`. Then we have the following map from colors to locations.

$$\{0 \mapsto \texttt{\%rcx},\ 1 \mapsto \texttt{-8(\%rbp)},\ 2 \mapsto \texttt{-16(\%rbp)}\}$$

Composing this mapping with the coloring, we arrive at the following assignment of variables to locations.

$$\{\texttt{v} \mapsto \texttt{-8(\%rbp)},\ \texttt{w} \mapsto \texttt{\%rcx},\ \texttt{x} \mapsto \texttt{-8(\%rbp)},\ \texttt{y} \mapsto \texttt{-16(\%rbp)},$$

$$\texttt{z} \mapsto \texttt{-8(\%rbp)},\ \texttt{t} \mapsto \texttt{\%rcx}\}$$

---

**Priority Queue**

A *priority queue* is a collection of items in which the removal of items is governed by priority. In a *min* queue, lower priority items are removed first. An implementation is in `priority_queue.rkt` of the support code.

(`make-pqueue` *cmp*) constructs an empty priority queue that uses the *cmp* predicate to determine whether its first argument has lower or equal priority to its second argument.

(`pqueue-count` *queue*) returns the number of items in the queue.

(`pqueue-push!` *queue item*) inserts the item into the queue and returns a handle for the item in the queue.

(`pqueue-pop!` *queue*) returns the item with the lowest priority.

(`pqueue-decrease-key!` *queue handle*) notifies the queue that the priority has decreased for the item associated with the given handle.

---

**Figure 3.11**
The priority queue data structure.

Adapt the code from the `assign_homes` pass (section 2.8) to replace the variables with their assigned location. Applying this assignment to our running example shown next, on the left, yields the program on the right.

```
movq $1, v                    movq $1, -8(%rbp)
movq $42, w                   movq $42, %rcx
movq v, x                     movq -8(%rbp), -8(%rbp)
addq $7, x                    addq $7, -8(%rbp)
movq x, y                     movq -8(%rbp), -16(%rbp)
movq x, z         ⇒           movq -8(%rbp), -8(%rbp)
addq w, z                     addq %rcx, -8(%rbp)
movq y, t                     movq -16(%rbp), %rcx
negq t                        negq %rcx
movq z, %rax                  movq -8(%rbp), %rax
addq t, %rax                  addq %rcx, %rax
jmp conclusion                jmp conclusion
```

**Exercise 3.4** Implement the `allocate_registers` pass. Create five programs that exercise all aspects of the register allocation algorithm, including spilling variables to the stack. Replace `assign_homes` in the list of `passes` in the `run-tests.rkt` script with the three new passes: `uncover_live`, `build_interference`, and `allocate_registers`. Temporarily remove the call to `compiler-tests`. Run the script to test the register allocator.

## 3.5  Patch Instructions

The remaining step in the compilation to x86 is to ensure that the instructions have at most one argument that is a memory access. In the running example, the instruction `movq -8(%rbp), -16(%rbp)` is problematic. Recall from section 2.9 that the fix is to first move -8(%rbp) into rax and then move rax into -16(%rbp). The moves from -8(%rbp) to -8(%rbp) are also problematic, but they can simply be deleted. In general, we recommend deleting all the trivial moves whose source and destination are the same location. The following is the output of patch_instructions on the running example.

```
movq $1, -8(%rbp)
movq $42, %rcx
movq -8(%rbp), -8(%rbp)
addq $7, -8(%rbp)
movq -8(%rbp), -16(%rbp)
movq -8(%rbp), -8(%rbp)          ⇒
addq %rcx, -8(%rbp)
movq -16(%rbp), %rcx
negq %rcx
movq -8(%rbp), %rax
addq %rcx, %rax
jmp conclusion
```

```
movq $1, -8(%rbp)
movq $42, %rcx
addq $7, -8(%rbp)
movq -8(%rbp), %rax
movq %rax, -16(%rbp)
addq %rcx, -8(%rbp)
movq -16(%rbp), %rcx
negq %rcx
movq -8(%rbp), %rax
addq %rcx, %rax
jmp conclusion
```

**Exercise 3.5** Update the patch_instructions compiler pass to delete trivial moves. Run the script to test the patch_instructions pass.

### 3.6 Prelude and Conclusion

Recall that this pass generates the prelude and conclusion instructions to satisfy the x86 calling conventions (section 3.1). With the addition of the register allocator, the callee-saved registers used by the register allocator must be saved in the prelude and restored in the conclusion. In the allocate_registers pass, add an entry to the *info* of X86Program named used_callee that stores the set of callee-saved registers that were assigned to variables. The prelude_and_conclusion pass can then access this information to decide which callee-saved registers need to be saved and restored. When calculating the amount to adjust the rsp in the prelude, make sure to take into account the space used for saving the callee-saved registers. Also, remember that the frame needs to be a multiple of 16 bytes! We recommend using the following equation for the amount $A$ to subtract from the rsp. Let $S$ be the number of stack locations used by spilled variables[1] and $C$ be the number of callee-saved registers that were allocated to variables. The *align* function rounds a number up to the nearest 16 bytes.

$$A = align(8S + 8C) - 8C$$

The reason we subtract $8C$ in this equation is that the prelude uses pushq to save each of the callee-saved registers, and pushq subtracts 8 from the rsp.

An overview of all the passes involved in register allocation is shown in figure 3.12.

---

1. Sometimes two or more spilled variables are assigned to the same stack location, so $S$ can be less than the number of spilled variables.

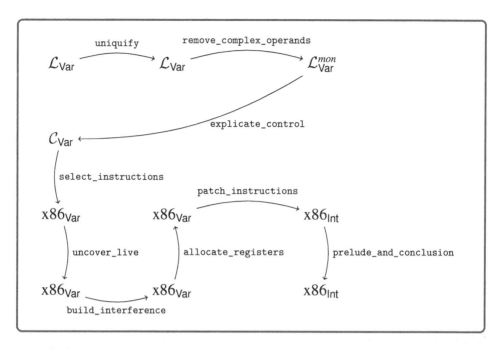

**Figure 3.12**
Diagram of the passes for $\mathcal{L}_{\text{Var}}$ with register allocation.

Figure 3.13 shows the x86 code generated for the running example (figure 3.1). To demonstrate both the use of registers and the stack, we limit the register allocator for this example to use just two registers: rcx (color 0) and rbx (color 1). In the prelude of the main function, we push rbx onto the stack because it is a callee-saved register and it was assigned to a variable by the register allocator. We subtract 8 from the rsp at the end of the prelude to reserve space for the one spilled variable. After that subtraction, the rsp is aligned to 16 bytes.

Moving on to the program proper, we see how the registers were allocated. Variables v, x, and z were assigned to rbx, and variables w and t was assigned to rcx. Variable y was spilled to the stack location -16(%rbp). Recall that the prelude saved the callee-save register rbx onto the stack. The spilled variables must be placed lower on the stack than the saved callee-save registers, so in this case y is placed at -16(%rbp).

In the conclusion, we undo the work that was done in the prelude. We move the stack pointer up by 8 bytes (the room for spilled variables), then pop the old values of rbx and rbp (callee-saved registers), and finish with retq to return control to the operating system.

**Exercise 3.6** Update the prelude_and_conclusion pass as described in this section. In the run-tests.rkt script, add prelude_and_conclusion to the list of passes and the call to compiler-tests. Run the script to test the complete compiler for $\mathcal{L}_{\text{Var}}$ that performs register allocation.

```
start:
        movq    $1, %rbx
        movq    $42, %rcx
        addq    $7, %rbx
        movq    %rbx, -16(%rbp)
        addq    %rcx, %rbx
        movq    -16(%rbp), %rcx
        negq    %rcx
        movq    %rbx, %rax
        addq    %rcx, %rax
        jmp conclusion

        .globl main
main:
        pushq   %rbp
        movq    %rsp, %rbp
        pushq   %rbx
        subq    $8, %rsp
        jmp start

conclusion:
        addq    $8, %rsp
        popq    %rbx
        popq    %rbp
        retq
```

**Figure 3.13**
The x86 output from the running example (figure 3.1), limiting allocation to just rbx and rcx.

## 3.7 Challenge: Move Biasing

This section describes an enhancement to the register allocator, called move biasing, for students who are looking for an extra challenge.

To motivate the need for move biasing we return to the running example, but this time we use all the general purpose registers. So, we have the following mapping of color numbers to registers.

$$\{0 \mapsto \%\text{rcx}, 1 \mapsto \%\text{rdx}, 2 \mapsto \%\text{rsi}, \dots \}$$

Using the same assignment of variables to color numbers that was produced by the register allocator described in the last section, we get the following program.

```
movq $1, v              movq $1, %rdx
movq $42, w             movq $42, %rcx
movq v, x               movq %rdx, %rdx
addq $7, x              addq $7, %rdx
movq x, y               movq %rdx, %rsi
movq x, z          ⇒    movq %rdx, %rdx
addq w, z               addq %rcx, %rdx
movq y, t               movq %rsi, %rcx
negq t                  negq %rcx
movq z, %rax            movq %rdx, %rax
addq t, %rax            addq %rcx, %rax
jmp conclusion          jmp conclusion
```

In this output code there are two `movq` instructions that can be removed because their source and target are the same. However, if we had put t, v, x, and y into the same register, we could instead remove three `movq` instructions. We can accomplish this by taking into account which variables appear in `movq` instructions with which other variables.

We say that two variables $p$ and $q$ are *move related* if they participate together in a `movq` instruction, that is, `movq` $p$, $q$ or `movq` $q$, $p$. Recall that we color variables that are more saturated before coloring variables that are less saturated, and in the case of equally saturated variables, we choose randomly. Now we break such ties by giving preference to variables that have an available color that is the same as the color of a move-related variable. Furthermore, when the register allocator chooses a color for a variable, it should prefer a color that has already been used for a move-related variable if one exists (and assuming that they do not interfere). This preference should not override the preference for registers over stack locations. So, this preference should be used as a tie breaker in choosing between two registers or in choosing between two stack locations.

We recommend representing the move relationships in a graph, similarly to how we represented interference. The following is the *move graph* for our running example.

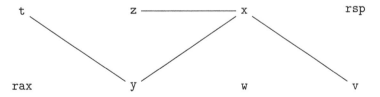

Now we replay the graph coloring, pausing to see the coloring of y. Recall the following configuration. The most saturated vertices were w and y.

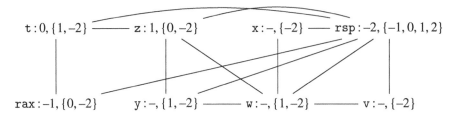

The last time, we chose to color w with 0. This time, we see that w is not move-related to any vertex, but y is move-related to t. So we choose to color y with 0, the same color as t.

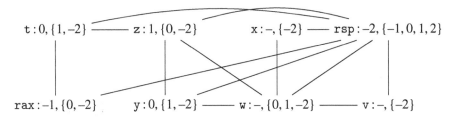

Now w is the most saturated, so we color it 2.

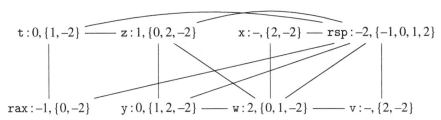

At this point, vertices x and v are most saturated, but x is move related to y and z, so we color x to 0 to match y. Finally, we color v to 0.

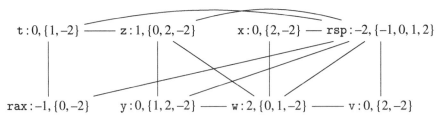

So, we have the following assignment of variables to registers.

$$\{v \mapsto \%\text{rcx}, w \mapsto \%\text{rsi}, x \mapsto \%\text{rcx}, y \mapsto \%\text{rcx}, z \mapsto \%\text{rdx}, t \mapsto \%\text{rcx}\}$$

We apply this register assignment to the running example shown next, on the left, to obtain the code in the middle. The patch_instructions then deletes the trivial moves to obtain the code on the right.

```
movq $1, v              movq $1, %rcx
movq $42, w             movq $42, %rsi              movq $1, %rcx
movq v, x               movq %rcx, %rcx             movq $42, %rsi
addq $7, x              addq $7, %rcx               addq $7, %rcx
movq x, y               movq %rcx, %rcx             movq %rcx, %rdx
movq x, z               movq %rcx, %rdx             addq %rsi, %rdx
addq w, z      ⇒        addq %rsi, %rdx    ⇒        negq %rcx
movq y, t               movq %rcx, %rcx             movq %rdx, %rax
negq t                  negq %rcx                   addq %rcx, %rax
movq z, %rax            movq %rdx, %rax             jmp conclusion
addq t, %rax            addq %rcx, %rax
jmp conclusion          jmp conclusion
```

**Exercise 3.7** Change your implementation of `allocate_registers` to take move biasing into account. Create two new tests that include at least one opportunity for move biasing, and visually inspect the output x86 programs to make sure that your move biasing is working properly. Make sure that your compiler still passes all the tests.

## 3.8 Further Reading

Early register allocation algorithms were developed for Fortran compilers in the 1950s (Horwitz et al. 1966; Backus 1978). The use of graph coloring began in the late 1970s and early 1980s with the work of Chaitin et al. (1981) on an optimizing compiler for PL/I. The algorithm is based on the following observation of Kempe (1879). If a graph $G$ has a vertex $v$ with degree lower than $k$, then $G$ is $k$ colorable if the subgraph of $G$ with $v$ removed is also $k$ colorable. To see why, suppose that the subgraph is $k$ colorable. At worst, the neighbors of $v$ are assigned different colors, but because there are fewer than $k$ neighbors, there will be one or more colors left over to use for coloring $v$ in $G$.

The algorithm of Chaitin et al. (1981) removes a vertex $v$ of degree less than $k$ from the graph and recursively colors the rest of the graph. Upon returning from the recursion, it colors $v$ with one of the available colors and returns. Chaitin (1982) augments this algorithm to handle spilling as follows. If there are no vertices of degree lower than $k$ then pick a vertex at random, spill it, remove it from the graph, and proceed recursively to color the rest of the graph.

Prior to coloring, Chaitin et al. (1981) merged variables that are move-related and that don't interfere with each other, in a process called *coalescing*. Although coalescing decreases the number of moves, it can make the graph more difficult to color. Briggs, Cooper, and Torczon (1994) proposed *conservative coalescing* in which two variables are merged only if they have fewer than $k$ neighbors of high degree. George and Appel (1996) observes that conservative coalescing is sometimes too conservative and made it more aggressive by iterating the coalescing with the removal of low-degree vertices. Attacking the problem from a different angle, Briggs, Cooper, and Torczon (1994) also proposed *biased coloring*, in which a variable is assigned to the same color as another move-related variable if possible, as discussed in section 3.7. The algorithm of Chaitin et al. (1981) and its successors iteratively performs coalescing, graph coloring, and spill code insertion until all variables have been assigned a location.

Briggs, Cooper, and Torczon (1994) observes that Chaitin (1982) sometimes spilled variables that don't have to be: a high-degree variable can be colorable if many of its neighbors are assigned the same color. Briggs, Cooper, and Torczon (1994) proposed *optimistic coloring*, in which a high-degree vertex is not immediately spilled. Instead the decision is deferred until after the recursive call, at which point it is apparent whether there is actually an available color or not. We observe that this algorithm is equivalent to the smallest-last ordering algorithm (Matula, Marble, and Isaacson 1972) if one takes the first $k$ colors to be registers and the rest to be stack locations. Earlier editions of the compiler course at Indiana University (Dybvig and Keep 2010) were based on the algorithm of Briggs, Cooper, and Torczon (1994).

The smallest-last ordering algorithm is one of many *greedy* coloring algorithms. A greedy coloring algorithm visits all the vertices in a particular order and assigns each one the first available color. An *offline* greedy algorithm chooses the ordering up front, prior to assigning colors. The algorithm of Chaitin et al. (1981) should be considered offline because the vertex ordering does not depend on the colors assigned. Other orderings are possible. For example, Chow and Hennessy (1984) ordered variables according to an estimate of runtime cost.

An *online* greedy coloring algorithm uses information about the current assignment of colors to influence the order in which the remaining vertices are colored. The saturation-based algorithm described in this chapter is one such algorithm. We choose to use saturation-based coloring because it is fun to introduce graph coloring via sudoku!

A register allocator may choose to map each variable to just one location, as in Chaitin et al. (1981), or it may choose to map a variable to one or more locations. The latter can be achieved by *live range splitting*, where a variable is replaced by several variables that each handle part of its live range (Chow and Hennessy 1984; Briggs, Cooper, and Torczon 1994; Cooper and Simpson 1998).

Palsberg (2007) observes that many of the interference graphs that arise from Java programs in the JoeQ compiler are *chordal*; that is, every cycle with four or more edges has an edge that is not part of the cycle but that connects two vertices on the cycle. Such graphs can be optimally colored by the greedy algorithm with a vertex ordering determined by maximum cardinality search.

In situations in which compile time is of utmost importance, such as in just-in-time compilers, graph coloring algorithms can be too expensive, and the linear scan algorithm of Poletto and Sarkar (1999) may be more appropriate.

# 4 Booleans and Conditionals

The $\mathcal{L}_{\text{Var}}$ language has only a single kind of value, the integers. In this chapter we add a second kind of value, the Booleans, to create the $\mathcal{L}_{\text{If}}$ language. In Racket, the Boolean values *true* and *false* are written #t and #f, respectively. The $\mathcal{L}_{\text{If}}$ language includes several operations that involve Booleans (and, or, not, eq?, <, etc.) and the if conditional expression . With the addition of if, programs can have nontrivial control flow which impacts explicate_control and liveness analysis. Also, because we now have two kinds of values, we need to handle programs that apply an operation to the wrong kind of value, such as (not 1).

There are two language design options for such situations. One option is to signal an error and the other is to provide a wider interpretation of the operation. The Racket language uses a mixture of these two options, depending on the operation and the kind of value. For example, the result of (not 1) is #f because Racket treats nonzero integers as if they were #t. On the other hand, (car 1) results in a runtime error in Racket because car expects a pair.

Typed Racket makes similar design choices as Racket, except that much of the error detection happens at compile time instead of runtime. Typed Racket accepts (not 1). But in the case of (car 1), Typed Racket reports a compile-time error because Racket expects the type of the argument to be of the form (Listof T) or (Pairof T1 T2).

The $\mathcal{L}_{\text{If}}$ language performs type checking during compilation just as Typed Racket. In chapter 9 we study the alternative choice, that is, a dynamically typed language like Racket. The $\mathcal{L}_{\text{If}}$ language is a subset of Typed Racket; for some operations we are more restrictive, for example, rejecting (not 1). We keep the type checker for $\mathcal{L}_{\text{If}}$ fairly simple because the focus of this book is on compilation and not type systems, about which there are already several excellent books (Pierce 2002, 2004; Harper 2016; Pierce et al. 2018).

This chapter is organized as follows. We begin by defining the syntax and interpreter for the $\mathcal{L}_{\text{If}}$ language (section 4.1). We then introduce the idea of type checking (aka semantic analysis) and define a type checker for $\mathcal{L}_{\text{If}}$ (section 4.2). To compile $\mathcal{L}_{\text{If}}$ we need to enlarge the intermediate language $\mathcal{C}_{\text{Var}}$ into $\mathcal{C}_{\text{If}}$ (section 4.3) and x86$_{\text{Int}}$ into x86$_{\text{If}}$ (section 4.4). The remaining sections of this chapter discuss how Booleans and conditional control flow require changes to the existing compiler passes and the addition of new ones. We introduce the shrink pass to translate some operators into others, thereby reducing the number of operators that need to be handled in

$$
\begin{array}{lcl}
\textit{type} & ::= & \texttt{Integer} \\
\textit{exp} & ::= & \textit{int} \mid (\texttt{read}) \mid (\text{-} \; \textit{exp}) \mid (\text{+} \; \textit{exp} \; \textit{exp}) \mid (\text{-} \; \textit{exp} \; \textit{exp}) \\
\textit{exp} & ::= & \textit{var} \mid (\texttt{let} \; ([\textit{var} \; \textit{exp}]) \; \textit{exp}) \\
\textit{type} & ::= & \texttt{Boolean} \\
\textit{bool} & ::= & \texttt{\#t} \mid \texttt{\#f} \\
\textit{cmp} & ::= & \texttt{eq?} \mid \texttt{<} \mid \texttt{<=} \mid \texttt{>} \mid \texttt{>=} \\
\textit{exp} & ::= & \textit{bool} \mid (\texttt{and} \; \textit{exp} \; \textit{exp}) \mid (\texttt{or} \; \textit{exp} \; \textit{exp}) \mid (\texttt{not} \; \textit{exp}) \\
 & \mid & (\textit{cmp} \; \textit{exp} \; \textit{exp}) \mid (\texttt{if} \; \textit{exp} \; \textit{exp} \; \textit{exp}) \\
\mathcal{L}_{\mathsf{If}} & ::= & \textit{exp}
\end{array}
$$

**Figure 4.1**
The concrete syntax of $\mathcal{L}_{\mathsf{If}}$, extending $\mathcal{L}_{\mathsf{Var}}$ (figure 2.1) with Booleans and conditionals.

later passes. The main event of this chapter is the `explicate_control` pass that is responsible for translating `if`s into conditional `goto`s (section 4.8). Regarding register allocation, there is the interesting question of how to handle conditional `goto`s during liveness analysis.

### 4.1   The $\mathcal{L}_{\mathsf{If}}$ Language

Definitions of the concrete syntax and abstract syntax of the $\mathcal{L}_{\mathsf{If}}$ language are shown in figures 4.1 and 4.2, respectively. The $\mathcal{L}_{\mathsf{If}}$ language includes all of $\mathcal{L}_{\mathsf{Var}}$ (shown in gray), the Boolean literals `#t` and `#f`, and the `if` expression. We expand the set of operators to include

1. the logical operators **and**, **or**, and **not**,
2. the `eq?` operation for comparing integers or Booleans for equality, and
3. the `<`, `<=`, `>`, and `>=` operations for comparing integers.

We reorganize the abstract syntax for the primitive operations given in figure 4.2, using only one grammar rule for all of them. This means that the grammar no longer checks whether the arity of an operator matches the number of arguments. That responsibility is moved to the type checker for $\mathcal{L}_{\mathsf{If}}$ (section 4.2).

Figure 4.3 shows the definition of the interpreter for $\mathcal{L}_{\mathsf{If}}$, which inherits from the interpreter for $\mathcal{L}_{\mathsf{Var}}$ (figure 2.4). The literals `#t` and `#f` evaluate to the corresponding Boolean values. The conditional expression (`if` $e_1$ $e_2$ $e_3$) evaluates expression $e_1$ and then either evaluates $e_2$ or $e_3$, depending on whether $e_1$ produced `#t` or `#f`. The logical operations **and**, **or**, and **not** behave according to propositional logic. In addition, the **and** and **or** operations perform *short-circuit evaluation*. That is, given the expression (`and` $e_1$ $e_2$), the expression $e_2$ is not evaluated if $e_1$ evaluates to `#f`. Similarly, given (`or` $e_1$ $e_2$), the expression $e_2$ is not evaluated if $e_1$ evaluates to `#t`.

With the increase in the number of primitive operations, the interpreter would become repetitive without some care. We refactor the case for `Prim`, moving the code that differs with each operation into the `interp_op` method shown in figure 4.4.

$$
\begin{array}{rcl}
\textit{type} & ::= & \texttt{Integer} \\
\textit{op} & ::= & \texttt{read} \mid \texttt{+} \mid \texttt{-} \\
\textit{exp} & ::= & (\texttt{Int}~\textit{int}) \mid (\texttt{Prim}~\textit{op}~(\textit{exp}\dots)) \\
\hline
\textit{exp} & ::= & (\texttt{Var}~\textit{var}) \mid (\texttt{Let}~\textit{var}~\textit{exp}~\textit{exp}) \\
\hline
\textit{type} & ::= & \texttt{Boolean} \\
\textit{bool} & ::= & \texttt{\#t} \mid \texttt{\#f} \\
\textit{cmp} & ::= & \texttt{eq?} \mid \texttt{<} \mid \texttt{<=} \mid \texttt{>} \mid \texttt{>=} \\
\textit{op} & ::= & \textit{cmp} \mid \texttt{and} \mid \texttt{or} \mid \texttt{not} \\
\textit{exp} & ::= & (\texttt{Bool}~\textit{bool}) \mid (\texttt{If}~\textit{exp}~\textit{exp}~\textit{exp}) \\
\mathcal{L}_{\textsf{If}} & ::= & (\texttt{Program '()}~\textit{exp})
\end{array}
$$

**Figure 4.2**
The abstract syntax of $\mathcal{L}_{\textsf{If}}$.

We handle the **and** and **or** operations separately because of their short-circuiting behavior.

### 4.2  Type Checking $\mathcal{L}_{\textsf{If}}$ Programs

It is helpful to think about type checking in two complementary ways. A type checker predicts the type of value that will be produced by each expression in the program. For $\mathcal{L}_{\textsf{If}}$, we have just two types, `Integer` and `Boolean`. So, a type checker should predict that

```
(+ 10 (- (+ 12 20)))
```

produces a value of type `Integer`, whereas

```
(and (not #f) #t)
```

produces a value of type `Boolean`.

A second way to think about type checking is that it enforces a set of rules about which operators can be applied to which kinds of values. For example, our type checker for $\mathcal{L}_{\textsf{If}}$ signals an error for the following expression:

```
(not (+ 10 (- (+ 12 20))))
```

The subexpression `(+ 10 (- (+ 12 20)))` has type `Integer`, but the type checker enforces the rule that the argument of **not** must be an expression of type `Boolean`.

We implement type checking using classes and methods because they provide the open recursion needed to reuse code as we extend the type checker in subsequent chapters, analogous to the use of classes and methods for the interpreters (section 2.1.1).

We separate the type checker for the $\mathcal{L}_{\textsf{Var}}$ subset into its own class, shown in figure 4.5. The type checker for $\mathcal{L}_{\textsf{If}}$ is shown in figure 4.6, and it inherits from the type checker for $\mathcal{L}_{\textsf{Var}}$. These type checkers are in the files **type-check-Lvar.rkt**

```
(define interp-Lif-class
  (class interp-Lvar-class
    (super-new)

    (define/public (interp_op op) ...)

    (define/override ((interp_exp env) e)
      (define recur (interp_exp env))
      (match e
        [(Bool b) b]
        [(If cnd thn els)
         (match (recur cnd)
           [#t (recur thn)]
           [#f (recur els)])]
        [(Prim 'and (list e1 e2))
         (match (recur e1)
           [#t (match (recur e2) [#t #t] [#f #f])]
           [#f #f])]
        [(Prim 'or (list e1 e2))
         (define v1 (recur e1))
         (match v1
           [#t #t]
           [#f (match (recur e2) [#t #t] [#f #f])])]
        [(Prim op args)
         (apply (interp_op op) (for/list ([e args]) (recur e)))]
        [else ((super interp_exp env) e)]))
  ))

  (define (interp_Lif p)
    (send (new interp-Lif-class) interp_program p))
```

**Figure 4.3**
Interpreter for the $\mathcal{L}_{\text{If}}$ language. (See figure 4.4 for interp-op.)

and `type-check-Lif.rkt` of the support code. Each type checker is a structurally recursive function over the AST. Given an input expression e, the type checker either signals an error or returns an expression and its type. It returns an expression because there are situations in which we want to change or update the expression.

Next we discuss the `type_check_exp` function of $\mathcal{L}_{\text{Var}}$ shown in figure 4.5. The type of an integer constant is `Integer`. To handle variables, the type checker uses the environment env to map variables to types. Consider the case for `let`. We type check the initializing expression to obtain its type T and then associate type T with the variable x in the environment used to type check the body of the `let`. Thus, when the type checker encounters a use of variable x, it can find its type in the environment. Regarding primitive operators, we recursively analyze the arguments and then invoke `type_check_op` to check whether the argument types are allowed.

```
(define/public (interp_op op)
  (match op
    ['+ fx+]
    ['- fx-]
    ['read read-fixnum]
    ['not (lambda (v) (match v [#t #f] [#f #t]))]
    ['eq? (lambda (v1 v2)
            (cond [(or (and (fixnum? v1) (fixnum? v2))
                       (and (boolean? v1) (boolean? v2))
                       (and (vector? v1) (vector? v2)))
                   (eq? v1 v2)]))]
    ['< (lambda (v1 v2)
          (cond [(and (fixnum? v1) (fixnum? v2))
                 (< v1 v2)]))]
    ['<= (lambda (v1 v2)
           (cond [(and (fixnum? v1) (fixnum? v2))
                  (<= v1 v2)]))]
    ['> (lambda (v1 v2)
          (cond [(and (fixnum? v1) (fixnum? v2))
                 (> v1 v2)]))]
    ['>= (lambda (v1 v2)
           (cond [(and (fixnum? v1) (fixnum? v2))
                  (>= v1 v2)]))]
    [else (error 'interp_op "unknown operator")]))
```

**Figure 4.4**
Interpreter for the primitive operators in the $\mathcal{L}_{\mathsf{If}}$ language.

Several auxiliary methods are used in the type checker. The method
`operator-types` defines a dictionary that maps the operator names to their
parameter and return types. The `type-equal?` method determines whether two
types are equal, which for now simply dispatches to `equal?` (deep equality). The
`check-type-equal?` method triggers an error if the two types are not equal. The
`type-check-op` method looks up the operator in the `operator-types` dictionary
and then checks whether the argument types are equal to the parameter types. The
result is the return type of the operator.

The definition of the type checker for $\mathcal{L}_{\mathsf{If}}$ is shown in figure 4.6. The type of a
Boolean constant is `Boolean`. The `operator-types` function adds dictionary entries
for the new operators. The equality operator requires the two arguments to have
the same type, and therefore we handle it separately from the other operators. The
condition of an `if` must be of `Boolean` type, and the two branches must have the
same type.

**Exercise 4.1** Create ten new test programs in $\mathcal{L}_{\mathsf{If}}$. Half the programs should have a
type error. For those programs, create an empty file with the same base name and
with file extension `.tyerr`. For example, if the test `cond_test_14.rkt` is expected

```
(define type-check-Lvar-class
  (class object%
    (super-new)

    (define/public (operator-types)
      '((+ . ((Integer Integer) . Integer))
        (- . ((Integer Integer) . Integer))
        (read . (() . Integer))))

    (define/public (type-equal? t1 t2) (equal? t1 t2))

    (define/public (check-type-equal? t1 t2 e)
      (unless (type-equal? t1 t2)
        (error 'type-check "~a != ~a\nin ~v" t1 t2 e)))

    (define/public (type-check-op op arg-types e)
      (match (dict-ref (operator-types) op)
        [`(,param-types . ,return-type)
         (for ([at arg-types] [pt param-types])
           (check-type-equal? at pt e))
         return-type]
        [else (error 'type-check-op "unrecognized ~a" op)]))

    (define/public (type-check-exp env)
      (lambda (e)
        (match e
          [(Int n) (values (Int n) 'Integer)]
          [(Var x) (values (Var x) (dict-ref env x))]
          [(Let x e body)
           (define-values (e^ Te) ((type-check-exp env) e))
           (define-values (b Tb) ((type-check-exp (dict-set env x Te)) body))
           (values (Let x e^ b) Tb)]
          [(Prim op es)
           (define-values (new-es ts)
             (for/lists (exprs types) ([e es]) ((type-check-exp env) e)))
           (values (Prim op new-es) (type-check-op op ts e))]
          [else (error 'type-check-exp "couldn't match" e)])))

    (define/public (type-check-program e)
      (match e
        [(Program info body)
         (define-values (body^ Tb) ((type-check-exp '()) body))
         (check-type-equal? Tb 'Integer body)
         (Program info body^)]
        [else (error 'type-check-Lvar "couldn't match ~a" e)]))
    ))

(define (type-check-Lvar p)
  (send (new type-check-Lvar-class) type-check-program p))
```

**Figure 4.5**
Type checker for the $\mathcal{L}_{\mathsf{Var}}$ language.

```
(define type-check-Lif-class
  (class type-check-Lvar-class
    (super-new)
    (inherit check-type-equal?)

    (define/override (operator-types)
      (append '((and . ((Boolean Boolean) . Boolean))
                (or . ((Boolean Boolean) . Boolean))
                (< . ((Integer Integer) . Boolean))
                (<= . ((Integer Integer) . Boolean))
                (> . ((Integer Integer) . Boolean))
                (>= . ((Integer Integer) . Boolean))
                (not . ((Boolean) . Boolean)))
              (super operator-types)))

    (define/override (type-check-exp env)
      (lambda (e)
        (match e
          [(Bool b) (values (Bool b) 'Boolean)]
          [(Prim 'eq? (list e1 e2))
           (define-values (e1^ T1) ((type-check-exp env) e1))
           (define-values (e2^ T2) ((type-check-exp env) e2))
           (check-type-equal? T1 T2 e)
           (values (Prim 'eq? (list e1^ e2^)) 'Boolean)]
          [(If cnd thn els)
           (define-values (cnd^ Tc) ((type-check-exp env) cnd))
           (define-values (thn^ Tt) ((type-check-exp env) thn))
           (define-values (els^ Te) ((type-check-exp env) els))
           (check-type-equal? Tc 'Boolean e)
           (check-type-equal? Tt Te e)
           (values (If cnd^ thn^ els^) Te)]
          [else ((super type-check-exp env) e)])))
    ))

(define (type-check-Lif p)
  (send (new type-check-Lif-class) type-check-program p))
```

**Figure 4.6**
Type checker for the $\mathcal{L}_{If}$ language.

to error, then create an empty file named `cond_test_14.tyerr`. This indicates to `interp-tests` and `compiler-tests` that a type error is expected. The other half of the test programs should not have type errors. In the `run-tests.rkt` script, change the second argument of `interp-tests` and `compiler-tests` to `type-check-Lif`, which causes the type checker to run prior to the compiler passes. Temporarily change the `passes` to an empty list and run the script, thereby checking that the new test programs either type check or do not, as intended. Run the test script to check that these test programs type check as expected.

$$
\begin{array}{lll}
atm & ::= & int \mid var \\
exp & ::= & atm \mid (\text{read}) \mid (- \ atm) \mid (+ \ atm \ atm) \mid (- \ atm \ atm) \\
stmt & ::= & var = exp; \\
tail & ::= & \text{return } exp; \mid stmt \ tail \\
\hline
atm & ::= & bool \\
cmp & ::= & \text{eq?} \mid < \mid <= \mid > \mid >= \\
exp & ::= & (\text{not } atm) \mid (cmp \ atm \ atm) \\
tail & ::= & \text{goto } label; \\
 & \mid & \text{if } (cmp \ atm \ atm) \text{ goto } label; \text{ else goto } label; \\
\mathcal{C}_{\text{If}} & ::= & (label: tail) \dots
\end{array}
$$

**Figure 4.7**
The concrete syntax of the $\mathcal{C}_{\text{If}}$ intermediate language, an extension of $\mathcal{C}_{\text{Var}}$ (figure 2.12).

$$
\begin{array}{lll}
atm & ::= & (\text{Int } int) \mid (\text{Var } var) \\
exp & ::= & atm \mid (\text{Prim 'read ()}) \mid (\text{Prim '- } (atm)) \\
 & \mid & (\text{Prim '+ } (atm \ atm)) \mid (\text{Prim '- } (atm \ atm)) \\
stmt & ::= & (\text{Assign (Var } var) \ exp) \\
tail & ::= & (\text{Return } exp) \mid (\text{Seq } stmt \ tail) \\
\hline
atm & ::= & (\text{Bool } bool) \\
cmp & ::= & \text{eq?} \mid < \mid <= \mid > \mid >= \\
exp & ::= & (\text{Prim 'not } (atm)) \mid (\text{Prim '}cmp \ (atm \ atm)) \\
tail & ::= & (\text{Goto } label) \\
 & \mid & (\text{IfStmt (Prim } cmp \ (atm \ atm)) \ (\text{Goto } label) \ (\text{Goto } label)) \\
\mathcal{C}_{\text{If}} & ::= & (\text{CProgram } info \ ((label . tail) \dots))
\end{array}
$$

**Figure 4.8**
The abstract syntax of $\mathcal{C}_{\text{If}}$, an extension of $\mathcal{C}_{\text{Var}}$ (figure 2.13).

## 4.3 The $\mathcal{C}_{\text{If}}$ Intermediate Language

The $\mathcal{C}_{\text{If}}$ language builds on $\mathcal{C}_{\text{Var}}$ by adding logical and comparison operators to the *exp* nonterminal and the literals #t and #f to the *arg* nonterminal. Regarding control flow, $\mathcal{C}_{\text{If}}$ adds goto and if statements to the *tail* nonterminal. The condition of an if statement is a comparison operation and the branches are goto statements, making it straightforward to compile if statements to x86. The CProgram construct contains an alist mapping labels to *tail* expressions. A goto statement transfers control to the *tail* expression corresponding to its label. Figure 4.7 defines the concrete syntax of the $\mathcal{C}_{\text{If}}$ intermediate language, and figure 4.8 defines its abstract syntax.

## 4.4 The x86$_{\text{If}}$ Language

To implement the new logical operations, the comparison operations, and the if expression, we delve further into the x86 language. Figures 4.9 and 4.10 present the

$$
\begin{array}{rcl}
reg & ::= & \texttt{rsp} \mid \texttt{rbp} \mid \texttt{rax} \mid \texttt{rbx} \mid \texttt{rcx} \mid \texttt{rdx} \mid \texttt{rsi} \mid \texttt{rdi} \mid \\
& & \texttt{r8} \mid \texttt{r9} \mid \texttt{r10} \mid \texttt{r11} \mid \texttt{r12} \mid \texttt{r13} \mid \texttt{r14} \mid \texttt{r15} \\
arg & ::= & \texttt{\$}\mathit{int} \mid \texttt{\%}\mathit{reg} \mid \mathit{int}\,(\texttt{\%}\mathit{reg}) \\
instr & ::= & \texttt{addq}\,\mathit{arg},\mathit{arg} \mid \texttt{subq}\,\mathit{arg},\mathit{arg} \mid \texttt{negq}\,\mathit{arg} \mid \texttt{movq}\,\mathit{arg},\mathit{arg} \mid \\
& & \texttt{pushq}\,\mathit{arg} \mid \texttt{popq}\,\mathit{arg} \mid \texttt{callq}\,\mathit{label} \mid \texttt{retq} \mid \texttt{jmp}\,\mathit{label} \mid \\
& & \mathit{label}\colon instr
\end{array}
$$

$$
\begin{array}{rcl}
bytereg & ::= & \texttt{ah} \mid \texttt{al} \mid \texttt{bh} \mid \texttt{bl} \mid \texttt{ch} \mid \texttt{cl} \mid \texttt{dh} \mid \texttt{dl} \\
arg & ::= & \texttt{\%}\mathit{bytereg} \\
cc & ::= & \texttt{e} \mid \texttt{ne} \mid \texttt{l} \mid \texttt{le} \mid \texttt{g} \mid \texttt{ge} \\
instr & ::= & \texttt{xorq}\ \mathit{arg},\ \mathit{arg} \mid \texttt{cmpq}\ \mathit{arg},\ \mathit{arg} \mid \texttt{set}cc\ \mathit{arg} \mid \texttt{movzbq}\ \mathit{arg},\ \mathit{arg} \\
& \mid & \texttt{jcc}\ \mathit{label} \\
\text{x86}_{\mathsf{If}} & ::= & \texttt{.globl main} \\
& & \texttt{main:}\ instr \ldots
\end{array}
$$

**Figure 4.9**
The concrete syntax of x86$_{\mathsf{If}}$ (extends x86$_{\mathsf{Int}}$ of figure 2.6).

definitions of the concrete and abstract syntax for the x86$_{\mathsf{If}}$ subset of x86, which includes instructions for logical operations, comparisons, and conditional jumps.

One challenge is that x86 does not provide an instruction that directly implements logical negation (**not** in $\mathcal{L}_{\mathsf{If}}$ and $\mathcal{C}_{\mathsf{If}}$). However, the **xorq** instruction can be used to encode **not**. The **xorq** instruction takes two arguments, performs a pairwise exclusive-or (**XOR**) operation on each bit of its arguments, and writes the results into its second argument. Recall the following truth table for exclusive-or:

|     | 0 | 1 |
| --- | --- | --- |
| 0 | 0 | 1 |
| 1 | 1 | 0 |

For example, applying **XOR** to each bit of the binary numbers 0011 and 0101 yields 0110. Notice that in the row of the table for the bit 1, the result is the opposite of the second bit. Thus, the **not** operation can be implemented by **xorq** with 1 as the first argument, as follows, where *arg* is the translation of *atm* to x86:

$$
var = (\texttt{not}\ atm);\qquad \Rightarrow\qquad
\begin{array}{l}
\texttt{movq}\ arg,var \\
\texttt{xorq}\ \texttt{\$1},var
\end{array}
$$

Next we consider the x86 instructions that are relevant for compiling the comparison operations. The **cmpq** instruction compares its two arguments to determine whether one argument is less than, equal to, or greater than the other argument. The **cmpq** instruction is unusual regarding the order of its arguments and where the result is placed. The argument order is backward: if you want to test whether $x < y$, then write **cmpq** $y$, $x$. The result of **cmpq** is placed in the special EFLAGS register. This register cannot be accessed directly, but it can be queried by a number of instructions, including the **set** instruction. The instruction **set**$cc\ d$ puts a

$$
\begin{array}{lcl}
reg & ::= & \texttt{rsp} \mid \texttt{rbp} \mid \texttt{rax} \mid \texttt{rbx} \mid \texttt{rcx} \mid \texttt{rdx} \mid \texttt{rsi} \mid \texttt{rdi} \mid \\
& & \texttt{r8} \mid \texttt{r9} \mid \texttt{r10} \mid \texttt{r11} \mid \texttt{r12} \mid \texttt{r13} \mid \texttt{r14} \mid \texttt{r15} \\
arg & ::= & (\texttt{Imm}\ int) \mid (\texttt{Reg}\ reg) \mid (\texttt{Deref}\ reg\ int) \\
instr & ::= & (\texttt{Instr addq}\ (arg\ arg)) \mid (\texttt{Instr subq}\ (arg\ arg)) \\
& \mid & (\texttt{Instr negq}\ (arg)) \mid (\texttt{Instr movq}\ (arg\ arg)) \\
& \mid & (\texttt{Instr pushq}\ (arg)) \mid (\texttt{Instr popq}\ (arg)) \\
& \mid & (\texttt{Callq}\ label\ int) \mid (\texttt{Retq}) \mid (\texttt{Jmp}\ label) \\
block & ::= & (\texttt{Block}\ info\ (instr \dots)) \\
\hline
bytereg & ::= & \texttt{ah} \mid \texttt{al} \mid \texttt{bh} \mid \texttt{bl} \mid \texttt{ch} \mid \texttt{cl} \mid \texttt{dh} \mid \texttt{dl} \\
arg & ::= & (\texttt{ByteReg}\ bytereg) \\
cc & ::= & \texttt{e} \mid \texttt{l} \mid \texttt{le} \mid \texttt{g} \mid \texttt{ge} \\
instr & ::= & (\texttt{Instr xorq}\ (arg\ arg)) \mid (\texttt{Instr cmpq}\ (arg\ arg)) \\
& \mid & (\texttt{Instr set}\ (cc\ arg)) \mid (\texttt{Instr movzbq}\ (arg\ arg)) \\
& \mid & (\texttt{JmpIf}\ 'cc'\ label) \\
\text{x86}_{\textsf{If}} & ::= & (\texttt{X86Program}\ info\ ((label\ .\ block) \dots))
\end{array}
$$

**Figure 4.10**
The abstract syntax of x86$_{\textsf{If}}$ (extends x86$_{\textsf{Int}}$ shown in figure 2.10).

1 or 0 into the destination $d$, depending on whether the contents of the EFLAGS register matches the condition code $cc$: e for equal, l for less, le for less-or-equal, g for greater, ge for greater-or-equal. The set instruction has a quirk in that its destination argument must be a single-byte register, such as al (l for lower bits) or ah (h for higher bits), which are part of the rax register. Thankfully, the movzbq instruction can be used to move from a single-byte register to a normal 64-bit register. The abstract syntax for the set instruction differs from the concrete syntax in that it separates the instruction name from the condition code.

The x86 instruction for conditional jump is relevant to the compilation of if expressions. The instruction j$cc$ $label$ updates the program counter to point to the instruction after $label$, depending on whether the result in the EFLAGS register matches the condition code $cc$; otherwise, the jump instruction falls through to the next instruction. Like the abstract syntax for set, the abstract syntax for conditional jump separates the instruction name from the condition code. For example, (JmpIf 'le 'foo) corresponds to jle foo. Because the conditional jump instruction relies on the EFLAGS register, it is common for it to be immediately preceded by a cmpq instruction to set the EFLAGS register.

### 4.5  Shrink the $\mathcal{L}_{\textsf{If}}$ Language

The $\mathcal{L}_{\textsf{If}}$ language includes several features that are easily expressible with other features. For example, and and or are expressible using if as follows.

$$
(\texttt{and}\ e_1\ e_2) \quad \Rightarrow \quad (\texttt{if}\ e_1\ e_2\ \texttt{\#f})
$$

$$
(\texttt{or}\ e_1\ e_2) \quad \Rightarrow \quad (\texttt{if}\ e_1\ \texttt{\#t}\ e_2)
$$

By performing these translations in the front end of the compiler, subsequent passes of the compiler do not need to deal with these features, thus making the passes shorter.

On the other hand, translations sometimes reduce the efficiency of the generated code by increasing the number of instructions. For example, expressing subtraction in terms of negation

$$(- \; e_1 \; e_2) \quad \Rightarrow \quad (+ \; e_1 \; (- \; e_2))$$

produces code with two x86 instructions (**negq** and **addq**) instead of just one (**subq**).

**Exercise 4.2** Implement the pass **shrink** to remove **and** and **or** from the language by translating them to **if** expressions in $\mathcal{L}_{\text{If}}$. Create four test programs that involve these operators. In the **run-tests.rkt** script, add the following entry for **shrink** to the list of passes (it should be the only pass at this point).

```
(list "shrink" shrink interp_Lif type-check-Lif)
```

This instructs **interp-tests** to run the interpreter **interp_Lif** and the type checker **type-check-Lif** on the output of **shrink**. Run the script to test your compiler on all the test programs.

## 4.6 Uniquify Variables

Add cases to **uniquify_exp** to handle Boolean constants and **if** expressions.

**Exercise 4.3** Update the **uniquify_exp** for $\mathcal{L}_{\text{If}}$ and add the following entry to the list of **passes** in the **run-tests.rkt** script:

```
(list "uniquify" uniquify interp_Lif type_check_Lif)
```

Run the script to test your compiler.

## 4.7 Remove Complex Operands

The output language of **remove_complex_operands** is $\mathcal{L}_{\text{if}}^{mon}$ (figure 4.11), the monadic normal form of $\mathcal{L}_{\text{If}}$. A Boolean constant is an atomic expression, but the **if** expression is not. All three subexpressions of an **if** are allowed to be complex expressions, but the operands of the **not** operator and comparison operators must be atomic.

Add cases to the **rco_exp** and **rco_atom** functions for the new features in $\mathcal{L}_{\text{If}}$. In recursively processing subexpressions, recall that you should invoke **rco_atom** when the output needs to be an *atm* (as specified in the grammar for $\mathcal{L}_{\text{if}}^{mon}$) and invoke **rco_exp** when the output should be *exp*. Regarding **if**, it is particularly important *not* to replace its condition with a temporary variable, because that would interfere with the generation of high-quality output in the upcoming **explicate_control** pass.

$$
\begin{array}{rcl}
atm & ::= & (\texttt{Int } int) \mid (\texttt{Var } var) \\
exp & ::= & atm \mid (\texttt{Prim 'read ()}) \\
 & \mid & (\texttt{Prim '- } (atm)) \mid (\texttt{Prim '+ } (atm\ atm)) \mid (\texttt{Prim '- } (atm\ atm)) \\
 & \mid & (\texttt{Let } var\ exp\ exp)
\end{array}
$$

$$
\begin{array}{rcl}
atm & ::= & (\texttt{Bool } bool) \\
exp & ::= & (\texttt{Prim not } (atm)) \mid (\texttt{Prim } cmp\ (atm\ atm)) \mid (\texttt{If } exp\ exp\ exp) \\
\mathcal{L}_{\mathsf{if}}^{mon} & ::= & (\texttt{Program () } exp)
\end{array}
$$

**Figure 4.11**
$\mathcal{L}_{\mathsf{if}}^{mon}$ is $\mathcal{L}_{\mathsf{if}}$ in monadic normal form (extends $\mathcal{L}_{\mathsf{Var}}^{mon}$ in figure 2.15).

**Exercise 4.4**  Add cases for Boolean constants and `if` to the `rco_atom` and `rco_exp` functions in `compiler.rkt`. Create three new $\mathcal{L}_{\mathsf{if}}$ programs that exercise the interesting code in this pass. In the `run-tests.rkt` script, add the following entry to the list of `passes` and then run the script to test your compiler.

```
(list "remove-complex" remove_complex_operands interp-Lif type-check-Lif)
```

## 4.8  Explicate Control

Recall that the purpose of `explicate_control` is to make the order of evaluation explicit in the syntax of the program. With the addition of `if`, this becomes more interesting. The `explicate_control` pass translates from $\mathcal{L}_{\mathsf{if}}$ to $\mathcal{C}_{\mathsf{if}}$. The main challenge to overcome is that the condition of an `if` can be an arbitrary expression in $\mathcal{L}_{\mathsf{if}}$, whereas in $\mathcal{C}_{\mathsf{if}}$ the condition must be a comparison.

As a motivating example, consider the following program that has an `if` expression nested in the condition of another `if`:

```
(let ([x (read)])
  (let ([y (read)])
    (if (if (< x 1) (eq? x 0) (eq? x 2))
        (+ y 2)
        (+ y 10))))
```

The naive way to compile `if` and the comparison operations would be to handle each of them in isolation, regardless of their context. Each comparison would be translated into a `cmpq` instruction followed by several instructions to move the result from the EFLAGS register into a general purpose register or stack location. Each `if` would be translated into a `cmpq` instruction followed by a conditional jump. The generated code for the inner `if` in this example would be as follows:

```
cmpq $1, x
setl %al
movzbq %al, tmp
cmpq $1, tmp
je then_branch_1
jmp else_branch_1
```

Notice that the three instructions starting with `setl` are redundant; the conditional jump could come immediately after the first `cmpq`.

Our goal is to compile `if` expressions so that the relevant comparison instruction appears directly before the conditional jump. For example, we want to generate the following code for the inner `if`:

```
cmpq $1, x
jl then_branch_1
jmp else_branch_1
```

One way to achieve this goal is to reorganize the code at the level of $\mathcal{L}_{If}$, pushing the outer `if` inside the inner one, yielding the following code:

```
(let ([x (read)])
  (let ([y (read)])
    (if (< x 1)
      (if (eq? x 0)
        (+ y 2)
        (+ y 10))
      (if (eq? x 2)
        (+ y 2)
        (+ y 10)))))
```

Unfortunately, this approach duplicates the two branches from the outer `if`, and a compiler must never duplicate code! After all, the two branches could be very large expressions.

How can we apply this transformation without duplicating code? In other words, how can two different parts of a program refer to one piece of code? The answer is that we must move away from abstract syntax *trees* and instead use *graphs*. At the level of x86 assembly, this is straightforward because we can label the code for each branch and insert jumps in all the places that need to execute the branch. In this way, jump instructions are edges in the graph and the basic blocks are the nodes. Likewise, our language $\mathcal{C}_{If}$ provides the ability to label a sequence of statements and to jump to a label via `goto`.

As a preview of what `explicate_control` will do, figure 4.12 shows the output of `explicate_control` on this example. Note how the condition of every `if` is a comparison operation and that we have not duplicated any code but instead have used labels and `goto` to enable sharing of code.

Recall that in section 2.6 we implement `explicate_control` for $\mathcal{L}_{Var}$ using two recursive functions, `explicate_tail` and `explicate_assign`. The former function

```
                                            start:
                                                x = (read);
                                                y = (read);
                                                if (< x 1)
                                                    goto block_4;
                                                else
                                                    goto block_5;
      (let ([x (read)])                     block_4:
        (let ([y (read)])                        if (eq? x 0)
          (if (if (< x 1)                            goto block_2;
                  (eq? x 0)          ⇒        else
                  (eq? x 2))                      goto block_3;
              (+ y 2)                       block_5:
              (+ y 10)))))                      if (eq? x 2)
                                                    goto block_2;
                                                else
                                                    goto block_3;
                                            block_2:
                                                return (+ y 2);
                                            block_3:
                                                return (+ y 10);
```

**Figure 4.12**
Translation from $\mathcal{L}_{If}$ to $\mathcal{C}_{If}$ via the `explicate_control`.

translates expressions in tail position, whereas the latter function translates expressions on the right-hand side of a let. With the addition of if expression to $\mathcal{L}_{If}$ we have a new kind of position to deal with: the predicate position of the if. We need another function, `explicate_pred`, that decides how to compile an if by analyzing its condition. So, `explicate_pred` takes an $\mathcal{L}_{If}$ expression and two $\mathcal{C}_{If}$ tails for the *then* branch and *else* branch and outputs a tail. In the following paragraphs we discuss specific cases in the `explicate_tail`, `explicate_assign`, and `explicate_pred` functions.

### 4.8.1 Explicate Tail and Assign

The `explicate_tail` and `explicate_assign` functions need additional cases for Boolean constants and if. The cases for if should recursively compile the two branches using either `explicate_tail` or `explicate_assign`, respectively. The cases should then invoke `explicate_pred` on the condition expression, passing in the generated code for the two branches. For example, consider the following program with an if in tail position.

```
(let ([x (read)])
  (if (eq? x 0) 42 777))
```

The two branches are recursively compiled to return statements. We then delegate to `explicate_pred`, passing the condition `(eq? x 0)` and the two return statements. We return to this example shortly when we discuss `explicate_pred`.

Next let us consider a program with an `if` on the right-hand side of a `let`.

```
(let ([y (read)])
  (let ([x (if (eq? y 0) 40 777)])
    (+ x 2)))
```

Note that the body of the inner `let` will have already been compiled to `return (+ x 2)`; and passed as the `cont` parameter of `explicate_assign`. We'll need to use `cont` to recursively process both branches of the `if`, and we do not want to duplicate code, so we generate the following block using an auxiliary function named `create_block`, discussed in the next section.

```
block_6:
  return (+ x 2)
```

We then use `goto block_6;` as the `cont` argument for compiling the branches. So the two branches compile to

$$
\begin{array}{ccc}
\texttt{x = 40;} & & \texttt{x = 777;} \\
\texttt{goto block\_6;} & \text{and} & \texttt{goto block\_6;}
\end{array}
$$

Finally, we delegate to `explicate_pred`, passing the condition `(eq? y 0)` and the previously presented code for the branches.

### 4.8.2  Create Block

We recommend implementing the `create_block` auxiliary function as follows, using a global variable `basic-blocks` to store a dictionary that maps labels to *tail* expressions. The main idea is that `create_block` generates a new label and then associates the given `tail` with the new label in the `basic-blocks` dictionary. The result of `create_block` is a `Goto` to the new label. However, if the given `tail` is already a `Goto`, then there is no need to generate a new label and entry in `basic-blocks`; we can simply return that `Goto`.

```
(define (create_block tail)
  (match tail
    [(Goto label) (Goto label)]
    [else
      (let ([label (gensym 'block)])
        (set! basic-blocks (cons (cons label tail) basic-blocks))
        (Goto label))]))
```

### 4.8.3  Explicate Predicate

The skeleton for the `explicate_pred` function is given in figure 4.13. It takes three parameters: (1) `cnd`, the condition expression of the `if`; (2) `thn`, the code generated by explicate for the *then* branch; and (3) `els`, the code generated by explicate for

```
(define (explicate_pred cnd thn els)
  (match cnd
    [(Var x) ___]
    [(Let x rhs body) ___]
    [(Prim 'not (list e)) ___]
    [(Prim op es) #:when (or (eq? op 'eq?) (eq? op '<))
     (IfStmt (Prim op es) (create_block thn)
             (create_block els))]
    [(Bool b) (if b thn els)]
    [(If cnd^ thn^ els^) ___]
    [else (error "explicate_pred unhandled case" cnd)]))
```

**Figure 4.13**
Skeleton for the `explicate_pred` auxiliary function.

the *else* branch. The `explicate_pred` function should match on **cnd** with a case for every kind of expression that can have type **Boolean**.

Consider the case for comparison operators. We translate the comparison to an **if** statement whose branches are **goto** statements created by applying **create_block** to the code generated for the **thn** and **els** branches. Let us illustrate this translation by returning to the program with an **if** expression in tail position, shown next. We invoke **explicate_pred** on its condition (eq? x 0).

```
(let ([x (read)])
  (if (eq? x 0) 42 777))
```

The two branches 42 and 777 were already compiled to **return** statements, from which we now create the following blocks:

```
block_1:
    return 42;
block_2:
    return 777;
```

After that, `explicate_pred` compiles the comparison (eq? x 0) to the following if statement:

```
if (eq? x 0)
   goto block_1;
else
   goto block_2;
```

Next consider the case for Boolean constants. We perform a kind of partial evaluation and output either the **thn** or **els** branch, depending on whether the constant is **#t** or **#f**. Let us illustrate this with the following program:

```
(if #t 42 777)
```

Again, the two branches 42 and 777 were compiled to `return` statements, so `explicate_pred` compiles the constant `#t` to the code for the *then* branch.

```
return 42;
```

This case demonstrates that we sometimes discard the `thn` or `els` blocks that are input to `explicate_pred`.

The case for `if` expressions in `explicate_pred` is particularly illuminating because it deals with the challenges discussed previously regarding nested `if` expressions (figure 4.12). The `thn^` and `els^` branches of the `if` inherit their context from the current one, that is, predicate context. So, you should recursively apply `explicate_pred` to the `thn^` and `els^` branches. For both of those recursive calls, pass `thn` and `els` as the extra parameters. Thus, `thn` and `els` may be used twice, once inside each recursive call. As discussed previously, to avoid duplicating code, we need to add them to the dictionary of basic blocks so that we can instead refer to them by name and execute them with a `goto`.

Figure 4.12 shows the output of the `remove_complex_operands` pass and then the `explicate_control` pass on the example program. We walk through the output program. Following the order of evaluation in the output of `remove_complex_operands`, we first have two calls to (`read`) and then the comparison (`< x 1`) in the predicate of the inner `if`. In the output of `explicate_control`, in the block labeled `start`, two assignment statements are followed by an `if` statement that branches to `block_4` or `block_5`. The blocks associated with those labels contain the translations of the code (`eq? x 0`) and (`eq? x 2`), respectively. In particular, we start `block_4` with the comparison (`eq? x 0`) and then branch to `block_2` or `block_3`, which correspond to the two branches of the outer `if`, that is, (`+ y 2`) and (`+ y 10`). The story for `block_5` is similar to that of `block_4`.

### 4.8.4 Interactions between Explicate and Shrink

The way in which the `shrink` pass transforms logical operations such as **and** and **or** can impact the quality of code generated by `explicate_control`. For example, consider the following program:

```
(if (and (eq? (read) 0) (eq? (read) 1))
    0
    42)
```

The **and** operation should transform into something that the `explicate_pred` function can analyze and descend through to reach the underlying `eq?` conditions. Ideally, for this program your `explicate_control` pass should generate code similar to the following:

```
start:
    tmp1 = (read);
    if (eq? tmp1 0) goto block40;
    else goto block39;
block40:
    tmp2 = (read);
    if (eq? tmp2 1) goto block38;
    else goto block39;
block38:
    return 0;
block39:
    return 42;
```

**Exercise 4.5** Implement the pass `explicate_control` by adding the cases for
Boolean constants and `if` to the `explicate_tail` and `explicate_assign` functions. Implement the auxiliary function `explicate_pred` for predicate contexts.
Create test cases that exercise all the new cases in the code for this pass. Add the
following entry to the list of **passes** in **run-tests.rkt**:

(list "explicate_control" explicate_control interp-Cif type-check-Cif)

and then run **run-tests.rkt** to test your compiler.

### 4.9   Select Instructions

The `select_instructions` pass translates $C_{If}$ to $x86^{Var}_{If}$. Recall that we implement
this pass using three auxiliary functions, one for each of the nonterminals *atm*, *stmt*,
and *tail* in $C_{If}$ (figure 4.8). For *atm*, we have new cases for the Booleans. We take
the usual approach of encoding them as integers.

$$\#t \quad \Rightarrow \quad 1 \qquad \#f \quad \Rightarrow \quad 0$$

For translating statements, we discuss some of the cases. The **not** operation can
be implemented in terms of `xorq`, as we discussed at the beginning of this section.
Given an assignment, if the left-hand-side variable is the same as the argument of
**not**, then just the `xorq` instruction suffices.

$$var = (not\ var); \quad \Rightarrow \quad xorq\ \$1,\ var$$

Otherwise, a `movq` is needed to adapt to the update-in-place semantics of x86. In
the following translation, let *arg* be the result of translating *atm* to x86.

$$var = (not\ atm); \quad \Rightarrow \quad \begin{array}{l} movq\ arg,\ var \\ xorq\ \$1,\ var \end{array}$$

Next consider the cases for equality comparisons. Translating this operation to
x86 is slightly involved due to the unusual nature of the `cmpq` instruction that we
discussed in section 4.4. We recommend translating an assignment with an equality
on the right-hand side into a sequence of three instructions.

$$var = ((\text{eq? } atm_1\ atm_2)); \quad \Rightarrow \quad \begin{array}{l} \texttt{cmpq } arg_2\text{, } arg_1 \\ \texttt{sete \%al} \\ \texttt{movzbq \%al, } var \end{array}$$

The translations for the other comparison operators are similar to this but use different condition codes for the **set** instruction.

Regarding the *tail* nonterminal, we have two new cases: **goto** and **if** statements. Both are straightforward to translate to x86. A **goto** statement becomes a jump instruction.

$$\texttt{goto } \ell; \quad \Rightarrow \quad \texttt{jmp } \ell$$

An **if** statement becomes a compare instruction followed by a conditional jump (for the *then* branch), and the fall-through is to a regular jump (for the *else* branch).

$$\begin{array}{l} \texttt{if (eq? } atm_1\ atm_2\texttt{)} \\ \quad \texttt{goto } \ell_1; \\ \texttt{else} \\ \quad \texttt{goto } \ell_2; \end{array} \quad \Rightarrow \quad \begin{array}{l} \texttt{cmpq } arg_2\text{, } arg_1 \\ \texttt{je } \ell_1 \\ \texttt{jmp } \ell_2 \end{array}$$

Again, the translations for the other comparison operators are similar to this but use different condition codes for the conditional jump instruction.

**Exercise 4.6** Expand your **select_instructions** pass to handle the new features of the $C_{If}$ language. Add the following entry to the list of **passes** in **run-tests.rkt**

```
(list "select_instructions" select_instructions interp-pseudo-x86-1)
```

Run the script to test your compiler on all the test programs.

## 4.10   Register Allocation

The changes required for compiling $\mathcal{L}_{If}$ affect liveness analysis, building the interference graph, and assigning homes, but the graph coloring algorithm itself does not change.

### 4.10.1   Liveness Analysis

Recall that for $\mathcal{L}_{Var}$ we implemented liveness analysis for a single basic block (section 3.2). With the addition of **if** expressions to $\mathcal{L}_{If}$, **explicate_control** produces many basic blocks.

The first question is, in what order should we process the basic blocks? Recall that to perform liveness analysis on a basic block we need to know the live-after set for the last instruction in the block. If a basic block has no successors (i.e., contains no jumps to other blocks), then it has an empty live-after set and we can immediately apply liveness analysis to it. If a basic block has some successors, then we need to complete liveness analysis on those blocks first. These ordering constraints are the reverse of a *topological order* on a graph representation of the program. In particular, the *control flow graph* (CFG) (Allen 1970) of a program has a node for each basic block and an edge for each jump from one block to another. It is straightforward to generate a CFG from the dictionary of basic blocks. One then transposes the CFG and applies the topological sort algorithm. We recommend using the `tsort` and `transpose` functions of the Racket `graph` package to accomplish this. As an aside, a topological ordering is only guaranteed to exist if the graph does not contain any cycles. This is the case for the control-flow graphs that we generate from $\mathcal{L}_{\text{If}}$ programs. However, in chapter 5 we add loops to create $\mathcal{L}_{\text{While}}$ and learn how to handle cycles in the control-flow graph.

You need to construct a directed graph to represent the control-flow graph. Do not use the `directed-graph` of the `graph` package because that allows at most one edge between each pair of vertices, whereas a control-flow graph may have multiple edges between a pair of vertices. The `multigraph.rkt` file in the support code implements a graph representation that allows multiple edges between a pair of vertices.

The next question is how to analyze jump instructions. Recall that in section 3.2 we maintain an alist named `label->live` that maps each label to the set of live locations at the beginning of its block. We use `label->live` to determine the live-before set for each (Jmp *label*) instruction. Now that we have many basic blocks, `label->live` needs to be updated as we process the blocks. In particular, after performing liveness analysis on a block, we take the live-before set of its first instruction and associate that with the block's label in the `label->live` alist.

In $x86_{\text{If}}^{\text{Var}}$ we also have the conditional jump (JmpIf *cc label*) to deal with. Liveness analysis for this instruction is particularly interesting because during compilation, we do not know which way a conditional jump will go. Thus we do not know whether to use the live-before set for the block associated with the *label* or the live-before set for the following instruction. However, there is no harm to the correctness of the generated code if we classify more locations as live than the ones that are truly live during one particular execution of the instruction. Thus, we can take the union of the live-before sets from the following instruction and from the mapping for *label* in `label->live`.

The auxiliary functions for computing the variables in an instruction's argument and for computing the variables read-from ($R$) or written-to ($W$) by an instruction need to be updated to handle the new kinds of arguments and instructions in $x86_{\text{If}}^{\text{Var}}$.

**Exercise 4.7** Update the `uncover_live` pass to apply liveness analysis to every basic block in the program. Add the following entry to the list of **passes** in the `run-tests.rkt` script:

```
(list "uncover_live" uncover_live interp-pseudo-x86-1)
```

### 4.10.2   Build the Interference Graph

Many of the new instructions in $x86_{\text{If}}^{\text{Var}}$ can be handled in the same way as the instructions in $x86_{\text{Var}}$. Some instructions, such as the `movzbq` instruction, require special care, similar to the `movq` instruction. Refer to rule number 1 in section 3.3.

**Exercise 4.8** Update the `build_interference` pass for $x86_{\text{If}}^{\text{Var}}$. Add the following entries to the list of **passes** in the `run-tests.rkt` script:

```
(list "build_interference" build_interference interp-pseudo-x86-1)
(list "allocate_registers" allocate_registers interp-pseudo-x86-1)
```

## 4.11  Patch Instructions

The new instructions `cmpq` and `movzbq` have some special restrictions that need to
be handled in the `patch_instructions` pass. The second argument of the `cmpq`
instruction must not be an immediate value (such as an integer). So, if you are
comparing two immediates, we recommend inserting a `movq` instruction to put the
second argument in `rax`. As usual, `cmpq` may have at most one memory reference.
The second argument of the `movzbq` must be a register.

**Exercise 4.9**  Update `patch_instructions` pass for x86$_\mathsf{If}^\mathsf{Var}$. Add the following entry
to the list of `passes` in `run-tests.rkt`, and then run this script to test your
compiler.

```
(list "patch_instructions" patch_instructions interp-x86-1)
```

Figure 4.14 shows a simple example program in $\mathcal{L}_\mathsf{If}$ translated to x86, showing the
results of `explicate_control`, `select_instructions`, and the final x86 assembly.
   Figure 4.15 lists all the passes needed for the compilation of $\mathcal{L}_\mathsf{If}$.

## 4.12  Challenge: Optimize Blocks and Remove Jumps

We discuss two optional challenges that involve optimizing the control-flow of the
program.

### 4.12.1  Optimize Blocks
The algorithm for `explicate_control` that we discussed in section 4.8 sometimes
generates too many blocks. It creates a basic block whenever a continuation *might*
get used more than once (for example, whenever the `cont` parameter is passed into
two or more recursive calls). However, some continuation arguments may not be
used at all. For example, consider the case for the constant `#t` in `explicate_pred`,
in which we discard the `els` continuation. The following example program falls into
this case, and it creates two unused blocks.

```
(if (eq? (read) 1) 42 0)             start:
                                          callq   read_int
⇓                                         movq    %rax, %rcx
                                          cmpq    $1, %rcx
start:                                    je block7952
    tmp7951 = (read);                     jmp block7953
    if (eq? tmp7951 1)               block7953:
      goto block7952;                     movq    $0, %rax
    else                                  jmp conclusion
      goto block7953;               block7952:
block7952:                                movq    $42, %rax
    return 42;                            jmp conclusion
block7953:
    return 0;                             .globl main
                           ⇒        main:
⇓                                         pushq   %rbp
                                          movq    %rsp, %rbp
start:                                    pushq   %r13
    callq read_int                        pushq   %r12
    movq %rax, tmp7951                     pushq   %rbx
    cmpq $1, tmp7951                       pushq   %r14
    je block7952                          subq    $0, %rsp
    jmp block7953                         jmp start
block7953:                          conclusion:
    movq $0, %rax                         addq    $0, %rsp
    jmp conclusion                        popq    %r14
block7952:                                popq    %rbx
    movq $42, %rax                        popq    %r12
    jmp conclusion                        popq    %r13
                                          popq    %rbp
                                          retq
```

**Figure 4.14**
Example compilation of an if expression to x86, showing the results of explicate_control,
select_instructions, and the final x86 assembly code.

```
                                     start:
                                         y = (read);
                                         goto block_5;
(let ([y (if #t                      block_5:
         (read)                          return (+ y 2);
         (if (eq? (read) 0)          block_6:
            777                          y = 777;
            (let ([x (read)])   ⇒        goto block_5;
               (+ 1 x))))])          block_7:
  (+ y 2))                              x = (read);
                                         y = (+ 1 x2);
                                         goto block_5;
```

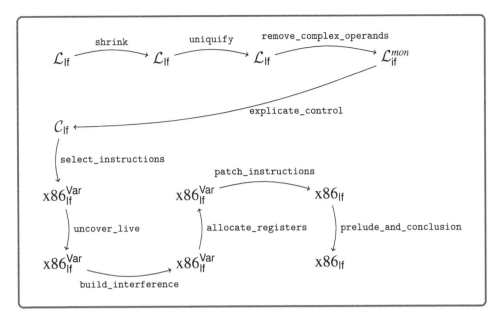

**Figure 4.15**
Diagram of the passes for $\mathcal{L}_{\text{If}}$, a language with conditionals.

   The question is, how can we decide whether to create a basic block? *Lazy evaluation* (Friedman and Wise 1976) can solve this conundrum by delaying the creation of a basic block until the point in time at which we know that it will be used. Racket provides support for lazy evaluation with the **racket/promise** package. The expression (**delay** $e_1 \ldots e_n$) creates a *promise* in which the evaluation of the expressions is postponed. When (**force** $p$) is applied to a promise $p$ for the first time, the expressions $e_1 \ldots e_n$ are evaluated and the result of $e_n$ is cached in the promise and returned. If **force** is applied again to the same promise, then the cached result is returned. If **force** is applied to an argument that is not a promise, **force** simply returns the argument.

   We use promises for the input and output of the functions **explicate_pred**, **explicate_assign**, and **explicate_tail**. So, instead of taking and returning *tail* expressions, they take and return promises. Furthermore, when we come to a situation in which a continuation might be used more than once, as in the case for **if** in **explicate_pred**, we create a delayed computation that creates a basic block for each continuation (if there is not already one) and then returns a **goto** statement to that basic block. When we come to a situation in which we have a promise but need an actual piece of code, for example, to create a larger piece of code with a constructor such as **Seq**, then insert a call to **force**. Also, we must modify the **create_block** function to begin with **delay** to create a promise. When forced, this promise forces the original promise. If that returns a **Goto** (because the block was already added to **basic-blocks**), then we return the **Goto**. Otherwise, we add the block to **basic-blocks** and return a **Goto** to the new label.

```
(let ([y (if #t
             (read)                          start:
             (if (eq? (read) 0)                y = (read);
                 777                   ⇒       goto block_5;
                 (let ([x (read)])     block_5:
                   (+ 1 x))))])              return (+ y 2);
      (+ y 2))
```

**Figure 4.16**
Translation from $\mathcal{L}_{If}$ to $\mathcal{C}_{If}$ via the improved `explicate_control`.

```
(define (create_block tail)
  (delay
    (define t (force tail))
    (match t
      [(Goto label) (Goto label)]
      [else
        (let ([label (gensym 'block)])
          (set! basic-blocks (cons (cons label t) basic-blocks))
          (Goto label))])))
```

Figure 4.16 shows the output of improved `explicate_control` on this example. As you can see, the number of basic blocks has been reduced from four blocks (see figure 4.12) to two blocks.

**Exercise 4.10** Implement the improvements to the `explicate_control` pass. Check that it removes trivial blocks in a few example programs. Then check that your compiler still passes all your tests.

### 4.12.2  Remove Jumps
There is an opportunity for removing jumps that is apparent in the example of figure 4.14. The `start` block ends with a jump to `block_5`, and there are no other jumps to `block_5` in the rest of the program. In this situation we can avoid the run-time overhead of this jump by merging `block_5` into the preceding block, which in this case is the `start` block. Figure 4.17 shows the output of `allocate_registers` on the left and the result of this optimization on the right.

**Exercise 4.11** Implement a pass named `remove_jumps` that merges basic blocks into their preceding basic block, when there is only one preceding block. The pass should translate from $x86_{If}^{Var}$ to $x86_{If}^{Var}$. In the `run-tests.rkt` script, add the following entry to the list of `passes` between `allocate_registers` and `patch_instructions`:

```
(list "remove_jumps" remove_jumps interp-pseudo-x86-1)
```

Run the script to test your compiler. Check that `remove_jumps` accomplishes the goal of merging basic blocks on several test programs.

```
start:                                    start:
    callq read_int                            callq read_int
    movq %rax, %rcx                            movq %rax, %rcx
    jmp block_5                     ⇒          movq %rcx, %rax
block_5:                                       addq $2, %rax
    movq %rcx, %rax                            jmp conclusion
    addq $2, %rax
    jmp conclusion
```

**Figure 4.17**
Merging basic blocks by removing unnecessary jumps.

## 4.13  Further Reading

The algorithm for the `explicate_control` pass is based on the `expose-basic-blocks` pass in the course notes of Dybvig and Keep (2010). It has similarities to the algorithms of Danvy (2003) and Appel and Palsberg (2003), and is related to translations into continuation passing style (van Wijngaarden 1966; Fischer 1972; Reynolds 1972; Plotkin 1975; Friedman, Wand, and Haynes 2001). The treatment of conditionals in the `explicate_control` pass is similar to short-cut Boolean evaluation (Logothetis and Mishra 1981; Aho et al. 2006; Clarke 1989; Danvy 2003) and the case-of-case transformation (Peyton Jones and Santos 1998).

# 5 Loops and Dataflow Analysis

In this chapter we study two features that are the hallmarks of imperative programming languages: loops and assignments to local variables. The following example demonstrates these new features by computing the sum of the first five positive integers:

```
(let ([sum 0])
  (let ([i 5])
    (begin
      (while (> i 0)
        (begin
          (set! sum (+ sum i))
          (set! i (- i 1))))
      sum)))
```

The `while` loop consists of a condition and a body.[1] The body is evaluated repeatedly so long as the condition remains true. The `set!` consists of a variable and a right-hand side expression. The `set!` updates value of the variable to the value of the right-hand side. The primary purpose of both the `while` loop and `set!` is to cause side effects, so they do not give a meaningful result value. Instead, their result is the `#<void>` value. The expression `(void)` is an explicit way to create the `#<void>` value, and it has type `Void`. The `#<void>` value can be passed around just like other values inside an $\mathcal{L}_{\mathsf{While}}$ program, and it can be compared for equality with another `#<void>` value. However, there are no other operations specific to the `#<void>` value in $\mathcal{L}_{\mathsf{While}}$. In contrast, Racket defines the `void?` predicate that returns `#t` when applied to `#<void>` and `#f` otherwise.[2] With the addition of side effect-producing features such as `while` loop and `set!`, it is helpful to include a language feature for sequencing side effects: the `begin` expression. It consists of one or more subexpressions that are evaluated left to right.

---

1. The `while` loop is not a built-in feature of the Racket language, but Racket includes many looping constructs and it is straightforward to define `while` as a macro.
2. Racket's `Void` type corresponds to what is often called the `Unit` type. Racket's `Void` type is inhabited by a single value `#<void>`, which corresponds to `unit` or `()` in the literature (Pierce 2002).

```
type   ::=  Integer
exp    ::=  int | (read) | (- exp) | (+ exp exp) | (- exp exp)
exp    ::=  var | (let ([var exp]) exp)
type   ::=  Boolean
bool   ::=  #t | #f
cmp    ::=  eq? | < | <= | > | >=
exp    ::=  bool | (and exp exp) | (or exp exp) | (not exp)
       |    (cmp exp exp) | (if exp exp exp)
type   ::=  Void
exp    ::=  (set! var exp) | (begin exp* exp) | (while exp exp) | (void)
ℒWhile ::=  exp
```

**Figure 5.1**
The concrete syntax of $\mathcal{L}_{\mathsf{While}}$, extending $\mathcal{L}_{\mathsf{If}}$ (figure 4.1).

```
type   ::=  Integer
op     ::=  read | + | -
exp    ::=  (Int int) | (Prim op (exp ... ))
exp    ::=  (Var var) | (Let var exp exp)
type   ::=  Boolean
bool   ::=  #t | #f
cmp    ::=  eq? | < | <= | > | >=
op     ::=  cmp | and | or | not
exp    ::=  (Bool bool) | (If exp exp exp)
type   ::=  Void
exp    ::=  (SetBang var exp) | (Begin exp* exp) | (WhileLoop exp exp) | (Void)
ℒWhile ::=  (Program '() exp)
```

**Figure 5.2**
The abstract syntax of $\mathcal{L}_{\mathsf{While}}$, extending $\mathcal{L}_{\mathsf{If}}$ (figure 4.2).

## 5.1   The $\mathcal{L}_{\mathsf{While}}$ Language

Figure 5.1 shows the definition of the concrete syntax of $\mathcal{L}_{\mathsf{While}}$, and figure 5.2 shows the definition of its abstract syntax. The definitional interpreter for $\mathcal{L}_{\mathsf{While}}$ is shown in figure 5.3. We add new cases for SetBang, WhileLoop, Begin, and Void, and we make changes to the cases for Var and Let regarding variables. To support assignment to variables and to make their lifetimes indefinite (see the second example in section 8.2), we box the value that is bound to each variable (in Let). The case for Var unboxes the value. Now we discuss the new cases. For SetBang, we find the variable in the environment to obtain a boxed value, and then we change it using set-box! to the result of evaluating the right-hand side. The result value of a SetBang is #<void>. For the WhileLoop, we repeatedly (1) evaluate the condition, and if the result is true, (2) evaluate the body. The result value of a while loop

```
(define interp-Lwhile-class
  (class interp-Lif-class
    (super-new)

    (define/override ((interp-exp env) e)
      (define recur (interp-exp env))
      (match e
        [(Let x e body)
         (define new-env (dict-set env x (box (recur e))))
         ((interp-exp new-env) body)]
        [(Var x) (unbox (dict-ref env x))]
        [(SetBang x rhs)
         (set-box! (dict-ref env x) (recur rhs))]
        [(WhileLoop cnd body)
         (define (loop)
           (cond [(recur cnd) (recur body) (loop)]
                 [else        (void)]))
         (loop)]
        [(Begin es body)
         (for ([e es]) (recur e))
         (recur body)]
        [(Void) (void)]
        [else ((super interp-exp env) e)]))
  ))

(define (interp-Lwhile p)
  (send (new interp-Lwhile-class) interp-program p))
```

**Figure 5.3**
Interpreter for $\mathcal{L}_{\text{While}}$.

is also #<void>. The (Begin *es body*) expression evaluates the subexpressions *es* for their effects and then evaluates and returns the result from *body*. The (Void) expression produces the #<void> value.

The definition of the type checker for $\mathcal{L}_{\text{While}}$ is shown in figure 5.4. The type checking of the SetBang expression requires the type of the variable and the right-hand side to agree. The result type is Void. For while, the condition must be a Boolean and the result type is Void. For Begin, the result type is the type of its last subexpression.

At first glance, the translation of these language features to x86 seems straight-forward because the $\mathcal{C}_{\text{If}}$ intermediate language already supports all the ingredients that we need: assignment, goto, conditional branching, and sequencing. However, there are complications that arise, which we discuss in the next section. After that we introduce the changes necessary to the existing passes.

## 5.2 Cyclic Control Flow and Dataflow Analysis

Up until this point, the programs generated in explicate_control were guaranteed to be acyclic. However, each while loop introduces a cycle. Does that matter?

```
(define type-check-Lwhile-class
  (class type-check-Lif-class
    (super-new)
    (inherit check-type-equal?)

    (define/override (type-check-exp env)
      (lambda (e)
        (define recur (type-check-exp env))
        (match e
          [(SetBang x rhs)
           (define-values (rhs^ rhsT) (recur rhs))
           (define varT (dict-ref env x))
           (check-type-equal? rhsT varT e)
           (values (SetBang x rhs^) 'Void)]
          [(WhileLoop cnd body)
           (define-values (cnd^ Tc) (recur cnd))
           (check-type-equal? Tc 'Boolean e)
           (define-values (body^ Tbody) ((type-check-exp env) body))
           (values (WhileLoop cnd^ body^) 'Void)]
          [(Begin es body)
           (define-values (es^ ts)
             (for/lists (l1 l2) ([e es]) (recur e)))
           (define-values (body^ Tbody) (recur body))
           (values (Begin es^ body^) Tbody)]
          [else ((super type-check-exp env) e)])))
  ))

(define (type-check-Lwhile p)
  (send (new type-check-Lwhile-class) type-check-program p))
```

**Figure 5.4**
Type checker for the $\mathcal{L}_{\mathsf{While}}$ language.

Indeed, it does. Recall that for register allocation, the compiler performs liveness analysis to determine which variables can share the same register. To accomplish this, we analyzed the control-flow graph in reverse topological order (section 4.10.1), but topological order is well defined only for acyclic graphs.

Let us return to the example of computing the sum of the first five positive integers. Here is the program after instruction selection but before register allocation.

```
(define (main) : Integer
   mainstart:                          block7:
      movq $0, sum                        addq i, sum
      movq $5, i                          movq $1, tmp4
      jmp block5                          negq tmp4
   block5:                                addq tmp4, i
      movq i, tmp3                        jmp block5
      cmpq tmp3, $0                    block8:
      jl block7                           movq $27, %rax
      jmp block8                          addq sum, %rax
                                          jmp mainconclusion)
```

Recall that liveness analysis works backward, starting at the end of each function. For this example we could start with `block8` because we know what is live at the beginning of the conclusion: only `rax` and `rsp`. So the live-before set for `block8` is {`rsp,sum`}. Next we might try to analyze `block5` or `block7`, but `block5` jumps to `block7` and vice versa, so it seems that we are stuck.

The way out of this impasse is to realize that we can compute an underapproximation of each live-before set by starting with empty live-after sets. By *underapproximation*, we mean that the set contains only variables that are live for some execution of the program, but the set may be missing some variables that are live. Next, the underapproximations for each block can be improved by (1) updating the live-after set for each block using the approximate live-before sets from the other blocks, and (2) performing liveness analysis again on each block. In fact, by iterating this process, the underapproximations eventually become the correct solutions! This approach of iteratively analyzing a control-flow graph is applicable to many static analysis problems and goes by the name *dataflow analysis*. It was invented by Kildall (1973) in his PhD thesis at the University of Washington.

Let us apply this approach to the previously presented example. We use the empty set for the initial live-before set for each block. Let $m_0$ be the following mapping from label names to sets of locations (variables and registers):

`mainstart: {}, block5: {}, block7: {}, block8: {}`

Using the above live-before approximations, we determine the live-after for each block and then apply liveness analysis to each block. This produces our next approximation $m_1$ of the live-before sets.

`mainstart: {}, block5: {i}, block7: {i, sum}, block8: {rsp, sum}`

For the second round, the live-after for `mainstart` is the current live-before for `block5`, which is {`i`}. Therefore the liveness analysis for `mainstart` computes the empty set. The live-after for `block5` is the union of the live-before sets for `block7` and `block8`, which is {`i, rsp, sum`}. So the liveness analysis for `block5` computes {`i, rsp, sum`}. The live-after for `block7` is the live-before for `block5` (from the previous iteration), which is {i}. So the liveness analysis for block7 remains {i, sum}. Together these yield the following approximation $m_2$ of the live-before sets:

```
mainstart: {}, block5: {i, rsp, sum}, block7: {i, sum}, block8: {rsp, sum}
```

In the preceding iteration, only block5 changed, so we can limit our attention to mainstart and block7, the two blocks that jump to block5. As a result, the live-before sets for mainstart and block7 are updated to include rsp, yielding the following approximation $m_3$:

```
mainstart: {rsp}, block5: {i,rsp,sum}, block7: {i,rsp,sum}, block8: {rsp,sum}
```

Because block7 changed, we analyze block5 once more, but its live-before set remains {i,rsp,sum}. At this point our approximations have converged, so $m_3$ is the solution.

This iteration process is guaranteed to converge to a solution by the Kleene fixed-point theorem, a general theorem about functions on lattices (Kleene 1952). Roughly speaking, a *lattice* is any collection that comes with a partial ordering $\sqsubseteq$ on its elements, a least element $\bot$ (pronounced *bottom*), and a join operator $\sqcup$.[3] When two elements are ordered $m_i \sqsubseteq m_j$, it means that $m_j$ contains at least as much information as $m_i$, so we can think of $m_j$ as a better-than-or-equal-to approximation in relation to $m_i$. The bottom element $\bot$ represents the complete lack of information, that is, the worst approximation. The join operator takes two lattice elements and combines their information; that is, it produces the least upper bound of the two.

A dataflow analysis typically involves two lattices: one lattice to represent abstract states and another lattice that aggregates the abstract states of all the blocks in the control-flow graph. For liveness analysis, an abstract state is a set of locations. We form the lattice $L$ by taking its elements to be sets of locations, the ordering to be set inclusion ($\subseteq$), the bottom to be the empty set, and the join operator to be set union. We form a second lattice $M$ by taking its elements to be mappings from the block labels to sets of locations (elements of $L$). We order the mappings point-wise, using the ordering of $L$. So, given any two mappings $m_i$ and $m_j$, $m_i \sqsubseteq_M m_j$ when $m_i(\ell) \subseteq m_j(\ell)$ for every block label $\ell$ in the program. The bottom element of $M$ is the mapping $\bot_M$ that sends every label to the empty set; that is, $\bot_M(\ell) = \emptyset$.

We can think of one iteration of liveness analysis applied to the whole program as being a function $f$ on the lattice $M$. It takes a mapping as input and computes a new mapping.

$$f(m_i) = m_{i+1}$$

Next let us think for a moment about what a final solution $m_s$ should look like. If we perform liveness analysis using the solution $m_s$ as input, we should get $m_s$ again

---

3. Technically speaking, we will be working with join semilattices.

as the output. That is, the solution should be a *fixed point* of the function $f$.

$$f(m_s) = m_s$$

Furthermore, the solution should include only locations that are forced to be there by performing liveness analysis on the program, so the solution should be the *least* fixed point.

The Kleene fixed-point theorem states that if a function $f$ is monotone (better inputs produce better outputs), then the least fixed point of $f$ is the least upper bound of the *ascending Kleene chain* obtained by starting at $\bot$ and iterating $f$, as follows:

$$\bot \sqsubseteq f(\bot) \sqsubseteq f(f(\bot)) \sqsubseteq \cdots \sqsubseteq f^n(\bot) \sqsubseteq \cdots$$

When a lattice contains only finitely long ascending chains, then every Kleene chain tops out at some fixed point after some number of iterations of $f$.

$$\bot \sqsubseteq f(\bot) \sqsubseteq f(f(\bot)) \sqsubseteq \cdots \sqsubseteq f^k(\bot) = f^{k+1}(\bot) = m_s$$

The liveness analysis is indeed a monotone function and the lattice $M$ has finitely long ascending chains because there are only a finite number of variables and blocks in the program. Thus we are guaranteed that iteratively applying liveness analysis to all blocks in the program will eventually produce the least fixed point solution.

Next let us consider dataflow analysis in general and discuss the generic work list algorithm (figure 5.5). The algorithm has four parameters: the control-flow graph `G`, a function `transfer` that applies the analysis to one block, and the `bottom` and `join` operators for the lattice of abstract states. The `analyze_dataflow` function is formulated as a *forward* dataflow analysis; that is, the inputs to the transfer function come from the predecessor nodes in the control-flow graph. However, liveness analysis is a *backward* dataflow analysis, so in that case one must supply the `analyze_dataflow` function with the transpose of the control-flow graph.

The algorithm begins by creating the bottom mapping, represented by a hash table. It then pushes all the nodes in the control-flow graph onto the work list (a queue). The algorithm repeats the `while` loop as long as there are items in the work list. In each iteration, a node is popped from the work list and processed. The `input` for the node is computed by taking the join of the abstract states of all the predecessor nodes. The `transfer` function is then applied to obtain the `output` abstract state. If the output differs from the previous state for this block, the mapping for this block is updated and its successor nodes are pushed onto the work list.

### 5.3 Mutable Variables and Remove Complex Operands

There is a subtle interaction between the `remove_complex_operands` pass, the addition of `set!`, and the left-to-right order of evaluation of Racket. Consider the following example:

```
(let ([x 2])
  (+ x (begin (set! x 40) x)))
```

```
(define (analyze_dataflow G transfer bottom join)
  (define mapping (make-hash))
  (for ([v (in-vertices G)])
    (dict-set! mapping v bottom))
  (define worklist (make-queue))
  (for ([v (in-vertices G)])
    (enqueue! worklist v))
  (define trans-G (transpose G))
  (while (not (queue-empty? worklist))
    (define node (dequeue! worklist))
    (define input (for/fold ([state bottom])
                            ([pred (in-neighbors trans-G node)])
                    (join state (dict-ref mapping pred))))
    (define output (transfer node input))
    (cond [(not (equal? output (dict-ref mapping node)))
           (dict-set! mapping node output)
           (for ([v (in-neighbors G node)])
             (enqueue! worklist v))]))
  mapping)
```

**Figure 5.5**
Generic work list algorithm for dataflow analysis.

The result of this program is 42 because the first read from x produces 2 and the second produces 40. However, if we naively apply the remove_complex_operands pass to this example we obtain the following program whose result is 80!

```
(let ([x 2])
  (let ([tmp (begin (set! x 40) x)])
    (+ x tmp)))
```

The problem is that with mutable variables, the ordering between reads and writes is important, and the remove_complex_operands pass moved the set! to happen before the first read of x.

We recommend solving this problem by giving special treatment to reads from mutable variables, that is, variables that occur on the left-hand side of a set!. We mark each read from a mutable variable with the form get! (GetBang in abstract syntax) to indicate that the read operation is effectful in that it can produce different results at different points in time. Let's apply this idea to the following variation that also involves a variable that is not mutated:

```
(let ([x 2])
  (let ([y 0])
    (+ y (+ x (begin (set! x 40) x)))))
```

We first analyze this program to discover that variable x is mutable but y is not. We then transform the program as follows, replacing each occurrence of x with (get! x):

```
(let ([x 2])
  (let ([y 0])
    (+ y (+ (get! x) (begin (set! x 40) (get! x))))))
```

Now that we have a clear distinction between reads from mutable and immutable variables, we can apply the `remove_complex_operands` pass, where reads from immutable variables are still classified as atomic expressions but reads from mutable variables are classified as complex. Thus, `remove_complex_operands` yields the following program:

```
(let ([x 2])
  (let ([y 0])
    (+ y (let ([t1 (get! x)])
           (let ([t2 (begin (set! x 40) (get! x))])
             (+ t1 t2))))))
```

The temporary variable `t1` gets the value of `x` before the `set!`, so it is 2. The temporary variable `t2` gets the value of `x` after the `set!`, so it is 40. We do not generate a temporary variable for the occurrence of `y` because it's an immutable variable. We want to avoid such unnecessary extra temporaries because they would needlessly increase the number of variables, making it more likely for some of them to be spilled. The result of this program is 42, the same as the result prior to `remove_complex_operands`.

The approach that we've sketched requires only a small modification to `remove_complex_operands` to handle `get!`. However, it requires a new pass, called `uncover-get!`, that we discuss in section 5.4.

As an aside, this problematic interaction between `set!` and the pass `remove_complex_operands` is particular to Racket and not its predecessor, the Scheme language. The key difference is that Scheme does not specify an order of evaluation for the arguments of an operator or function call (Sperber et al. 2009). Thus, a compiler for Scheme is free to choose any ordering: both 42 and 80 would be correct results for the example program. Interestingly, Racket is implemented on top of the Chez Scheme compiler (Dybvig 2006) and an approach similar to the one presented in this section (using extra `let` bindings to control the order of evaluation) is used in the translation from Racket to Scheme (Flatt et al. 2019).

Having discussed the complications that arise from adding support for assignment and loops, we turn to discussing the individual compilation passes.

## 5.4    Uncover `get!`

The goal of this pass is to mark uses of mutable variables so that `remove_complex_operands` can treat them as complex expressions and thereby preserve their ordering relative to the side effects in other operands. So, the first step is to collect all the mutable variables. We recommend creating an auxiliary function for this, named `collect-set!`, that recursively traverses expressions, returning the set of all variables that occur on the left-hand side of a `set!`. Here's an excerpt of its implementation.

```
(define (collect-set! e)
  (match e
    [(Var x) (set)]
    [(Int n) (set)]
    [(Let x rhs body)
     (set-union (collect-set! rhs) (collect-set! body))]
    [(SetBang var rhs)
     (set-union (set var) (collect-set! rhs))]
    ...))
```

By placing this pass after `uniquify`, we need not worry about variable shadowing, and our logic for `Let` can remain simple, as in this excerpt.

The second step is to mark the occurrences of the mutable variables with the new `GetBang` AST node (`get!` in concrete syntax). The following is an excerpt of the `uncover-get!-exp` function, which takes two parameters: the set of mutable variables `set!-vars` and the expression `e` to be processed. The case for `(Var x)` replaces it with `(GetBang x)` if it is a mutable variable or leaves it alone if not.

```
(define ((uncover-get!-exp set!-vars) e)
  (match e
    [(Var x)
     (if (set-member? set!-vars x)
         (GetBang x)
         (Var x))]
    ...))
```

To wrap things up, define the `uncover-get!` function for processing a whole program, using `collect-set!` to obtain the set of mutable variables and then `uncover-get!-exp` to replace their occurrences with `GetBang`.

## 5.5 Remove Complex Operands

The new language forms, `get!`, `set!`, `begin`, and `while` are all complex expressions. The subexpressions of `set!`, `begin`, and `while` are allowed to be complex. Figure 5.6 defines the output language $\mathcal{L}_{\text{While}}^{mon}$ of this pass.

As usual, when a complex expression appears in a grammar position that needs to be atomic, such as the argument of a primitive operator, we must introduce a temporary variable and bind it to the complex expression. This approach applies, unchanged, to handle the new language forms. For example, in the following code there are two `begin` expressions appearing as arguments to the + operator. The output of `rco_exp` is then shown, in which the `begin` expressions have been bound to temporary variables. Recall that `let` expressions in $\mathcal{L}_{\text{While}}^{mon}$ are allowed to have arbitrary expressions in their right-hand side expression, so it is fine to place `begin` there.

$$
\begin{array}{lll}
\textit{atm} & ::= & \text{(Int } \textit{int}\text{)} \mid \text{(Var } \textit{var}\text{)} \\
\textit{exp} & ::= & \textit{atm} \mid \text{(Prim 'read ())} \\
& \mid & \text{(Prim '- } (\textit{atm})\text{)} \mid \text{(Prim '+ } (\textit{atm atm})\text{)} \mid \text{(Prim '- } (\textit{atm atm})\text{)} \\
& \mid & \text{(Let } \textit{var exp exp}\text{)}
\end{array}
$$

$$
\begin{array}{lll}
\textit{atm} & ::= & \text{(Bool } \textit{bool}\text{)} \\
\textit{exp} & ::= & \text{(Prim not } (\textit{atm})\text{)} \mid \text{(Prim } \textit{cmp} \text{ } (\textit{atm atm})\text{)} \mid \text{(If } \textit{exp exp exp}\text{)}
\end{array}
$$

$$
\begin{array}{lll}
\textit{atm} & ::= & \text{(Void)} \\
\textit{exp} & ::= & \text{(GetBang } \textit{var}\text{)} \mid \text{(SetBang } \textit{var exp}\text{)} \mid \text{(Begin } (\textit{exp} \dots) \text{ } \textit{exp}\text{)} \\
& \mid & \text{(WhileLoop } \textit{exp exp}\text{)} \\
\mathcal{L}_{\text{While}}^{mon} & ::= & \text{(Program '() } \textit{exp}\text{)}
\end{array}
$$

**Figure 5.6**
$\mathcal{L}_{\text{While}}^{mon}$ is $\mathcal{L}_{\text{While}}$ in monadic normal form.

```
                                        (let ([x2 10])
                                        (let ([y3 0])
   (let ([x2 10])                       (let ([tmp4 (begin
   (let ([y3 0])                                     (set! y3 (read))
     (+ (+ (begin                                    x2)])
           (set! y3 (read))             (let ([tmp5 (begin
           (get! x2))         ⇒                       (set! x2 (read))
         (begin                                       y3)])
           (set! x2 (read))             (let ([tmp6 (+ tmp4 tmp5)])
           (get! y3)))                  (let ([tmp7 x2])
       (get! x2))))                       (+ tmp6 tmp7)))))))
```

## 5.6   Explicate Control and $\mathcal{C}_\circlearrowleft$

Recall that in the `explicate_control` pass we define one helper function for each kind of position in the program. For the $\mathcal{L}_{\text{Var}}$ language of integers and variables, we needed assignment and tail positions. The `if` expressions of $\mathcal{L}_{\text{If}}$ introduced predicate positions. For $\mathcal{L}_{\text{While}}$, the `begin` expression introduces yet another kind of position: effect position. Except for the last subexpression, the subexpressions inside a `begin` are evaluated only for their effect. Their result values are discarded. We can generate better code by taking this fact into account.

The output language of `explicate_control` is $\mathcal{C}_\circlearrowleft$ (figure 5.7), which is nearly identical to $\mathcal{C}_{\text{If}}$. The only syntactic differences are the addition of (Void) and that `read` may appear as a statement. The most significant difference between the programs generated by `explicate_control` in chapter 4 versus `explicate_control` in this chapter is that the control-flow graphs of the latter may contain cycles.

The new auxiliary function `explicate_effect` takes an expression (in an effect position) and the code for its continuation. The function returns a *tail* that includes the generated code for the input expression followed by the continuation. If the expression is obviously pure, that is, never causes side effects, then the expression can be removed, so the result is just the continuation. The case for

$$
\begin{array}{lll}
atm & ::= & (\text{Int } int) \mid (\text{Var } var) \\
exp & ::= & atm \mid (\text{Prim 'read ()}) \mid (\text{Prim '- } (atm)) \\
    & \mid & (\text{Prim '+ } (atm\ atm)) \mid (\text{Prim '- } (atm\ atm)) \\
stmt & ::= & (\text{Assign (Var } var)\ exp) \\
tail & ::= & (\text{Return } exp) \mid (\text{Seq } stmt\ tail) \\
\hline
atm & ::= & (\text{Bool } bool) \\
cmp & ::= & \text{eq? } \mid < \mid <= \mid > \mid >= \\
exp & ::= & (\text{Prim 'not } (atm)) \mid (\text{Prim '} cmp\ (atm\ atm)) \\
tail & ::= & (\text{Goto } label) \\
     & \mid & (\text{IfStmt (Prim } cmp\ (atm\ atm))\ (\text{Goto } label)\ (\text{Goto } label)) \\
\hline
atm & ::= & \textbf{(Void)} \\
stmt & ::= & \textbf{(Prim 'read ())} \\
\mathcal{C}_{\circlearrowleft} & ::= & \textbf{(CProgram } \textit{info } ((\textit{label} . \textit{tail}) \dots )) \\
\end{array}
$$

**Figure 5.7**
The abstract syntax of $\mathcal{C}_{\circlearrowleft}$, extending $\mathcal{C}_{\text{If}}$ (figure 4.8).

(WhileLoop *cnd body*) expressions is interesting; the generated code is depicted in the following diagram:

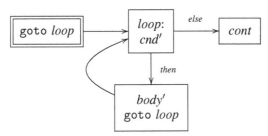

We start by creating a fresh label *loop* for the top of the loop. Next, recursively process the *body* (in effect position) with a goto to *loop* as the continuation, producing *body′*. Process the *cnd* (in predicate position) with *body′* as the *then* branch and the continuation block as the *else* branch. The result should be added to the dictionary of basic-blocks with the label *loop*. The result for the whole while loop is a goto to the *loop* label.

The auxiliary functions for tail, assignment, and predicate positions need to be updated. The three new language forms, while, set!, and begin, can appear in assignment and tail positions. Only begin may appear in predicate positions; the other two have result type Void.

## 5.7  Select Instructions

Only two small additions are needed in the select_instructions pass to handle the changes to $\mathcal{C}_{\circlearrowleft}$. First, to handle the addition of (Void) we simply translate it to 0. Second, read may appear as a stand-alone statement instead of appearing only on the right-hand side of an assignment statement. The code generation is nearly identical to the one for assignment; just leave off the instruction for moving the result into the left-hand side.

## 5.8   Register Allocation

As discussed in section 5.2, the presence of loops in $\mathcal{L}_{\mathsf{While}}$ means that the control-flow graphs may contain cycles, which complicates the liveness analysis needed for register allocation. We recommend using the generic `analyze_dataflow` function that was presented at the end of section 5.2 to perform liveness analysis, replacing the code in `uncover_live` that processed the basic blocks in topological order (section 4.10.1).

The `analyze_dataflow` function has the following four parameters.

1. The first parameter `G` should be passed the transpose of the control-flow graph.
2. The second parameter `transfer` should be passed a function that applies liveness analysis to a basic block. It takes two parameters: the label for the block to analyze and the live-after set for that block. The transfer function should return the live-before set for the block. Also, as a side effect, it should update the block's *info* with the liveness information for each instruction. To implement the `transfer` function, you should be able to reuse the code you already have for analyzing basic blocks.
3. The third and fourth parameters of `analyze_dataflow` are `bottom` and `join` for the lattice of abstract states, that is, sets of locations. For liveness analysis, the bottom of the lattice is the empty set, and the join operator is set union.

Figure 5.8 provides an overview of all the passes needed for the compilation of $\mathcal{L}_{\mathsf{While}}$.

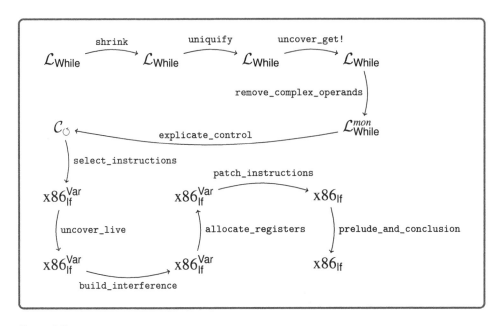

**Figure 5.8**
Diagram of the passes for $\mathcal{L}_{\mathsf{While}}$.

# 6 Tuples and Garbage Collection

In this chapter we study the implementation of tuples, called vectors in Racket. A tuple is a fixed-length sequence of elements in which each element may have a different type. This language feature is the first to use the computer's *heap*, because the lifetime of a tuple is indefinite; that is, a tuple lives forever from the programmer's viewpoint. Of course, from an implementer's viewpoint, it is important to reclaim the space associated with a tuple when it is no longer needed, which is why we also study *garbage collection* techniques in this chapter.

Section 6.1 introduces the $\mathcal{L}_{\mathsf{Tup}}$ language, including its interpreter and type checker. The $\mathcal{L}_{\mathsf{Tup}}$ language extends the $\mathcal{L}_{\mathsf{While}}$ language (chapter 5) with tuples. Section 6.2 describes a garbage collection algorithm based on copying live tuples back and forth between two halves of the heap. The garbage collector requires coordination with the compiler so that it can find all the live tuples. Sections 6.3 through 6.8 discuss the necessary changes and additions to the compiler passes, including a new compiler pass named `expose_allocation`.

## 6.1 The $\mathcal{L}_{\mathsf{Tup}}$ Language

Figure 6.1 shows the definition of the concrete syntax for $\mathcal{L}_{\mathsf{Tup}}$, and figure 6.2 shows the definition of the abstract syntax. The $\mathcal{L}_{\mathsf{Tup}}$ language includes the forms `vector` for creating a tuple, `vector-ref` for reading an element of a tuple, `vector-set!` for writing to an element of a tuple, and `vector-length` for obtaining the number of elements of a tuple. The following program shows an example use of tuples. It creates a tuple t containing the elements 40, #t, and another tuple that contains just 2. The element at index 1 of t is #t, so the *then* branch of the if is taken. The element at index 0 of t is 40, to which we add 2, the element at index 0 of the tuple. The result of the program is 42.

```
(let ([t (vector 40 #t (vector 2))])
  (if (vector-ref t 1)
      (+ (vector-ref t 0)
         (vector-ref (vector-ref t 2) 0))
      44))
```

Tuples raise several interesting new issues. First, variable binding performs a shallow copy in dealing with tuples, which means that different variables can refer

$$
\begin{array}{lll}
type & ::= & \texttt{Integer} \\
exp & ::= & int \mid (\texttt{read}) \mid (\texttt{-}\ exp) \mid (\texttt{+}\ exp\ exp) \mid (\texttt{-}\ exp\ exp) \\
\hline
exp & ::= & var \mid (\texttt{let}\ ([var\ exp])\ exp) \\
\hline
type & ::= & \texttt{Boolean} \\
bool & ::= & \texttt{\#t} \mid \texttt{\#f} \\
cmp & ::= & \texttt{eq?} \mid \texttt{<} \mid \texttt{<=} \mid \texttt{>} \mid \texttt{>=} \\
exp & ::= & bool \mid (\texttt{and}\ exp\ exp) \mid (\texttt{or}\ exp\ exp) \mid (\texttt{not}\ exp) \\
& \mid & (cmp\ exp\ exp) \mid (\texttt{if}\ exp\ exp\ exp) \\
\hline
type & ::= & \texttt{Void} \\
exp & ::= & (\texttt{set!}\ var\ exp) \mid (\texttt{begin}\ exp^*\ exp) \mid (\texttt{while}\ exp\ exp) \mid (\texttt{void}) \\
\hline
type & ::= & (\texttt{Vector}\ type^*) \\
exp & ::= & (\texttt{vector}\ exp^*) \mid (\texttt{vector-length}\ exp) \\
& \mid & (\texttt{vector-ref}\ exp\ int) \mid (\texttt{vector-set!}\ exp\ int\ exp) \\
\mathcal{L}_{\textsf{Tup}} & ::= & exp
\end{array}
$$

**Figure 6.1**
The concrete syntax of $\mathcal{L}_{\textsf{Tup}}$, extending $\mathcal{L}_{\textsf{While}}$ (figure 5.1).

$$
\begin{array}{lll}
type & ::= & \texttt{Integer} \\
op & ::= & \texttt{read} \mid \texttt{+} \mid \texttt{-} \\
exp & ::= & (\texttt{Int}\ int) \mid (\texttt{Prim}\ op\ (exp\ldots)) \\
\hline
exp & ::= & (\texttt{Var}\ var) \mid (\texttt{Let}\ var\ exp\ exp) \\
\hline
type & ::= & \texttt{Boolean} \\
bool & ::= & \texttt{\#t} \mid \texttt{\#f} \\
cmp & ::= & \texttt{eq?} \mid \texttt{<} \mid \texttt{<=} \mid \texttt{>} \mid \texttt{>=} \\
op & ::= & cmp \mid \texttt{and} \mid \texttt{or} \mid \texttt{not} \\
exp & ::= & (\texttt{Bool}\ bool) \mid (\texttt{If}\ exp\ exp\ exp) \\
\hline
type & ::= & \texttt{Void} \\
exp & ::= & (\texttt{SetBang}\ var\ exp) \mid (\texttt{Begin}\ exp^*\ exp) \mid (\texttt{WhileLoop}\ exp\ exp) \mid (\texttt{Void}) \\
\hline
type & ::= & (\texttt{Vector}\ type^*) \\
op & ::= & \texttt{vector} \mid \texttt{vector-length} \\
exp & ::= & (\texttt{Prim}\ \texttt{vector-ref}\ (exp\ (\texttt{Int}\ int))) \\
& \mid & (\texttt{Prim}\ \texttt{vector-set!}\ (exp\ (\texttt{Int}\ int)\ exp)) \\
\mathcal{L}_{\textsf{Tup}} & ::= & (\texttt{Program}\ \texttt{'()}\ exp)
\end{array}
$$

**Figure 6.2**
The abstract syntax of $\mathcal{L}_{\textsf{Tup}}$.

to the same tuple; that is, two variables can be *aliases* for the same entity. Consider the following example, in which t1 and t2 refer to the same tuple value and t3 refers to a different tuple value with equal elements. The result of the program is 42.

```
(let ([t1 (vector 3 7)])
  (let ([t2 t1])
    (let ([t3 (vector 3 7)])
      (if (and (eq? t1 t2) (not (eq? t1 t3)))
          42
          0)))))
```

Whether two variables are aliased or not affects what happens when the underlying tuple is mutated. Consider the following example in which t1 and t2 again
refer to the same tuple value.

```
(let ([t1 (vector 3 7)])
  (let ([t2 t1])
    (let ([_ (vector-set! t2 0 42)])
      (vector-ref t1 0))))
```

The mutation through t2 is visible in referencing the tuple from t1, so the result
of this program is 42.

The next issue concerns the lifetime of tuples. When does a tuple's lifetime end?
Notice that $\mathcal{L}_{\mathrm{Tup}}$ does not include an operation for deleting tuples. Furthermore,
the lifetime of a tuple is not tied to any notion of static scoping. For example, the
following program returns 42 even though the variable w goes out of scope prior to
the vector-ref that reads from the vector to which it was bound.

```
(let ([v (vector (vector 44))])
  (let ([x (let ([w (vector 42)])
             (let ([_ (vector-set! v 0 w)])
               0))])
    (+ x (vector-ref (vector-ref v 0) 0))))
```

From the perspective of programmer-observable behavior, tuples live forever.
However, if they really lived forever then many long-running programs would run
out of memory. To solve this problem, the language's runtime system performs
automatic garbage collection.

Figure 6.3 shows the definitional interpreter for the $\mathcal{L}_{\mathrm{Tup}}$ language. We define
the vector, vector-ref, vector-set!, and vector-length operations for $\mathcal{L}_{\mathrm{Tup}}$
in terms of the corresponding operations in Racket. One subtle point is that the
vector-set! operation returns the #<void> value.

Figure 6.4 shows the type checker for $\mathcal{L}_{\mathrm{Tup}}$. The type of a tuple is a Vector type
that contains a type for each of its elements. To create the s-expression for the
Vector type, we use the unquote-splicing operator ,@ to insert the list t* without
its usual start and end parentheses. The type of accessing the ith element of a
tuple is the ith element type of the tuple's type, if there is one. If not, an error is
signaled. Note that the index i is required to be a constant integer (and not, for
example, a call to read) so that the type checker can determine the element's type
given the tuple type. Regarding writing an element to a tuple, the element's type
must be equal to the ith element type of the tuple's type. The result type is Void.

```
(define interp-Lvec-class
  (class interp-Lwhile-class
    (super-new)

    (define/override (interp-op op)
      (match op
        ['eq? (lambda (v1 v2)
                (cond [(or (and (fixnum? v1) (fixnum? v2))
                           (and (boolean? v1) (boolean? v2))
                           (and (vector? v1) (vector? v2))
                           (and (void? v1) (void? v2)))
                       (eq? v1 v2)]))]
        ['vector vector]
        ['vector-length vector-length]
        ['vector-ref vector-ref]
        ['vector-set! vector-set!]
        [else (super interp-op op)]
        ))

    (define/override ((interp-exp env) e)
      (match e
        [(HasType e t) ((interp-exp env) e)]
        [else ((super interp-exp env) e)]
        ))
    ))

(define (interp-Lvec p)
  (send (new interp-Lvec-class) interp-program p))
```

**Figure 6.3**
Interpreter for the $\mathcal{L}_{\mathsf{Tup}}$ language.

## 6.2  Garbage Collection

Garbage collection is a runtime technique for reclaiming space on the heap that
will not be used in the future of the running program. We use the term *object* to
refer to any value that is stored in the heap, which for now includes only tuples.[1]
Unfortunately, it is impossible to know precisely which objects will be accessed in
the future and which will not. Instead, garbage collectors overapproximate the set of
objects that will be accessed by identifying which objects can possibly be accessed.
The running program can directly access objects that are in registers and on the
procedure call stack. It can also transitively access the elements of tuples, starting
with a tuple whose address is in a register or on the procedure call stack. We define

---

1. The term *object* as it is used in the context of object-oriented programming has a more specific
meaning than the way in which we use the term here.

```
(define type-check-Lvec-class
  (class type-check-Lif-class
    (super-new)
    (inherit check-type-equal?)

    (define/override (type-check-exp env)
      (lambda (e)
        (define recur (type-check-exp env))
        (match e
          [(Prim 'vector es)
           (define-values (e* t*) (for/lists (e* t*) ([e es]) (recur e)))
           (define t `(Vector ,@t*))
           (values (Prim 'vector e*) t)]
          [(Prim 'vector-ref (list e1 (Int i)))
           (define-values (e1^ t) (recur e1))
           (match t
             [`(Vector ,ts ...)
              (unless (and (0 . <= . i) (i . < . (length ts)))
                (error 'type-check "index ~a out of bounds\nin ~v" i e))
              (values (Prim 'vector-ref (list e1^ (Int i))) (list-ref ts i))]
             [else (error 'type-check "expect Vector, not ~a\nin ~v" t e)])]
          [(Prim 'vector-set! (list e1 (Int i) elt) )
           (define-values (e-vec t-vec) (recur e1))
           (define-values (e-elt^ t-elt) (recur elt))
           (match t-vec
             [`(Vector ,ts ...)
              (unless (and (0 . <= . i) (i . < . (length ts)))
                (error 'type-check "index ~a out of bounds\nin ~v" i e))
              (check-type-equal? (list-ref ts i) t-elt e)
              (values (Prim 'vector-set! (list e-vec (Int i) e-elt^)) 'Void)]
             [else (error 'type-check "expect Vector, not ~a\nin ~v" t-vec e)])]
          [(Prim 'vector-length (list e))
           (define-values (e^ t) (recur e))
           (match t
             [`(Vector ,ts ...)
              (values (Prim 'vector-length (list e^)) 'Integer)]
             [else (error 'type-check "expect Vector, not ~a\nin ~v" t e)])]
          [(Prim 'eq? (list arg1 arg2))
           (define-values (e1 t1) (recur arg1))
           (define-values (e2 t2) (recur arg2))
           (match* (t1 t2)
             [(`(Vector ,ts1 ...) `(Vector ,ts2 ...)) (void)]
             [(other wise) (check-type-equal? t1 t2 e)])
           (values (Prim 'eq? (list e1 e2)) 'Boolean)]
          [else ((super type-check-exp env) e)]
          )))
    ))

(define (type-check-Lvec p)
  (send (new type-check-Lvec-class) type-check-program p))
```

**Figure 6.4**
Type checker for the $\mathcal{L}_{\text{Tup}}$ language.

the *root set* to be all the tuple addresses that are in registers or on the procedure call stack. We define the *live objects* to be the objects that are reachable from the root set. Garbage collectors reclaim the space that is allocated to objects that are no longer live. That means that some objects may not get reclaimed as soon as they could be, but at least garbage collectors do not reclaim the space dedicated to objects that will be accessed in the future! The programmer can influence which objects get reclaimed by causing them to become unreachable.

So the goal of the garbage collector is twofold:

1. to preserve all the live objects, and
2. to reclaim the memory of everything else, that is, the *garbage*.

### 6.2.1  Two-Space Copying Collector

Here we study a relatively simple algorithm for garbage collection that is the basis of many state-of-the-art garbage collectors (Lieberman and Hewitt 1983; Ungar 1984; Jones and Lins 1996; Detlefs et al. 2004; Dybvig 2006; Tene, Iyengar, and Wolf 2011). In particular, we describe a two-space copying collector (Wilson 1992) that uses Cheney's algorithm to perform the copy (Cheney 1970). Figure 6.5 gives a coarse-grained depiction of what happens in a two-space collector, showing two time steps, prior to garbage collection (on the top) and after garbage collection (on the bottom). In a two-space collector, the heap is divided into two parts named the FromSpace and the ToSpace. Initially, all allocations go to the FromSpace until there is not enough room for the next allocation request. At that point, the garbage collector goes to work to make room for the next allocation.

A copying collector makes more room by copying all the live objects from the FromSpace into the ToSpace and then performs a sleight of hand, treating the ToSpace as the new FromSpace and the old FromSpace as the new ToSpace. In the example shown in figure 6.5, the root set consists of three pointers, one in a register and two on the stack. All the live objects have been copied to the ToSpace (the right-hand side of figure 6.5) in a way that preserves the pointer relationships. For example, the pointer in the register still points to a tuple that in turn points to two other tuples. There are four tuples that are not reachable from the root set and therefore do not get copied into the ToSpace.

The exact situation shown in figure 6.5 cannot be created by a well-typed program in $\mathcal{L}_{\mathsf{Tup}}$ because it contains a cycle. However, creating cycles will be possible once we get to $\mathcal{L}_{\mathsf{Dyn}}$ (chapter 9). We design the garbage collector to deal with cycles to begin with, so we will not need to revisit this issue.

### 6.2.2  Graph Copying via Cheney's Algorithm

Let us take a closer look at the copying of the live objects. The allocated objects and pointers can be viewed as a graph, and we need to copy the part of the graph that is reachable from the root set. To make sure that we copy all the reachable vertices in the graph, we need an exhaustive graph traversal algorithm, such as depth-first search or breadth-first search (Moore 1959; Cormen et al. 2001). Recall that such algorithms take into account the possibility of cycles by marking which

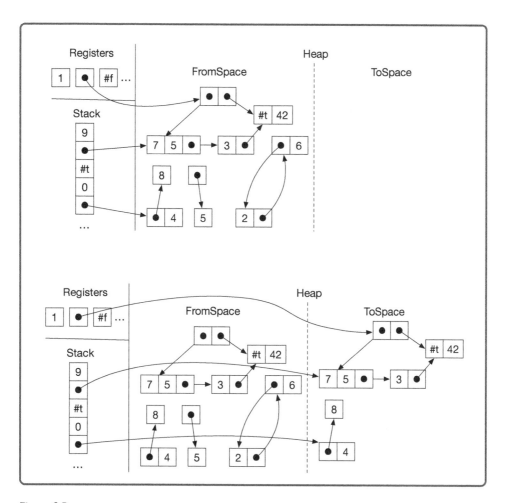

**Figure 6.5**
A copying collector in action.

vertices have already been visited, so to ensure termination of the algorithm. These search algorithms also use a data structure such as a stack or queue as a to-do list to keep track of the vertices that need to be visited. We use breadth-first search and a trick due to Cheney (1970) for simultaneously representing the queue and copying tuples into the ToSpace.

Figure 6.6 shows several snapshots of the ToSpace as the copy progresses. The queue is represented by a chunk of contiguous memory at the beginning of the ToSpace, using two pointers to track the front and the back of the queue, called the *free pointer* and the *scan pointer*, respectively. The algorithm starts by copying all tuples that are immediately reachable from the root set into the ToSpace to form the initial queue. When we copy a tuple, we mark the old tuple to indicate that it has been visited. We discuss how this marking is accomplished in section 6.2.3. Note that any pointers inside the copied tuples in the queue still point back to the FromSpace. Once the initial queue has been created, the algorithm enters a loop in which it repeatedly processes the tuple at the front of the queue and pops it off the queue. To process a tuple, the algorithm copies all the objects that are directly reachable from it to the ToSpace, placing them at the back of the queue. The algorithm then updates the pointers in the popped tuple so that they point to the newly copied objects.

As shown in figure 6.6, in the first step we copy the tuple whose second element is 42 to the back of the queue. The other pointer goes to a tuple that has already been copied, so we do not need to copy it again, but we do need to update the pointer to the new location. This can be accomplished by storing a *forwarding pointer* to the new location in the old tuple, when we initially copied the tuple into the ToSpace. This completes one step of the algorithm. The algorithm continues in this way until the queue is empty; that is, when the scan pointer catches up with the free pointer.

### 6.2.3  Data Representation

The garbage collector places some requirements on the data representations used by our compiler. First, the garbage collector needs to distinguish between pointers and other kinds of data such as integers. The following are several ways to accomplish this:

1. Attach a tag to each object that identifies what type of object it is (McCarthy 1960).
2. Store different types of objects in different regions (Steele 1977).
3. Use type information from the program to either (a) generate type-specific code for collecting, or (b) generate tables that guide the collector (Appel 1989; Goldberg 1991; Diwan, Moss, and Hudson 1992).

Dynamically typed languages, such as Racket, need to tag objects in any case, so option 1 is a natural choice for those languages. However, $\mathcal{L}_{\mathsf{Tup}}$ is a statically typed language, so it would be unfortunate to require tags on every object, especially small and pervasive objects like integers and Booleans. Option 3 is the best-performing choice for statically typed languages, but it comes with a relatively high implementation complexity. To keep this chapter within a reasonable scope of complexity, we recommend a combination of options 1 and 2, using separate strategies for the stack and the heap.

Regarding the stack, we recommend using a separate stack for pointers, which we call the *root stack* (aka *shadow stack*) (Siebert 2001; Henderson 2002; Baker et al. 2009). That is, when a local variable needs to be spilled and is of type `Vector`, we put it on the root stack instead of putting it on the procedure call stack. Furthermore, we always spill tuple-typed variables if they are live during a call to the collector, thereby ensuring that no pointers are in registers during a collection. Figure 6.7 reproduces the example shown in figure 6.5 and contrasts it with the data layout using a root stack. The root stack contains the two pointers from the regular stack and also the pointer in the second register.

The problem of distinguishing between pointers and other kinds of data also arises inside each tuple on the heap. We solve this problem by attaching a tag, an extra 64 bits, to each tuple. Figure 6.8 shows a zoomed-in view of the tags for two

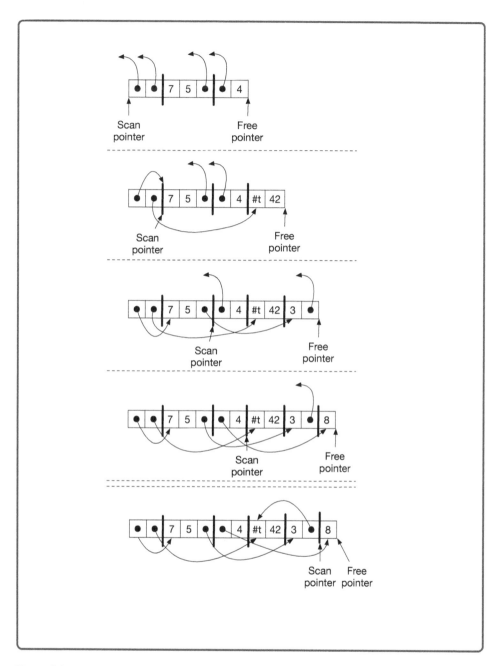

**Figure 6.6**
Depiction of the Cheney algorithm copying the live tuples.

of the tuples in the example given in figure 6.5. Note that we have drawn the bits in a big-endian way, from right to left, with bit location 0 (the least significant bit) on the far right, which corresponds to the direction of the x86 shifting instructions salq (shift left) and sarq (shift right). Part of each tag is dedicated to specifying

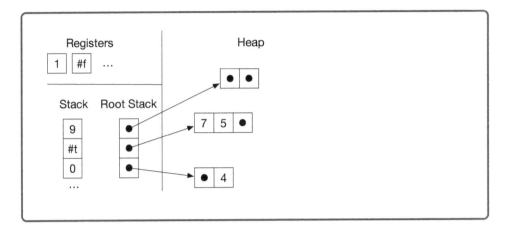

**Figure 6.7**
Maintaining a root stack to facilitate garbage collection.

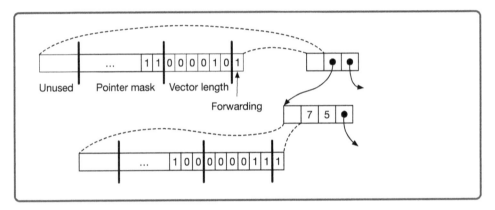

**Figure 6.8**
Representation of tuples in the heap.

which elements of the tuple are pointers, the part labeled *pointer mask*. Within the pointer mask, a 1 bit indicates that there is a pointer, and a 0 bit indicates some other kind of data. The pointer mask starts at bit location 7. We limit tuples to a maximum size of fifty elements, so we need 50 bits for the pointer mask.[2] The tag also contains two other pieces of information. The length of the tuple (number of elements) is stored in bits at locations 1 through 6. Finally, the bit at location 0 indicates whether the tuple has yet to be copied to the ToSpace. If the bit has value 1, then this tuple has not yet been copied. If the bit has value 0, then the entire tag is a forwarding pointer. (The lower 3 bits of a pointer are always zero in any case, because our tuples are 8-byte aligned.)

---

2. A production-quality compiler would handle arbitrarily sized tuples and use a more complex approach.

```
void initialize(uint64_t rootstack_size, uint64_t heap_size);
void collect(int64_t** rootstack_ptr, uint64_t bytes_requested);
int64_t* free_ptr;
int64_t* fromspace_begin;
int64_t* fromspace_end;
int64_t** rootstack_begin;
```

**Figure 6.9**
The compiler's interface to the garbage collector.

### 6.2.4  Implementation of the Garbage Collector

An implementation of the copying collector is provided in the `runtime.c` file. Figure 6.9 defines the interface to the garbage collector that is used by the compiler. The `initialize` function creates the FromSpace, ToSpace, and root stack and should be called in the prelude of the `main` function. The arguments of `initialize` are the root stack size and the heap size. Both need to be multiples of sixty-four, and $16,384$ is a good choice for both. The `initialize` function puts the address of the beginning of the FromSpace into the global variable `free_ptr`. The global variable `fromspace_end` points to the address that is one past the last element of the FromSpace. We use half-open intervals to represent chunks of memory (Dijkstra 1982). The `rootstack_begin` variable points to the first element of the root stack.

As long as there is room left in the FromSpace, your generated code can allocate tuples simply by moving the `free_ptr` forward. The amount of room left in the FromSpace is the difference between the `fromspace_end` and the `free_ptr`. The `collect` function should be called when there is not enough room left in the FromSpace for the next allocation. The `collect` function takes a pointer to the current top of the root stack (one past the last item that was pushed) and the number of bytes that need to be allocated. The `collect` function performs the copying collection and leaves the heap in a state such that there is enough room for the next allocation.

The introduction of garbage collection has a nontrivial impact on our compiler passes. We introduce a new compiler pass named `expose_allocation` that elaborates the code for allocating tuples. We also make significant changes to `select_instructions`, `build_interference`, `allocate_registers`, and `prelude_and_conclusion` and make minor changes in several more passes.

The following program serves as our running example. It creates two tuples, one nested inside the other. Both tuples have length one. The program accesses the element in the inner tuple.

```
(vector-ref (vector-ref (vector (vector 42)) 0) 0)
```

## 6.3 Expose Allocation

The pass `expose_allocation` lowers tuple creation into making a conditional call to the collector followed by allocating the appropriate amount of memory and initializing it. We choose to place the `expose_allocation` pass before `remove_complex_operands` because it generates code that contains complex operands.

The output of `expose_allocation` is a language $\mathcal{L}_{\text{Alloc}}$ that replaces tuple creation with new lower-level forms that we use in the translation of tuple creation.

$$exp \quad ::= \quad \cdots \mid (\text{collect } int) \mid (\text{allocate } int\ type) \mid (\text{global-value } name)$$

The (`collect` $n$) form runs the garbage collector, requesting that it make sure that there are $n$ bytes ready to be allocated. During instruction selection, the (`collect` $n$) form will become a call to the `collect` function in `runtime.c`. The (`allocate` $n$ $type$) form obtains memory for $n$ elements (and space at the front for the 64-bit tag), but the elements are not initialized. The $type$ parameter is the type of the tuple: (`Vector` $type_1 \ldots type_n$) where $type_i$ is the type of the $i$th element. The (`global-value` $name$) form reads the value of a global variable, such as `free_ptr`.

The type information that you need for (`allocate` $n$ $type$) can be obtained by running the `type-check-Lvec-has-type` type checker immediately before the `expose_allocation` pass. This version of the type checker places a special AST node of the form (`HasType` $e$ $type$) around each tuple creation. The concrete syntax for `HasType` is `has-type`.

The following shows the transformation of tuple creation into (1) a sequence of temporary variable bindings for the initializing expressions, (2) a conditional call to `collect`, (3) a call to `allocate`, and (4) the initialization of the tuple. The *len* placeholder refers to the length of the tuple, and *bytes* is the total number of bytes that need to be allocated for the tuple, which is 8 for the tag plus *len* times 8.

```
(has-type (vector e₀ ... eₙ₋₁) type)
⟹
  (let ([x₀ e₀]) ... (let ([xₙ₋₁ eₙ₋₁])
  (let ([_ (if (< (+ (global-value free_ptr) bytes)
                  (global-value fromspace_end))
               (void)
               (collect bytes))])
  (let ([v (allocate len type)])
  (let ([_ (vector-set! v 0 x₀)]) ...
  (let ([_ (vector-set! v n-1 xₙ₋₁)])
    v) ... )))) ...)
```

The sequencing of the initializing expressions $e_0, \ldots, e_{n-1}$ prior to the `allocate` is important because they may trigger garbage collection and we cannot have an allocated but uninitialized tuple on the heap during a collection.

Figure 6.10 shows the output of the `expose_allocation` pass on our running example.

```
(vector-ref
 (vector-ref
  (let ([vecinit6
         (let ([_4 (if (< (+ (global-value free_ptr) 16)
                          (global-value fromspace_end))
                       (void)
                       (collect 16))])
           (let ([alloc2 (allocate 1 (Vector Integer))])
           (let ([_3 (vector-set! alloc2 0 42)])
             alloc2)))])
   (let ([_8 (if (< (+ (global-value free_ptr) 16)
                    (global-value fromspace_end))
                 (void)
                 (collect 16))])
   (let ([alloc5 (allocate 1 (Vector (Vector Integer)))])
   (let ([_7 (vector-set! alloc5 0 vecinit6)])
     alloc5))))
  0)
 0)
```

**Figure 6.10**
Output of the `expose_allocation` pass.

$$
\begin{array}{rcl}
atm & ::= & (\text{Int } int) \mid (\text{Var } var) \\
exp & ::= & atm \mid (\text{Prim 'read ()}) \\
    & \mid & (\text{Prim '- } (atm)) \mid (\text{Prim '+ } (atm\ atm)) \mid (\text{Prim '- } (atm\ atm)) \\
    & \mid & (\text{Let } var\ exp\ exp) \\
\hline
atm & ::= & (\text{Bool } bool) \\
exp & ::= & (\text{Prim not } (atm)) \mid (\text{Prim } cmp\ (atm\ atm)) \mid (\text{If } exp\ exp\ exp) \\
atm & ::= & (\text{Void}) \\
exp & ::= & (\text{GetBang } var) \mid (\text{SetBang } var\ exp) \mid (\text{Begin } (exp\ \ldots)\ exp) \\
    & \mid & (\text{WhileLoop } exp\ exp) \\
\hline
exp & ::= & (\text{Collect } int)) \mid (\text{Allocate } int\ type) \mid (\text{GlobalValue } var) \\
\mathcal{L}^{mon}_{\text{Alloc}} & ::= & (\text{Program '() } exp)
\end{array}
$$

**Figure 6.11**
$\mathcal{L}^{mon}_{\text{Alloc}}$ is $\mathcal{L}_{\text{Alloc}}$ in monadic normal form.

## 6.4   Remove Complex Operands

The forms `collect`, `allocate`, and `global_value` should be treated as complex
operands. Figure 6.11 shows the grammar for the output language $\mathcal{L}^{mon}_{\text{Alloc}}$ of this
pass, which is $\mathcal{L}_{\text{Alloc}}$ in monadic normal form.

| | | |
|---|---|---|
| *atm* | ::= | (Int *int*) \| (Var *var*) |
| *exp* | ::= | *atm* \| (Prim 'read ()) \| (Prim '- (*atm*)) |
| | \| | (Prim '+ (*atm atm*)) \| (Prim '- (*atm atm*)) |
| *stmt* | ::= | (Assign (Var *var*) *exp*) |
| *tail* | ::= | (Return *exp*) \| (Seq *stmt tail*) |
| *atm* | ::= | (Bool *bool*) |
| *cmp* | ::= | eq? \| < \| <= \| > \| >= |
| *exp* | ::= | (Prim 'not (*atm*)) \| (Prim '*cmp* (*atm atm*)) |
| *tail* | ::= | (Goto *label*) |
| | \| | (IfStmt (Prim *cmp* (*atm atm*)) (Goto *label*) (Goto *label*)) |
| *atm* | ::= | (Void) |
| *stmt* | ::= | (Prim 'read ()) |
| *exp* | ::= | (Allocate *int type*) |
| | \| | (Prim vector-ref (*atm* (Int *int*))) |
| | \| | (Prim vector-set! (*atm* (Int *int*) *atm*)) |
| | \| | (Prim vector-length (*atm*)) |
| | \| | (GlobalValue *var*) |
| *stmt* | ::= | (Prim vector-set! (*atm* (Int *int*) *atm*)) |
| | \| | (Collect *int*) |
| $C_{\text{Tup}}$ | ::= | (CProgram *info* ((*label* . *tail*) … )) |

**Figure 6.12**
The abstract syntax of $C_{\text{Tup}}$, extending $C_{\circlearrowright}$ (figure 5.7).

## 6.5  Explicate Control and the $C_{\text{Tup}}$ Language

The output of `explicate_control` is a program in the intermediate language $C_{\text{Tup}}$, for which figure 6.12 shows the definition of the abstract syntax. The new expressions of $C_{\text{Tup}}$ include `allocate`, `vector-ref`, and `vector-set!`, and `global_value`. $C_{\text{Tup}}$ also includes the new `collect` statement. The `explicate_control` pass can treat these new forms much like the other forms that we've already encountered. The output of the `explicate_control` pass on the running example is shown on the left side of figure 6.15 in the next section.

## 6.6  Select Instructions and the x86$_{\text{Global}}$ Language

In this pass we generate x86 code for most of the new operations that are needed to compile tuples, including `Allocate`, `Collect`, and accessing tuple elements. We compile `GlobalValue` to `Global` because the latter has a different concrete syntax (see figures 6.13 and 6.14).

The tuple read and write forms translate into `movq` instructions. (The +1 in the offset serves to move past the tag at the beginning of the tuple representation.)

```
lhs = (vector-ref tup n);
⟹
movq tup', %r11
movq 8(n + 1)(%r11), lhs'
```

```
lhs = (vector-set! tup n rhs);
⟹
movq tup', %r11
movq rhs', 8(n + 1)(%r11)
movq $0, lhs'
```

The *lhs'*, *tup'*, and *rhs'* are obtained by translating from $C_{\mathsf{Tup}}$ to x86. The move of *tup'* to register r11 ensures that the offset expression 8(n + 1)(%r11) contains a register operand. This requires removing r11 from consideration by the register allocating.

Why not use rax instead of r11? Suppose that we instead used rax. Then the generated code for tuple assignment would be

```
movq tup', %rax
movq rhs', 8(n + 1)(%rax)
```

Next, suppose that *rhs'* ends up as a stack location, so patch_instructions would insert a move through rax as follows:

```
movq tup', %rax
movq rhs', %rax
movq %rax, 8(n + 1)(%rax)
```

However, this sequence of instructions does not work because we're trying to use rax for two different values (*tup'* and *rhs'*) at the same time!

The vector-length operation should be translated into a sequence of instructions that read the tag of the tuple and extract the 6 bits that represent the tuple length, which are the bits starting at index 1 and going up to and including bit 6. The x86 instructions andq (for bitwise-and) and sarq (shift right) can be used to accomplish this.

We compile the allocate form to operations on the free_ptr, as shown next. This approach is called *inline allocation* because it implements allocation without a function call by simply incrementing the allocation pointer. It is much more efficient than calling a function for each allocation. The address in the free_ptr is the next free address in the FromSpace, so we copy it into r11 and then move it forward by enough space for the tuple being allocated, which is 8(*len* + 1) bytes because each element is 8 bytes (64 bits) and we use 8 bytes for the tag. We then initialize the *tag* and finally copy the address in r11 to the left-hand side. Refer to figure 6.8 to see how the tag is organized. We recommend using the Racket operations bitwise-ior and arithmetic-shift to compute the tag during compilation. The type annotation in the allocate form is used to determine the pointer mask region of the tag. The addressing mode free_ptr(%rip) essentially stands for the address of the free_ptr global variable using a special instruction-pointer-relative addressing

$$
\begin{array}{rcl}
reg & ::= & \text{rsp | rbp | rax | rbx | rcx | rdx | rsi | rdi |} \\
    &     & \text{r8 | r9 | r10 | r11 | r12 | r13 | r14 | r15} \\
arg & ::= & \$\mathit{int} \text{ | \%} \mathit{reg} \text{ | } \mathit{int} (\%\mathit{reg}) \\
instr & ::= & \text{addq } \mathit{arg}, \mathit{arg} \text{ | subq } \mathit{arg}, \mathit{arg} \text{ | negq } \mathit{arg} \text{ | movq } \mathit{arg}, \mathit{arg} \text{ |} \\
      &     & \text{pushq } \mathit{arg} \text{ | popq } \mathit{arg} \text{ | callq } \mathit{label} \text{ | retq | jmp } \mathit{label} \text{ |} \\
      &     & \mathit{label}: \mathit{instr}
\end{array}
$$

$$
\begin{array}{rcl}
\mathit{bytereg} & ::= & \text{ah | al | bh | bl | ch | cl | dh | dl} \\
\mathit{arg} & ::= & \text{\%} \mathit{bytereg} \\
\mathit{cc} & ::= & \text{e | ne | l | le | g | ge} \\
\mathit{instr} & ::= & \text{xorq } \mathit{arg}, \mathit{arg} \text{ | cmpq } \mathit{arg}, \mathit{arg} \text{ | set} \mathit{cc} \text{ } \mathit{arg} \text{ | movzbq } \mathit{arg}, \mathit{arg} \\
 & | & \text{j} \mathit{cc} \text{ } \mathit{label}
\end{array}
$$

$$
\begin{array}{rcl}
\mathit{arg} & ::= & \mathit{label}(\text{\%rip}) \\
\text{x86}_{\text{Global}} & ::= & \text{.globl main} \\
 & & \text{main: } \mathit{instr}^{*}
\end{array}
$$

**Figure 6.13**
The concrete syntax of x86$_{\text{Global}}$ (extends x86$_{\text{If}}$ shown in figure 4.9).

mode of the x86-64 processor. In particular, the assembler computes the distance $d$ between the address of `free_ptr` and where the `rip` would be at that moment and then changes the `free_ptr(%rip)` argument to $d$`(%rip)`, which at runtime will compute the address of `free_ptr`.

```
lhs = (allocate len (Vector type...));
⟹
movq free_ptr(%rip), %r11
addq 8(len + 1), free_ptr(%rip)
movq $tag, 0(%r11)
movq %r11, lhs'
```

The `collect` form is compiled to a call to the `collect` function in the runtime. The arguments to `collect` are (1) the top of the root stack, and (2) the number of bytes that need to be allocated. We use another dedicated register, `r15`, to store the pointer to the top of the root stack. Therefore `r15` is not available for use by the register allocator.

```
(collect bytes)
⟹
movq %r15, %rdi
movq $bytes, %rsi
callq collect
```

The definitions of the concrete and abstract syntax of the x86$_{\text{Global}}$ language are shown in figures 6.13 and 6.14. It differs from x86$_{\text{If}}$ only in the addition of global variables. Figure 6.15 shows the output of the `select_instructions` pass on the running example.

$$
\begin{array}{lcl}
reg & ::= & \texttt{rsp} \mid \texttt{rbp} \mid \texttt{rax} \mid \texttt{rbx} \mid \texttt{rcx} \mid \texttt{rdx} \mid \texttt{rsi} \mid \texttt{rdi} \mid \\
    &     & \texttt{r8} \mid \texttt{r9} \mid \texttt{r10} \mid \texttt{r11} \mid \texttt{r12} \mid \texttt{r13} \mid \texttt{r14} \mid \texttt{r15} \\
arg & ::= & (\texttt{Imm}\ int) \mid (\texttt{Reg}\ reg) \mid (\texttt{Deref}\ reg\ int) \\
instr & ::= & (\texttt{Instr addq}\ (arg\ arg)) \mid (\texttt{Instr subq}\ (arg\ arg)) \\
      & \mid & (\texttt{Instr negq}\ (arg)) \mid (\texttt{Instr movq}\ (arg\ arg)) \\
      & \mid & (\texttt{Instr pushq}\ (arg)) \mid (\texttt{Instr popq}\ (arg)) \\
      & \mid & (\texttt{Callq}\ label\ int) \mid (\texttt{Retq}) \mid (\texttt{Jmp}\ label) \\
block & ::= & (\texttt{Block}\ info\ (instr \dots)) \\
\hline
bytereg & ::= & \texttt{ah} \mid \texttt{al} \mid \texttt{bh} \mid \texttt{bl} \mid \texttt{ch} \mid \texttt{cl} \mid \texttt{dh} \mid \texttt{dl} \\
arg & ::= & (\texttt{ByteReg}\ bytereg) \\
cc & ::= & \texttt{e} \mid \texttt{l} \mid \texttt{le} \mid \texttt{g} \mid \texttt{ge} \\
instr & ::= & (\texttt{Instr xorq}\ (arg\ arg)) \mid (\texttt{Instr cmpq}\ (arg\ arg)) \\
      & \mid & (\texttt{Instr set}\ (cc\ arg)) \mid (\texttt{Instr movzbq}\ (arg\ arg)) \\
      & \mid & (\texttt{JmpIf}\ 'cc'\ label) \\
\hline
arg & ::= & (\texttt{Global}\ label) \\
\text{x86}_{\text{Global}} & ::= & (\texttt{X86Program}\ info\ ((label\ .\ block) \dots)) \\
\end{array}
$$

**Figure 6.14**
The abstract syntax of x86$_{\text{Global}}$ (extends x86$_{\text{If}}$ shown in figure 4.10).

```
                                                        start:
                                                          movq free_ptr(%rip), tmp9
                                                          movq tmp9, tmp0
                                                          addq $16, tmp0
                                                          movq fromspace_end(%rip), tmp1
                                                          cmpq tmp1, tmp0
                                                          jl block0
                                                          jmp block1
                                                        block0:
                                                          movq $0, _4
                                                          jmp block9
                                                        block1:
                                                          movq %r15, %rdi
                                                          movq $16, %rsi
                                                          callq collect
                                                          jmp block9
                                                        block9:
                                                          movq free_ptr(%rip), %r11
                                                          addq $16, free_ptr(%rip)
                                                          movq $3, 0(%r11)
   start:                                                movq %r11, alloc2
     tmp9 = (global-value free_ptr);                     movq alloc2, %r11
     tmp0 = (+ tmp9 16);                                 movq $42, 8(%r11)
     tmp1 = (global-value fromspace_end);                movq $0, _3
     if (< tmp0 tmp1)                                    movq alloc2, vecinit6
       goto block0;                                      movq free_ptr(%rip), tmp2
     else                                                movq tmp2, tmp3
         goto block1;                                    addq $16, tmp3
   block0:                                               movq fromspace_end(%rip), tmp4
     _4 = (void);                                        cmpq tmp4, tmp3
     goto block9;                                        jl block7
   block1:                                               jmp block8
     (collect 16)                                      block7:
     goto block9;                                        movq $0, _8
   block9:                                               jmp block6
     alloc2 = (allocate 1 (Vector Integer));   ⇒       block8:
     _3 = (vector-set! alloc2 0 42);                     movq %r15, %rdi
     vecinit6 = alloc2;                                  movq $16, %rsi
     tmp2 = (global-value free_ptr);                     callq collect
     tmp3 = (+ tmp2 16);                                 jmp block6
     tmp4 = (global-value fromspace_end);              block6:
     if (< tmp3 tmp4)                                    movq free_ptr(%rip), %r11
       goto block7;                                      addq $16, free_ptr(%rip)
     else                                                movq $131, 0(%r11)
         goto block8;                                    movq %r11, alloc5
   block7:                                               movq alloc5, %r11
     _8 = (void);                                        movq vecinit6, 8(%r11)
     goto block6;                                        movq $0, _7
   block8:                                               movq alloc5, %r11
     (collect 16)                                        movq 8(%r11), tmp5
     goto block6;                                        movq tmp5, %r11
   block6:                                               movq 8(%r11), %rax
     alloc5 = (allocate 1 (Vector (Vector Integer)));    jmp conclusion
     _7 = (vector-set! alloc5 0 vecinit6);
     tmp5 = (vector-ref alloc5 0);
     return (vector-ref tmp5 0);
```

**Figure 6.15**
Output of the explicate_control (*left*) and select_instructions (*right*) passes on the running example.

## 6.7   Register Allocation

As discussed previously in this chapter, the garbage collector needs to access all the pointers in the root set, that is, all variables that are tuples. It will be the responsibility of the register allocator to make sure that

1. the root stack is used for spilling tuple-typed variables, and
2. if a tuple-typed variable is live during a call to the collector, it must be spilled to ensure that it is visible to the collector.

The latter responsibility can be handled during construction of the interference graph, by adding interference edges between the call-live tuple-typed variables and all the callee-saved registers. (They already interfere with the caller-saved registers.) The type information for variables is in the `Program` form, so we recommend adding another parameter to the `build_interference` function to communicate this alist.

The spilling of tuple-typed variables to the root stack can be handled after graph coloring, in choosing how to assign the colors (integers) to registers and stack locations. The `Program` output of this pass changes to also record the number of spills to the root stack.

## 6.8   Prelude and Conclusion

Figure 6.16 shows the output of the `prelude_and_conclusion` pass on the running example. In the prelude of the `main` function, we allocate space on the root stack to make room for the spills of tuple-typed variables. We do so by incrementing the root stack pointer (`r15`), taking care that the root stack grows up instead of down. For the running example, there was just one spill, so we increment `r15` by 8 bytes. In the conclusion we subtract 8 bytes from `r15`.

One issue that deserves special care is that there may be a call to `collect` prior to the initializing assignments for all the variables in the root stack. We do not want the garbage collector to mistakenly determine that some uninitialized variable is a pointer that needs to be followed. Thus, we zero out all locations on the root stack in the prelude of `main`. In figure 6.16, the instruction `movq $0, 0(%r15)` is sufficient to accomplish this task because there is only one spill. In general, we have to clear as many words as there are spills of tuple-typed variables. The garbage collector tests each root to see if it is null prior to dereferencing it.

Figure 6.17 gives an overview of all the passes needed for the compilation of $\mathcal{L}_{\text{Tup}}$.

```
        .globl main
main:
    pushq %rbp
    movq %rsp, %rbp
    subq $0, %rsp
    movq $65536, %rdi
    movq $65536, %rsi
    callq initialize
    movq rootstack_begin(%rip), %r15
    movq $0, 0(%r15)
    addq $8, %r15
    jmp start
conclusion:
    subq $8, %r15
    addq $0, %rsp
    popq %rbp
    retq
```

**Figure 6.16**
The prelude and conclusion generated by the `prelude_and_conclusion` pass for the running example.

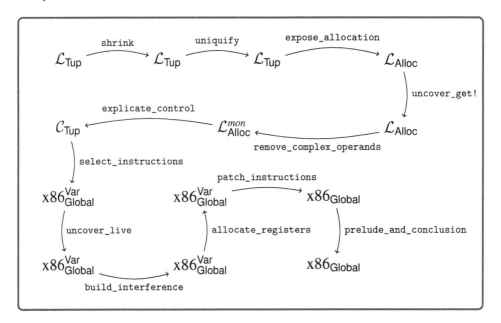

**Figure 6.17**
Diagram of the passes for $\mathcal{L}_{\mathsf{Tup}}$, a language with tuples.

```
type   ::=  Integer
 exp   ::=  int | (read) | (- exp) | (+ exp exp) | (- exp exp)
 exp   ::=  var | (let ([var exp]) exp)
type   ::=  Boolean
bool   ::=  #t | #f
cmp    ::=  eq? | < | <= | > | >=
 exp   ::=  bool | (and exp exp) | (or exp exp) | (not exp)
        |  (cmp exp exp) | (if exp exp exp)
type   ::=  Void
 exp   ::=  (set! var exp) | (begin exp* exp) | (while exp exp) | (void)
type   ::=  (Vector type*)
 exp   ::=  (vector exp*) | (vector-length exp)
        |  (vector-ref exp int) | (vector-set! exp int exp)
type   ::=  var
exp    ::=  (var exp ... )
def    ::=  (struct var ([var : type] ... ) #:mutable)
L_Struct ::=  def ... exp
```

**Figure 6.18**
The concrete syntax of $\mathcal{L}_{\text{Struct}}$, extending $\mathcal{L}_{\text{Tup}}$ (figure 6.1).

### 6.9 Challenge: Simple Structures

The language $\mathcal{L}_{\text{Struct}}$ extends $\mathcal{L}_{\text{Tup}}$ with support for simple structures. The definition of its concrete syntax is shown in figure 6.18, and the abstract syntax is shown in figure 6.19. Recall that a **struct** in Typed Racket is a user-defined data type that contains named fields and that is heap allocated, similarly to a vector. The following is an example of a structure definition, in this case the definition of a **point** type:

```
(struct point ([x : Integer] [y : Integer]) #:mutable)
```

An instance of a structure is created using function-call syntax, with the name of the structure in the function position, as follows:

```
(point 7 12)
```

Function-call syntax is also used to read a field of a structure. The function name is formed by the structure name, a dash, and the field name. The following example uses **point-x** and **point-y** to access the x and y fields of two point instances:

```
(let ([pt1 (point 7 12)])
  (let ([pt2 (point 4 3)])
    (+ (- (point-x pt1) (point-x pt2))
       (- (point-y pt1) (point-y pt2)))))
```

```
type   ::=  Integer
exp    ::=  (Int int) | (Prim 'read ())
       |    (Prim '- (exp)) | (Prim '+ (exp exp)) | (Prim '- (exp exp))
exp    ::=  (Var var) | (Let var exp exp)
type   ::=  Boolean
bool   ::=  #t | #f
cmp    ::=  eq? | < | <= | > | >=
op     ::=  cmp | and | or | not
exp    ::=  (Bool bool) | (If exp exp exp)
type   ::=  Void
exp    ::=  (SetBang var exp) | (Begin exp* exp) | (WhileLoop exp exp) | (Void)
type   ::=  (Vector type*)
op     ::=  vector | vector-length
exp    ::=  (Prim vector-ref (exp (Int int)))
       |    (Prim vector-set! (exp (Int int) exp))
type   ::=  (Var var)
exp    ::=  (Apply var exp ... )
def    ::=  (StructDef var ([var : type] ... ))
L_Struct ::= (ProgramDefsExp '() (def ... )) exp
```

**Figure 6.19**
The abstract syntax of $\mathcal{L}_{\text{Struct}}$, extending $\mathcal{L}_{\text{Tup}}$ (figure 6.2).

Similarly, to write to a field of a structure, use its set function, whose name starts with set-, followed by the structure name, then a dash, then the field name, and finally with an exclamation mark. The following example uses set-point-x! to change the x field from 7 to 42:

```
(let ([pt (point 7 12)])
  (let ([_ (set-point-x! pt 42)])
    (point-x pt)))
```

**Exercise 6.1** Create a type checker for $\mathcal{L}_{\text{Struct}}$ by extending the type checker for $\mathcal{L}_{\text{Tup}}$. Extend your compiler with support for simple structures, compiling $\mathcal{L}_{\text{Struct}}$ to x86 assembly code. Create five new test cases that use structures, and test your compiler.

```
  type  ::=  Integer
  exp   ::=  int | (read) | (- exp) | (+ exp exp) | (- exp exp)
  exp   ::=  var | (let ([var exp]) exp)
  type  ::=  Boolean
  bool  ::=  #t | #f
  cmp   ::=  eq? | < | <= | > | >=
  exp   ::=  bool | (and exp exp) | (or exp exp) | (not exp)
         |  (cmp exp exp) | (if exp exp exp)
  type  ::=  Void
  exp   ::=  (set! var exp) | (begin exp* exp) | (while exp exp) | (void)
  type  ::=  (Vector type*)
  exp   ::=  (vector exp*) | (vector-length exp)
         |  (vector-ref exp int) | (vector-set! exp int exp)
  type  ::=  (Vectorof type)
  exp   ::=  (* exp exp) | (make-vector exp exp)
  𝓛Array ::=  exp
```

**Figure 6.20**
The concrete syntax of $\mathcal{L}_{\text{Array}}$, extending $\mathcal{L}_{\text{Tup}}$ (figure 6.1).

## 6.10  Challenge: Arrays

In this chapter we have studied tuples, that is, heterogeneous sequences of elements whose length is determined at compile time. This challenge is also about sequences, but this time the length is determined at runtime and all the elements have the same type (they are homogeneous). We use the term *array* for this latter kind of sequence. The Racket language does not distinguish between tuples and arrays; they are both represented by vectors. However, Typed Racket distinguishes between tuples and arrays: the **Vector** type is for tuples, and the **Vectorof** type is for arrays.

Figure 6.20 presents the definition of the concrete syntax for $\mathcal{L}_{\text{Array}}$, and figure 6.21 presents the definition of the abstract syntax, extending $\mathcal{L}_{\text{Tup}}$ with the **Vectorof** type and the **make-vector** primitive operator for creating an array, whose arguments are the length of the array and an initial value for all the elements in the array. The **vector-length**, **vector-ref**, and **vector-ref!** operators that we defined for tuples become overloaded for use with arrays. We include integer multiplication in $\mathcal{L}_{\text{Array}}$ because it is useful in many examples involving arrays such as computing the inner product of two arrays (figure 6.22).

Figure 6.23 shows the definition of the type checker for $\mathcal{L}_{\text{Array}}$. The result type of **make-vector** is (Vectorof T), where T is the type of the initializing expression. The length expression is required to have type **Integer**. The type checking of the operators **vector-length**, **vector-ref**, and **vector-set!** is updated to handle the situation in which the vector has type **Vectorof**. In these cases we translate the operators to their **vectorof** form so that later passes can easily distinguish between operations on tuples versus arrays. We override the **operator-types** method to

$$
\begin{array}{lll}
\textit{type} & ::= & \texttt{Integer} \\
\textit{exp} & ::= & (\texttt{Int}\ \textit{int})\ |\ (\texttt{Prim 'read ()}) \\
& | & (\texttt{Prim '- }(\textit{exp}))\ |\ (\texttt{Prim '+ }(\textit{exp exp}))\ |\ (\texttt{Prim '- }(\textit{exp exp})) \\
\hline
\textit{exp} & ::= & (\texttt{Var}\ \textit{var})\ |\ (\texttt{Let}\ \textit{var exp exp}) \\
\hline
\textit{type} & ::= & \texttt{Boolean} \\
\textit{bool} & ::= & \texttt{\#t}\ |\ \texttt{\#f} \\
\textit{cmp} & ::= & \texttt{eq?}\ |\ \texttt{<}\ |\ \texttt{<=}\ |\ \texttt{>}\ |\ \texttt{>=} \\
\textit{op} & ::= & \textit{cmp}\ |\ \texttt{and}\ |\ \texttt{or}\ |\ \texttt{not} \\
\textit{exp} & ::= & (\texttt{Bool}\ \textit{bool})\ |\ (\texttt{If}\ \textit{exp exp exp}) \\
\hline
\textit{type} & ::= & \texttt{Void} \\
\textit{exp} & ::= & (\texttt{SetBang}\ \textit{var exp})\ |\ (\texttt{Begin}\ \textit{exp}^*\ \textit{exp})\ |\ (\texttt{WhileLoop}\ \textit{exp exp})\ |\ (\texttt{Void}) \\
\hline
\textit{type} & ::= & (\texttt{Vector}\ \textit{type}^*) \\
\textit{op} & ::= & \texttt{vector}\ |\ \texttt{vector-length} \\
\textit{exp} & ::= & (\texttt{Prim vector-ref }(\textit{exp}\ (\texttt{Int}\ \textit{int}))) \\
& | & (\texttt{Prim vector-set! }(\textit{exp}\ (\texttt{Int}\ \textit{int})\ \textit{exp})) \\
\hline
\textit{type} & ::= & (\textbf{Vectorof}\ \textit{type}) \\
\textit{exp} & ::= & (\texttt{Prim '* }(\textit{exp exp}))\ |\ (\texttt{make-vector}\ \textit{exp exp}) \\
\mathcal{L}_{\text{Array}} & ::= & \textit{exp}
\end{array}
$$

**Figure 6.21**
The abstract syntax of $\mathcal{L}_{\text{Array}}$, extending $\mathcal{L}_{\text{Tup}}$ (figure 6.2).

```
(let ([A (make-vector 2 2)])
(let ([B (make-vector 2 3)])
(let ([i 0])
(let ([prod 0])
(begin
  (while (< i n)
    (begin
      (set! prod (+ prod (* (vector-ref A i)
                            (vector-ref B i))))
      (set! i (+ i 1))))
  prod)))))
```

**Figure 6.22**
Example program that computes the inner product.

provide the type signature for multiplication: it takes two integers and returns an integer.

The definition of the interpreter for $\mathcal{L}_{\text{Array}}$ is shown in figure 6.24. The `make-vector` operator is interpreted using Racket's `make-vector` function, and multiplication is interpreted using `fx*`, which is multiplication for `fixnum` integers. In the `resolve` pass (section 6.10.2) we translate array access operations into `vectorof-ref` and `vectorof-set!` operations, which we interpret using `vector` operations with additional bounds checks that signal a `trapped-error`.

```
(define type-check-Lvecof-class
  (class type-check-Lvec-class
    (super-new)
    (inherit check-type-equal?)

    (define/override (operator-types)
      (append '((* . ((Integer Integer) . Integer)))
              (super operator-types)))

    (define/override (type-check-exp env)
      (lambda (e)
        (define recur (type-check-exp env))
        (match e
          [(Prim 'make-vector (list e1 e2))
           (define-values (e1^ t1) (recur e1))
           (define-values (e2^ elt-type) (recur e2))
           (define vec-type `(Vectorof ,elt-type))
           (values (Prim 'make-vector (list e1^ e2^)) vec-type)]
          [(Prim 'vector-ref (list e1 e2))
           (define-values (e1^ t1) (recur e1))
           (define-values (e2^ t2) (recur e2))
           (match* (t1 t2)
             [(`(Vectorof ,elt-type) 'Integer)
              (values (Prim 'vectorof-ref (list e1^ e2^)) elt-type)]
             [(other wise) ((super type-check-exp env) e)])]
          [(Prim 'vector-set! (list e1 e2 e3))
           (define-values (e-vec t-vec) (recur e1))
           (define-values (e2^ t2) (recur e2))
           (define-values (e-arg^ t-arg) (recur e3))
           (match t-vec
             [`(Vectorof ,elt-type)
              (check-type-equal? elt-type t-arg e)
              (values (Prim 'vectorof-set! (list e-vec e2^ e-arg^)) 'Void)]
             [else ((super type-check-exp env) e)])]
          [(Prim 'vector-length (list e1))
           (define-values (e1^ t1) (recur e1))
           (match t1
             [`(Vectorof ,t)
              (values (Prim 'vectorof-length (list e1^)) 'Integer)]
             [else ((super type-check-exp env) e)])]
          [else ((super type-check-exp env) e)])))
    ))

(define (type-check-Lvecof p)
  (send (new type-check-Lvecof-class) type-check-program p))
```

**Figure 6.23**
Type checker for the $\mathcal{L}_{\mathsf{Array}}$ language.

## 6.10.1 Data Representation

Just as with tuples, we store arrays on the heap, which means that the garbage collector will need to inspect arrays. An immediate thought is to use the same representation for arrays that we use for tuples. However, we limit tuples to a length of fifty so that their length and pointer mask can fit into the 64-bit tag at

```
(define interp-Lvecof-class
  (class interp-Lvec-class
    (super-new)

    (define/override (interp-op op)
      (match op
        ['make-vector make-vector]
        ['vectorof-length vector-length]
        ['vectorof-ref
         (lambda (v i)
           (if (< i (vector-length v))
               (vector-ref v i)
               (error 'trapped-error "index ~a out of bounds\nin ~v" i v)))]
        ['vectorof-set!
         (lambda (v i e)
           (if (< i (vector-length v))
               (vector-set! v i e)
               (error 'trapped-error "index ~a out of bounds\nin ~v" i v)))]
        [else (super interp-op op)]))
    ))

(define (interp-Lvecof p)
  (send (new interp-Lvecof-class) interp-program p))
```

**Figure 6.24**
Interpreter for $\mathcal{L}_{\mathsf{Array}}$.

the beginning of each tuple (section 6.2.3). We intend arrays to allow millions of elements, so we need more bits to store the length. However, because arrays are homogeneous, we need only 1 bit for the pointer mask instead of 1 bit per array element. Finally, the garbage collector must be able to distinguish between tuples and arrays, so we need to reserve one bit for that purpose. We arrive at the following layout for the 64-bit tag at the beginning of an array:

- The right-most bit is the forwarding bit, just as in a tuple. A 0 indicates that it is a forwarding pointer, and a 1 indicates that it is not.
- The next bit to the left is the pointer mask. A 0 indicates that none of the elements are pointers to the heap, and a 1 indicates that all the elements are pointers.
- The next 60 bits store the length of the array.
- The bit at position 62 distinguishes between a tuple (0) and an array (1).
- The left-most bit is reserved as explained in chapter 10.

In the following subsections we provide hints regarding how to update the passes to handle arrays.

### 6.10.2 Overload Resolution
As noted previously, with the addition of arrays, several operators have become *overloaded*; that is, they can be applied to values of more than one type. In this

case, the element access and length operators can be applied to both tuples and arrays. This kind of overloading is quite common in programming languages, so many compilers perform *overload resolution* to handle it. The idea is to translate each overloaded operator into different operators for the different types.

Implement a new pass named `resolve`. Translate the reading of an array element into a call to `vectorof-ref` and the writing of an array element to `vectorof-set!` Translate calls to `vector-length` into `vectorof-length`. When these operators are applied to tuples, leave them as is.

### 6.10.3  Bounds Checking

Recall that the interpreter for $\mathcal{L}_{\mathsf{Array}}$ signals a `trapped-error` when there is an array access that is out of bounds. Therefore your compiler is obliged to also catch these errors during execution and halt, signaling an error. We recommend inserting a new pass named `check_bounds` that inserts code around each `vectorof-ref` and `vectorof-set!` operation to ensure that the index is greater than or equal to zero and less than the array's length. If not, the program should halt, for which we recommend using a new primitive operation named `exit`.

### 6.10.4  Expose Allocation

This pass should translate array creation into lower-level operations. In particular, the new AST node (`AllocateArray` *exp type*) is analogous to the `Allocate` AST node for tuples. The *type* argument must be (`Vectorof` T), where $T$ is the element type for the array. The `AllocateArray` AST node allocates an array of the length specified by the *exp* (of type `Integer`), but does not initialize the elements of the array. Generate code in this pass to initialize the elements analogous to the case for tuples.

### 6.11  Uncover get!

Add cases for `AllocateArray` to `collect-set!` and `uncover-get!-exp`.

### 6.11.1  Remove Complex Operands

Add cases in the `rco_atom` and `rco_exp` for `AllocateArray`. In particular, an `AllocateArray` node is complex, and its subexpression must be atomic.

### 6.11.2  Explicate Control

Add cases for `AllocateArray` to `explicate_tail` and `explicate_assign`.

### 6.11.3  Select Instructions

Generate instructions for `AllocateArray` similar to those for `Allocate` given in section 6.6 except that the tag at the front of the array should instead use the representation discussed in section 6.10.1.

Regarding `vectorof-length`, extract the length from the tag.

The instructions generated for accessing an element of an array differ from those for a tuple (section 6.6) in that the index is not a constant so you need to generate instructions that compute the offset at runtime.

Compile the `exit` primitive into a call to the `exit` function of the C standard library, with an argument of 255.

**Exercise 6.2** Implement a compiler for the $\mathcal{L}_{Array}$ language by extending your compiler for $\mathcal{L}_{While}$. Test your compiler on a half dozen new programs, including the one shown in figure 6.22 and also a program that multiplies two matrices. Note that although matrices are two-dimensional arrays, they can be encoded into one-dimensional arrays by laying out each row in the array, one after the next.

### 6.12 Challenge: Generational Collection

The copying collector described in section 6.2 can incur significant runtime overhead because the call to `collect` takes time proportional to all the live data. One way to reduce this overhead is to reduce how much data is inspected in each call to `collect`. In particular, researchers have observed that recently allocated data is more likely to become garbage then data that has survived one or more previous calls to `collect`. This insight motivated the creation of *generational garbage collectors* that (1) segregate data according to its age into two or more generations; (2) allocate less space for younger generations, so collecting them is faster, and more space for the older generations; and (3) perform collection on the younger generations more frequently than on older generations (Wilson 1992).

For this challenge assignment, the goal is to adapt the copying collector implemented in `runtime.c` to use two generations, one for young data and one for old data. Each generation consists of a FromSpace and a ToSpace. The following is a sketch of how to adapt the `collect` function to use the two generations:

1. Copy the young generation's FromSpace to its ToSpace and then switch the role of the ToSpace and FromSpace.
2. If there is enough space for the requested number of bytes in the young FromSpace, then return from `collect`.
3. If there is not enough space in the young FromSpace for the requested bytes, then move the data from the young generation to the old one with the following steps:
   a. If there is enough room in the old FromSpace, copy the young FromSpace to the old FromSpace and then return.
   b. If there is not enough room in the old FromSpace, then collect the old generation by copying the old FromSpace to the old ToSpace and swap the roles of the old FromSpace and ToSpace.
   c. If there is enough room now, copy the young FromSpace to the old FromSpace and return. Otherwise, allocate a larger FromSpace and ToSpace for the old generation. Copy the young FromSpace and the old FromSpace into the larger FromSpace for the old generation and then return.

We recommend that you generalize the `cheney` function so that it can be used for all the copies mentioned: between the young FromSpace and ToSpace, between the old FromSpace and ToSpace, and between the young FromSpace and old FromSpace. This can be accomplished by adding parameters to `cheney` that replace its use of the global variables `fromspace_begin`, `fromspace_end`, `tospace_begin`, and `tospace_end`.

Note that the collection of the young generation does not traverse the old generation. This introduces a potential problem: there may be young data that is reachable only through pointers in the old generation. If these pointers are not taken into account, the collector could throw away young data that is live! One solution, called *pointer recording*, is to maintain a set of all the pointers from the old generation into the new generation and consider this set as part of the root set. To maintain this set, the compiler must insert extra instructions around every `vector-set!`. If the vector being modified is in the old generation, and if the value being written is a pointer into the new generation, then that pointer must be added to the set. Also, if the value being overwritten was a pointer into the new generation, then that pointer should be removed from the set.

**Exercise 6.3** Adapt the `collect` function in `runtime.c` to implement generational garbage collection, as outlined in this section. Update the code generation for `vector-set!` to implement pointer recording. Make sure that your new compiler and runtime execute without error on your test suite.

## 6.13  Further Reading

Appel (1990) describes many data representation approaches including the ones used in the compilation of Standard ML.

There are many alternatives to copying collectors (and their bigger siblings, the generational collectors) with regard to garbage collection, such as mark-and-sweep (McCarthy 1960) and reference counting (Collins 1960). The strengths of copying collectors are that allocation is fast (just a comparison and pointer increment), there is no fragmentation, cyclic garbage is collected, and the time complexity of collection depends only on the amount of live data and not on the amount of garbage (Wilson 1992). The main disadvantages of a two-space copying collector is that it uses a lot of extra space and takes a long time to perform the copy, though these problems are ameliorated in generational collectors. Racket programs tend to allocate many small objects and generate a lot of garbage, so copying and generational collectors are a good fit. Garbage collection is an active research topic, especially concurrent garbage collection (Tene, Iyengar, and Wolf 2011). Researchers are continuously developing new techniques and revisiting old trade-offs (Blackburn, Cheng, and McKinley 2004; Jones, Hosking, and Moss 2011; Shahriyar et al. 2013; Cutler and Morris 2015; Shidal et al. 2015; Österlund and Löwe 2016; Jacek and Moss 2019; Gamari and Dietz 2020). Researchers meet every year at the International Symposium on Memory Management to present these findings.

# 7 Functions

This chapter studies the compilation of a subset of Typed Racket in which only top-level function definitions are allowed. This kind of function appears in the C programming language, and it serves as an important stepping-stone to implementing lexically scoped functions in the form of **lambda** abstractions, which is the topic of chapter 8.

## 7.1 The $\mathcal{L}_{\mathsf{Fun}}$ Language

The concrete syntax and abstract syntax for function definitions and function application are shown in figures 7.1 and 7.2, with which we define the $\mathcal{L}_{\mathsf{Fun}}$ language. Programs in $\mathcal{L}_{\mathsf{Fun}}$ begin with zero or more function definitions. The function names from these definitions are in scope for the entire program, including all the function definitions, and therefore the ordering of function definitions does not matter. The concrete syntax for function application is (*exp exp* ... ), where the first expression must evaluate to a function and the remaining expressions are the arguments. The abstract syntax for function application is (**Apply** *exp exp**).

Functions are first-class in the sense that a function pointer is data and can be stored in memory or passed as a parameter to another function. Thus, there is a function type, written

$$(type_1 \;\; \cdots \;\; type_n \; \text{->} \; type_r)$$

for a function whose $n$ parameters have the types $type_1$ through $type_n$ and whose return type is $type_R$. The main limitation of these functions (with respect to Racket functions) is that they are not lexically scoped. That is, the only external entities that can be referenced from inside a function body are other globally defined functions. The syntax of $\mathcal{L}_{\mathsf{Fun}}$ prevents function definitions from being nested inside each other.

The program shown in figure 7.3 is a representative example of defining and using functions in $\mathcal{L}_{\mathsf{Fun}}$. We define a function **map** that applies some other function **f** to both elements of a tuple and returns a new tuple containing the results. We also define a function **inc**. The program applies **map** to **inc** and (**vector 0 41**). The result is (**vector 1 42**), from which we return 42.

The definitional interpreter for $\mathcal{L}_{\mathsf{Fun}}$ is shown in figure 7.4. The case for the **ProgramDefsExp** AST is responsible for setting up the mutual recursion between

| *type* | ::= | Integer |
| *exp* | ::= | *int* \| (read) \| (- *exp*) \| (+ *exp* *exp*) \| (- *exp* *exp*) |
| *exp* | ::= | *var* \| (let ([*var* *exp*]) *exp*) |
| *type* | ::= | Boolean |
| *bool* | ::= | #t \| #f |
| *cmp* | ::= | eq? \| < \| <= \| > \| >= |
| *exp* | ::= | *bool* \| (and *exp* *exp*) \| (or *exp* *exp*) \| (not *exp*) |
| | \| | (*cmp* *exp* *exp*) \| (if *exp* *exp* *exp*) |
| *type* | ::= | Void |
| *exp* | ::= | (set! *var* *exp*) \| (begin *exp*\* *exp*) \| (while *exp* *exp*) \| (void) |
| *type* | ::= | (Vector *type*\*) |
| *exp* | ::= | (vector *exp*\*) \| (vector-length *exp*) |
| | \| | (vector-ref *exp* *int*) \| (vector-set! *exp* *int* *exp*) |
| *type* | ::= | (*type* ... -> *type*) |
| *exp* | ::= | (*exp* *exp* ... ) |
| *def* | ::= | (define (*var* [*var*:*type*] ... ) : *type* *exp*) |
| $\mathcal{L}_{\text{Fun}}$ | ::= | *def* ... *exp* |

**Figure 7.1**
The concrete syntax of $\mathcal{L}_{\text{Fun}}$, extending $\mathcal{L}_{\text{Tup}}$ (figure 6.1).

| *type* | ::= | Integer |
| *op* | ::= | read \| + \| - |
| *exp* | ::= | (Int *int*) \| (Prim *op* (*exp* ... )) |
| *exp* | ::= | (Var *var*) \| (Let *var* *exp* *exp*) |
| *type* | ::= | Boolean |
| *bool* | ::= | #t \| #f |
| *cmp* | ::= | eq? \| < \| <= \| > \| >= |
| *op* | ::= | *cmp* \| and \| or \| not |
| *exp* | ::= | (Bool *bool*) \| (If *exp* *exp* *exp*) |
| *type* | ::= | Void |
| *exp* | ::= | (SetBang *var* *exp*) \| (Begin *exp*\* *exp*) \| (WhileLoop *exp* *exp*) \| (Void) |
| *type* | ::= | (Vector *type*\*) |
| *op* | ::= | vector \| vector-length |
| *exp* | ::= | (Prim vector-ref (*exp* (Int *int*))) |
| | \| | (Prim vector-set! (*exp* (Int *int*) *exp*)) |
| *type* | ::= | (*type* ... -> *type*) |
| *exp* | ::= | (Apply *exp* *exp* ... ) |
| *def* | ::= | (Def *var* ([*var*:*type*]... ) *type* '() *exp*) |
| $\mathcal{L}_{\text{Fun}}$ | ::= | (ProgramDefsExp '() (*def* ... )) *exp* |

**Figure 7.2**
The abstract syntax of $\mathcal{L}_{\text{Fun}}$, extending $\mathcal{L}_{\text{Tup}}$ (figure 6.2).

```
(define (map [f : (Integer -> Integer)] [v : (Vector Integer Integer)])
        : (Vector Integer Integer)
  (vector (f (vector-ref v 0)) (f (vector-ref v 1))))

(define (inc [x : Integer]) : Integer
  (+ x 1))

(vector-ref (map inc (vector 0 41)) 1)
```

**Figure 7.3**
Example of using functions in $\mathcal{L}_{\mathsf{Fun}}$.

the top-level function definitions. We use the classic back-patching approach that uses mutable variables and makes two passes over the function definitions (Kelsey, Clinger, and Rees 1998). In the first pass we set up the top-level environment using a mutable cons cell for each function definition. Note that the lambda value for each function is incomplete; it does not yet include the environment. Once the top-level environment has been constructed, we iterate over it and update the lambda values to use the top-level environment. To interpret a function application, we match the result of the function expression to obtain a function value. We then extend the function's environment with the mapping of parameters to argument values. Finally, we interpret the body of the function in this extended environment.

The type checker for $\mathcal{L}_{\mathsf{Fun}}$ is shown in figure 7.5. Similarly to the interpreter, the case for the ProgramDefsExp AST is responsible for setting up the mutual recursion between the top-level function definitions. We begin by create a mapping env from every function name to its type. We then type check the program using this mapping. In the case for function application, we match the type of the function expression to a function type and check that the types of the argument expressions are equal to the function's parameter types. The type of the application as a whole is the return type from the function type.

```
(define interp-Lfun-class
  (class interp-Lvec-class
    (super-new)

    (define/override ((interp-exp env) e)
      (define recur (interp-exp env))
      (match e
        [(Apply fun args)
         (define fun-val (recur fun))
         (define arg-vals (for/list ([e args]) (recur e)))
         (match fun-val
           [`(function (,xs ...) ,body ,fun-env)
            (define params-args (for/list ([x xs] [arg arg-vals])
                                  (cons x (box arg))))
            (define new-env (append params-args fun-env))
            ((interp-exp new-env) body)]
           [else
            (error 'interp-exp "expected function, not ~a" fun-val)])]
        [else ((super interp-exp env) e)]
        ))

    (define/public (interp-def d)
      (match d
        [(Def f (list `[,xs : ,ps] ...) rt _ body)
         (cons f (box `(function ,xs ,body ())))]))

    (define/override (interp-program p)
      (match p
        [(ProgramDefsExp info ds body)
         (let ([top-level (for/list ([d ds]) (interp-def d))])
           (for/list ([f (in-dict-values top-level)])
             (set-box! f (match (unbox f)
                           [`(function ,xs ,body ())
                            `(function ,xs ,body ,top-level)])))
           ((interp-exp top-level) body))]))
    ))

(define (interp-Lfun p)
  (send (new interp-Lfun-class) interp-program p))
```

**Figure 7.4**
Interpreter for the $\mathcal{L}_{\mathsf{Fun}}$ language.

```
(define type-check-Lfun-class
  (class type-check-Lvec-class
    (super-new)
    (inherit check-type-equal?)

    (define/public (type-check-apply env e es)
      (define-values (e^ ty) ((type-check-exp env) e))
      (define-values (e* ty*) (for/lists (e* ty*) ([e (in-list es)])
                                ((type-check-exp env) e)))
      (match ty
        [`(,ty^* ... -> ,rt)
         (for ([arg-ty ty*] [param-ty ty^*])
           (check-type-equal? arg-ty param-ty (Apply e es)))
         (values e^ e* rt)]))

    (define/override (type-check-exp env)
      (lambda (e)
        (match e
          [(FunRef f n)
           (values (FunRef f n) (dict-ref env f))]
          [(Apply e es)
           (define-values (e^ es^ rt) (type-check-apply env e es))
           (values (Apply e^ es^) rt)]
          [(Call e es)
           (define-values (e^ es^ rt) (type-check-apply env e es))
           (values (Call e^ es^) rt)]
          [else ((super type-check-exp env) e)])))

    (define/public (type-check-def env)
      (lambda (e)
        (match e
          [(Def f (and p:t* (list `[,xs : ,ps] ...)) rt info body)
           (define new-env (append (map cons xs ps) env))
           (define-values (body^ ty^) ((type-check-exp new-env) body))
           (check-type-equal? ty^ rt body)
           (Def f p:t* rt info body^)])))

    (define/public (fun-def-type d)
      (match d
        [(Def f (list `[,xs : ,ps] ...) rt info body) `(,@ps -> ,rt)]))

    (define/override (type-check-program e)
      (match e
        [(ProgramDefsExp info ds body)
         (define env (for/list ([d ds])
                       (cons (Def-name d) (fun-def-type d))))
         (define ds^ (for/list ([d ds]) ((type-check-def env) d)))
         (define-values (body^ ty) ((type-check-exp env) body))
         (check-type-equal? ty 'Integer body)
         (ProgramDefsExp info ds^ body^)]))))

(define (type-check-Lfun p)
  (send (new type-check-Lfun-class) type-check-program p))
```

**Figure 7.5**
Type checker for the $\mathcal{L}_{\text{Fun}}$ language.

## 7.2   Functions in x86

The x86 architecture provides a few features to support the implementation of functions. We have already seen that there are labels in x86 so that one can refer to the location of an instruction, as is needed for jump instructions. Labels can also be used to mark the beginning of the instructions for a function. Going further, we can obtain the address of a label by using the `leaq` instruction. For example, the following puts the address of the `inc` label into the `rbx` register:

```
leaq inc(%rip), %rbx
```

Recall from section 6.6 that `inc(%rip)` is an example of instruction-pointer-relative addressing.

In section 2.2 we used the `callq` instruction to jump to functions whose locations were given by a label, such as `read_int`. To support function calls in this chapter we instead jump to functions whose location are given by an address in a register; that is, we use *indirect function calls*. The x86 syntax for this is a `callq` instruction that requires an asterisk before the register name.

```
callq *%rbx
```

### 7.2.1   Calling Conventions

The `callq` instruction provides partial support for implementing functions: it pushes the return address on the stack and it jumps to the target. However, `callq` does not handle

1. parameter passing,
2. pushing frames on the procedure call stack and popping them off, or
3. determining how registers are shared by different functions.

Regarding parameter passing, recall that the x86-64 calling convention for Unix-based systems uses the following six registers to pass arguments to a function, in the given order:

```
rdi rsi rdx rcx r8 r9
```

If there are more than six arguments, then the calling convention mandates using space on the frame of the caller for the rest of the arguments. However, to ease the implementation of efficient tail calls (section 7.2.2), we arrange never to need more than six arguments. The return value of the function is stored in register `rax`.

Regarding frames and the procedure call stack, recall from section 2.2 that the stack grows down and each function call uses a chunk of space on the stack called a frame. The caller sets the stack pointer, register `rsp`, to the last data item in its frame. The callee must not change anything in the caller's frame, that is, anything that is at or above the stack pointer. The callee is free to use locations that are below the stack pointer.

Recall that we store variables of tuple type on the root stack. So, the prelude of a function needs to move the root stack pointer `r15` up according to the number

| Caller View | Callee View | Contents | Frame |
|---|---|---|---|
| 8(%rbp) | | return address | |
| 0(%rbp) | | old rbp | |
| -8(%rbp) | | callee-saved 1 | Caller |
| ... | | ... | |
| $-8j$(%rbp) | | callee-saved $j$ | |
| $-8(j+1)$(%rbp) | | local variable 1 | |
| ... | | ... | |
| $-8(j+k)$(%rbp) | | local variable $k$ | |
| | 8(%rbp) | return address | |
| | 0(%rbp) | old rbp | |
| | -8(%rbp) | callee-saved 1 | Callee |
| | ... | ... | |
| | $-8n$(%rbp) | callee-saved $n$ | |
| | $-8(n+1)$(%rbp) | local variable 1 | |
| | ... | ... | |
| | $-8(n+m)$(%rbp) | local variable $m$ | |

**Figure 7.6**
Memory layout of caller and callee frames.

of variables of tuple type and the conclusion needs to move the root stack pointer back down. Also, the prelude must initialize to 0 this frame's slots in the root stack to signal to the garbage collector that those slots do not yet contain a valid pointer. Otherwise the garbage collector will interpret the garbage bits in those slots as memory addresses and try to traverse them, causing serious mayhem!

Regarding the sharing of registers between different functions, recall from section 3.1 that the registers are divided into two groups, the caller-saved registers and the callee-saved registers. The caller should assume that all the caller-saved registers are overwritten with arbitrary values by the callee. For that reason we recommend in section 3.1 that variables that are live during a function call should not be assigned to caller-saved registers.

On the flip side, if the callee wants to use a callee-saved register, the callee must save the contents of those registers on their stack frame and then put them back prior to returning to the caller. For that reason we recommend in section 3.1 that if the register allocator assigns a variable to a callee-saved register, then the prelude of the **main** function must save that register to the stack and the conclusion of **main** must restore it. This recommendation now generalizes to all functions.

Recall that the base pointer, register **rbp**, is used as a point of reference within a frame, so that each local variable can be accessed at a fixed offset from the base pointer (section 2.2). Figure 7.6 shows the general layout of the caller and callee frames.

### 7.2.2  Efficient Tail Calls

In general, the amount of stack space used by a program is determined by the longest chain of nested function calls. That is, if function $f_1$ calls $f_2$, $f_2$ calls $f_3$, and so on to $f_n$, then the amount of stack space is linear in $n$. The depth $n$ can grow quite large if functions are recursive. However, in some cases we can arrange to use only a constant amount of space for a long chain of nested function calls.

A *tail call* is a function call that happens as the last action in a function body. For example, in the following program, the recursive call to `tail_sum` is a tail call:

```
(define (tail_sum [n : Integer] [r : Integer]) : Integer
  (if (eq? n 0)
      r
      (tail_sum (- n 1) (+ n r))))

(+ (tail_sum 3 0) 36)
```

At a tail call, the frame of the caller is no longer needed, so we can pop the caller's frame before making the tail call. With this approach, a recursive function that makes only tail calls ends up using a constant amount of stack space. Functional languages like Racket rely heavily on recursive functions, so the definition of Racket *requires* that all tail calls be optimized in this way.

Some care is needed with regard to argument passing in tail calls. As mentioned, for arguments beyond the sixth, the convention is to use space in the caller's frame for passing arguments. However, for a tail call we pop the caller's frame and can no longer use it. An alternative is to use space in the callee's frame for passing arguments. However, this option is also problematic because the caller and callee's frames overlap in memory. As we begin to copy the arguments from their sources in the caller's frame, the target locations in the callee's frame might collide with the sources for later arguments! We solve this problem by using the heap instead of the stack for passing more than six arguments (section 7.5).

As mentioned, for a tail call we pop the caller's frame prior to making the tail call. The instructions for popping a frame are the instructions that we usually place in the conclusion of a function. Thus, we also need to place such code immediately before each tail call. These instructions include restoring the callee-saved registers, so it is fortunate that the argument passing registers are all caller-saved registers.

One note remains regarding which instruction to use to make the tail call. When the callee is finished, it should not return to the current function but instead return to the function that called the current one. Thus, the return address that is already on the stack is the right one, and we should not use `callq` to make the tail call because that would overwrite the return address. Instead we simply use the `jmp` instruction. As with the indirect function call, we write an *indirect jump* with a register prefixed with an asterisk. We recommend using `rax` to hold the jump target because the conclusion can overwrite just about everything else.

```
jmp *%rax
```

## 7.3   Shrink $\mathcal{L}_{\mathsf{Fun}}$

The `shrink` pass performs a minor modification to ease the later passes. This pass introduces an explicit `main` function that gobbles up all the top-level statements of the module. It also changes the top `ProgramDefsExp` form to `ProgramDefs`.

```
   (ProgramDefsExp info (def ... ) exp)
⇒ (ProgramDefs info (def ...  mainDef))
```

where *mainDef* is

```
(Def 'main '() 'Integer '() exp')
```

## 7.4   Reveal Functions and the $\mathcal{L}_{\mathsf{FunRef}}$ Language

The syntax of $\mathcal{L}_{\mathsf{Fun}}$ is inconvenient for purposes of compilation in that it conflates the use of function names and local variables. This is a problem because we need to compile the use of a function name differently from the use of a local variable. In particular, we use `leaq` to convert the function name (a label in x86) to an address in a register. Thus, we create a new pass that changes function references from (`Var` $f$) to (`FunRef` $f$ $n$) where $n$ is the arity of the function. This pass is named `reveal_functions` and the output language is $\mathcal{L}_{\mathsf{FunRef}}$.

Placing this pass after `uniquify` will make sure that there are no local variables and functions that share the same name. The `reveal_functions` pass should come before the `remove_complex_operands` pass because function references should be categorized as complex expressions.

## 7.5   Limit Functions

Recall that we wish to limit the number of function parameters to six so that we do not need to use the stack for argument passing, which makes it easier to implement efficient tail calls. However, because the input language $\mathcal{L}_{\mathsf{Fun}}$ supports arbitrary numbers of function arguments, we have some work to do! The `limit_functions` pass transforms functions and function calls that involve more than six arguments to pass the first five arguments as usual, but it packs the rest of the arguments into a tuple and passes it as the sixth argument.[1]

Each function definition with seven or more parameters is transformed as follows:

```
(Def f ([x₁:T₁]  ...  [xₙ:Tₙ]) Tᵣ info body)
```
$$\Rightarrow$$
```
(Def f ([x₁:T₁]  ...  [x₅:T₅] [tup : (Vector T₆ ... Tₙ)]) Tᵣ info body')
```

where the *body* is transformed into *body'* by replacing the occurrences of each parameter $x_i$ where $i > 5$ with the $k$th element of the tuple, where $k = i - 6$.

---

1. The implementation this pass can be postponed to last because you can test the rest of the passes on functions with six or fewer parameters.

$$
\begin{array}{lll}
\textit{atm} & ::= & (\texttt{Int}\ \textit{int})\ |\ (\texttt{Var}\ \textit{var}) \\
\textit{exp} & ::= & \textit{atm}\ |\ (\texttt{Prim}\ \texttt{'read}\ ()) \\
 & | & (\texttt{Prim}\ \texttt{'-}\ (\textit{atm}))\ |\ (\texttt{Prim}\ \texttt{'+}\ (\textit{atm}\ \textit{atm}))\ |\ (\texttt{Prim}\ \texttt{'-}\ (\textit{atm}\ \textit{atm})) \\
 & | & (\texttt{Let}\ \textit{var}\ \textit{exp}\ \textit{exp})
\end{array}
$$

$$
\begin{array}{lll}
\textit{atm} & ::= & (\texttt{Bool}\ \textit{bool}) \\
\textit{exp} & ::= & (\texttt{Prim}\ \texttt{not}\ (\textit{atm}))\ |\ (\texttt{Prim}\ \textit{cmp}\ (\textit{atm}\ \textit{atm}))\ |\ (\texttt{If}\ \textit{exp}\ \textit{exp}\ \textit{exp})
\end{array}
$$

$$
\begin{array}{lll}
\textit{atm} & ::= & (\texttt{Void}) \\
\textit{exp} & ::= & (\texttt{GetBang}\ \textit{var})\ |\ (\texttt{SetBang}\ \textit{var}\ \textit{exp})\ |\ (\texttt{Begin}\ (\textit{exp}\ \dots)\ \textit{exp}) \\
 & | & (\texttt{WhileLoop}\ \textit{exp}\ \textit{exp})
\end{array}
$$

$$
\begin{array}{lll}
\textit{exp} & ::= & (\texttt{Collect}\ \textit{int}))\ |\ (\texttt{Allocate}\ \textit{int}\ \textit{type})\ |\ (\texttt{GlobalValue}\ \textit{var})
\end{array}
$$

$$
\begin{array}{lll}
\textit{type} & ::= & (\textit{type}\ \dots\ \texttt{->}\ \textit{type}) \\
\textit{exp} & ::= & (\texttt{FunRef}\ \textit{label}\ \textit{int})\ |\ (\texttt{Apply}\ \textit{atm}\ \textit{atm}\ \dots) \\
\textit{def} & ::= & (\texttt{Def}\ \textit{var}\ ([\textit{var}\colon\textit{type}]\ \dots)\ \textit{type}\ \texttt{'()}\ \textit{exp}) \\
\mathcal{L}^{mon}_{\mathsf{FunRef}} & ::= & (\texttt{ProgramDefsExp}\ \texttt{'()}\ (\textit{def}\ \dots))\ \textit{exp})
\end{array}
$$

**Figure 7.7**
$\mathcal{L}^{mon}_{\mathsf{FunRef}}$ is $\mathcal{L}_{\mathsf{FunRef}}$ in monadic normal form.

$$(\texttt{Var}\ x_i)\ \Rightarrow\ (\texttt{Prim}\ \texttt{'vector-ref}\ (\texttt{list}\ \texttt{tup}\ (\texttt{Int}\ k)))$$

For function calls with too many arguments, the `limit_functions` pass transforms them in the following way:

$$(e_0\ e_1\ \dots\ e_n) \qquad\qquad \Rightarrow \qquad (e_0\ e_1 \dots e_5\ (\texttt{vector}\ e_6 \dots e_n))$$

## 7.6    Remove Complex Operands

The primary decisions to make for this pass are whether to classify **FunRef** and **Apply** as either atomic or complex expressions. Recall that an atomic expression ends up as an immediate argument of an x86 instruction. Function application translates to a sequence of instructions, so **Apply** must be classified as a complex expression. On the other hand, the arguments of **Apply** should be atomic expressions. Regarding **FunRef**, as discussed previously, the function label needs to be converted to an address using the `leaq` instruction. Thus, even though **FunRef** seems rather simple, it needs to be classified as a complex expression so that we generate an assignment statement with a left-hand side that can serve as the target of the `leaq`.

The output of this pass, $\mathcal{L}^{mon}_{\mathsf{FunRef}}$ (figure 7.7), extends $\mathcal{L}^{mon}_{\mathsf{Alloc}}$ (figure 6.11) with **FunRef** and **Apply** in the grammar for expressions and augments programs to include a list of function definitions.

## 7.7    Explicate Control and the $\mathcal{C}_{\mathsf{Fun}}$ Language

Figure 7.8 defines the abstract syntax for $\mathcal{C}_{\mathsf{Fun}}$, the output of `explicate_control`. The auxiliary functions for assignment and tail contexts should be updated with

$$
\begin{array}{lll}
\textit{atm} & ::= & (\texttt{Int } \textit{int}) \mid (\texttt{Var } \textit{var}) \\
\textit{exp} & ::= & \textit{atm} \mid (\texttt{Prim 'read ()}) \mid (\texttt{Prim '- } (\textit{atm})) \\
& \mid & (\texttt{Prim '+ } (\textit{atm atm})) \mid (\texttt{Prim '- } (\textit{atm atm})) \\
\textit{stmt} & ::= & (\texttt{Assign (Var } \textit{var}) \textit{ exp}) \\
\textit{tail} & ::= & (\texttt{Return } \textit{exp}) \mid (\texttt{Seq } \textit{stmt tail}) \\
\hline
\textit{atm} & ::= & (\texttt{Bool } \textit{bool}) \\
\textit{cmp} & ::= & \texttt{eq?} \mid \texttt{<} \mid \texttt{<=} \mid \texttt{>} \mid \texttt{>=} \\
\textit{exp} & ::= & (\texttt{Prim 'not } (\textit{atm})) \mid (\texttt{Prim '} \textit{cmp } (\textit{atm atm})) \\
\textit{tail} & ::= & (\texttt{Goto } \textit{label}) \\
& \mid & (\texttt{IfStmt (Prim } \textit{cmp } (\textit{atm atm})) \texttt{ (Goto } \textit{label}) \texttt{ (Goto } \textit{label})) \\
\hline
\textit{atm} & ::= & (\texttt{Void}) \\
\textit{stmt} & ::= & (\texttt{Prim 'read ()}) \\
\hline
\textit{exp} & ::= & (\texttt{Allocate } \textit{int type}) \\
& \mid & (\texttt{Prim vector-ref } (\textit{atm } (\texttt{Int } \textit{int}))) \\
& \mid & (\texttt{Prim vector-set! } (\textit{atm } (\texttt{Int } \textit{int}) \textit{ atm})) \\
& \mid & (\texttt{Prim vector-length } (\textit{atm})) \\
& \mid & (\texttt{GlobalValue } \textit{var}) \\
\textit{stmt} & ::= & (\texttt{Prim vector-set! } (\textit{atm } (\texttt{Int } \textit{int}) \textit{ atm})) \\
& \mid & (\texttt{Collect } \textit{int}) \\
\hline
\textit{exp} & ::= & (\textbf{FunRef } \textit{label int}) \mid (\textbf{Call } \textit{atm } (\textit{atm} \dots)) \\
\textit{tail} & ::= & (\textbf{TailCall } \textit{atm atm} \dots) \\
\textit{def} & ::= & (\textbf{Def } \textit{label } ([\textit{var}:\textit{type}] \dots) \textit{ type info } ((\textit{label} . \textit{tail}) \dots)) \\
\mathcal{C}_{\textsf{Fun}} & ::= & (\textbf{ProgramDefs } \textit{info } (\textit{def} \dots))
\end{array}
$$

**Figure 7.8**
The abstract syntax of $\mathcal{C}_{\textsf{Fun}}$, extending $\mathcal{C}_{\textsf{Tup}}$ (figure 6.12).

cases for `Apply` and `FunRef` and the function for predicate context should be updated for `Apply` but not `FunRef`. (A `FunRef` cannot be a Boolean.) In assignment and predicate contexts, `Apply` becomes `Call`, whereas in tail position `Apply` becomes `TailCall`. We recommend defining a new auxiliary function for processing function definitions. This code is similar to the case for `Program` in $\mathcal{L}_{\textsf{Tup}}$. The top-level `explicate_control` function that handles the `ProgramDefs` form of $\mathcal{L}_{\textsf{Fun}}$ can then apply this new function to all the function definitions.

$$
\begin{array}{rcl}
reg & ::= & \texttt{rsp} \mid \texttt{rbp} \mid \texttt{rax} \mid \texttt{rbx} \mid \texttt{rcx} \mid \texttt{rdx} \mid \texttt{rsi} \mid \texttt{rdi} \mid \\
& & \texttt{r8} \mid \texttt{r9} \mid \texttt{r10} \mid \texttt{r11} \mid \texttt{r12} \mid \texttt{r13} \mid \texttt{r14} \mid \texttt{r15} \\
arg & ::= & \$int \mid \%reg \mid int(\%reg) \\
instr & ::= & \texttt{addq}\,arg,arg \mid \texttt{subq}\,arg,arg \mid \texttt{negq}\,arg \mid \texttt{movq}\,arg,arg \mid \\
& & \texttt{pushq}\,arg \mid \texttt{popq}\,arg \mid \texttt{callq}\,label \mid \texttt{retq} \mid \texttt{jmp}\,label \mid \\
& & label : instr
\end{array}
$$

$$
\begin{array}{rcl}
bytereg & ::= & \texttt{ah} \mid \texttt{al} \mid \texttt{bh} \mid \texttt{bl} \mid \texttt{ch} \mid \texttt{cl} \mid \texttt{dh} \mid \texttt{dl} \\
arg & ::= & \%bytereg \\
cc & ::= & \texttt{e} \mid \texttt{ne} \mid \texttt{l} \mid \texttt{le} \mid \texttt{g} \mid \texttt{ge} \\
instr & ::= & \texttt{xorq}\,arg, arg \mid \texttt{cmpq}\,arg, arg \mid \texttt{set}cc\,arg \mid \texttt{movzbq}\,arg, arg \\
& \mid & \texttt{j}cc\,label
\end{array}
$$

$$
\begin{array}{rcl}
arg & ::= & label(\%\texttt{rip})
\end{array}
$$

$$
\begin{array}{rcl}
instr & ::= & \texttt{callq} * arg \mid \texttt{tailjmp}\,arg \mid \texttt{leaq}\,arg, \%reg \\
block & ::= & instr^{+} \\
def & ::= & \texttt{.globl .align}\ 8\ label\,(label : block)^{*} \\
\text{x86}^{\text{Def}}_{\text{callq}*} & ::= & def^{*}
\end{array}
$$

**Figure 7.9**
The concrete syntax of $\text{x86}^{\text{Def}}_{\text{callq}*}$ (extends $\text{x86}_{\text{Global}}$ of figure 6.13).

## 7.8 Select Instructions and the $\text{x86}^{\text{Def}}_{\text{callq}*}$ Language

The output of select instructions is a program in the $\text{x86}^{\text{Def}}_{\text{callq}*}$ language; the definition of its concrete syntax is shown in figure 7.9, and the definition of its abstract syntax is shown in figure 7.10. We use the **align** directive on the labels of function definitions to make sure the bottom three bits are zero, which we put to use in chapter 9. We discuss the new instructions as needed in this section.

An assignment of a function reference to a variable becomes a load-effective-address instruction as follows, where $lhs'$ is the translation of $lhs$ from $atm$ in $C_{\text{Fun}}$ to $arg$ in $\text{x86}^{\text{Var,Def}}_{\text{callq}*}$. The **FunRef** becomes a **Global** AST node, whose concrete syntax is instruction-pointer-relative addressing.

$$lhs = (\texttt{fun-ref}\ f\ n); \qquad \Rightarrow \qquad \texttt{leaq}\ f(\%\texttt{rip}),\ lhs'$$

Regarding function definitions, we need to remove the parameters and instead perform parameter passing using the conventions discussed in section 7.2. That is, the arguments are passed in registers. We recommend turning the parameters into local variables and generating instructions at the beginning of the function to move from the argument-passing registers (section 7.2.1) to these local variables.

$$(\texttt{Def}\ f\ \texttt{'(}[x_1 : T_1]\ [x_2 : T_2]\ \ldots\ \texttt{)}\ T_r\ info\ B)$$
$$\Rightarrow$$
$$(\texttt{Def}\ f\ \texttt{'()}\ \texttt{'Integer}\ info'\ B')$$

The basic blocks $B'$ are the same as $B$ except that the **start** block is modified to add the instructions for moving from the argument registers to the parameter

$$reg ::= \text{rsp} \mid \text{rbp} \mid \text{rax} \mid \text{rbx} \mid \text{rcx} \mid \text{rdx} \mid \text{rsi} \mid \text{rdi} \mid$$
$$\text{r8} \mid \text{r9} \mid \text{r10} \mid \text{r11} \mid \text{r12} \mid \text{r13} \mid \text{r14} \mid \text{r15}$$
$$arg ::= (\texttt{Imm } int) \mid (\texttt{Reg } reg) \mid (\texttt{Deref } reg\ int)$$
$$instr ::= (\texttt{Instr addq } (arg\ arg)) \mid (\texttt{Instr subq } (arg\ arg))$$
$$\mid\ (\texttt{Instr negq } (arg)) \mid (\texttt{Instr movq } (arg\ arg))$$
$$\mid\ (\texttt{Instr pushq } (arg)) \mid (\texttt{Instr popq } (arg))$$
$$\mid\ (\texttt{Callq } label\ int) \mid (\texttt{Retq}) \mid (\texttt{Jmp } label)$$
$$block ::= (\texttt{Block } info\ (instr \ldots))$$

---

$$bytereg ::= \text{ah} \mid \text{al} \mid \text{bh} \mid \text{bl} \mid \text{ch} \mid \text{cl} \mid \text{dh} \mid \text{dl}$$
$$arg ::= (\texttt{ByteReg } bytereg)$$
$$cc ::= \text{e} \mid \text{l} \mid \text{le} \mid \text{g} \mid \text{ge}$$
$$instr ::= (\texttt{Instr xorq } (arg\ arg)) \mid (\texttt{Instr cmpq } (arg\ arg))$$
$$\mid\ (\texttt{Instr set } (cc\ arg)) \mid (\texttt{Instr movzbq } (arg\ arg))$$
$$\mid\ (\texttt{JmpIf } 'cc'\ label)$$

---

$$arg ::= (\texttt{Global } label)$$

---

$$instr ::= (\texttt{IndirectCallq } arg\ int) \mid (\texttt{TailJmp } arg\ int)$$
$$\mid\ (\texttt{Instr 'leaq } (arg\ (\texttt{Reg } reg)))$$
$$block ::= (\texttt{Block } info\ (instr \ldots))$$
$$def ::= (\texttt{Def } label\ '()\ type\ info\ ((label\ .\ block) \ldots))$$
$$\text{x86}^{\text{Def}}_{\text{callq}*} ::= (\texttt{X86Program } info\ (def \ldots))$$

**Figure 7.10**
The abstract syntax of $\text{x86}^{\text{Def}}_{\text{callq}*}$ (extends $\text{x86}_{\text{Global}}$ of figure 6.14).

variables. So the `start` block of $B$ shown on the left of the following is changed to the code on the right:

$$
\begin{array}{ccc}
\begin{array}{l}
\texttt{start:} \\
\quad instr_1 \\
\quad \ldots \\
\quad instr_n
\end{array}
&
\Rightarrow
&
\begin{array}{l}
f\texttt{start:} \\
\quad \texttt{movq \%rdi, } x_1 \\
\quad \texttt{movq \%rsi, } x_2 \\
\quad \ldots \\
\quad instr_1 \\
\quad \ldots \\
\quad instr_n
\end{array}
\end{array}
$$

Recall that we use the label `start` for the initial block of a program, and in section 2.7 we recommend labeling the conclusion of the program with `conclusion`, so that (`Return` *Arg*) can be compiled to an assignment to `rax` followed by a jump to `conclusion`. With the addition of function definitions, there is a start block and conclusion for each function, but their labels need to be unique. We recommend prepending the function's name to `start` and `conclusion`, respectively, to obtain unique labels.

The interpreter for $\text{x86}^{\text{Def}}_{\text{callq}*}$ needs to be given the number of parameters the function expects, but the parameters are no longer in the syntax of function definitions. Instead, add an entry to *info* that maps `num-params` to the number of parameters to construct *info'*.

By changing the parameters to local variables, we are giving the register allocator control over which registers or stack locations to use for them. If you implement the move-biasing challenge (section 3.7), the register allocator will try to assign the parameter variables to the corresponding argument register, in which case the `patch_instructions` pass will remove the `movq` instruction. This happens in the example translation given in figure 7.12 in section 7.12, in the **add** function. Also, note that the register allocator will perform liveness analysis on this sequence of move instructions and build the interference graph. So, for example, $x_1$ will be marked as interfering with `rsi`, and that will prevent the mapping of $x_1$ to `rsi`, which is good because otherwise the first `movq` would overwrite the argument in `rsi` that is needed for $x_2$.

Next, consider the compilation of function calls. In the mirror image of the handling of parameters in function definitions, the arguments are moved to the argument-passing registers. Note that the function is not given as a label, but its address is produced by the argument $arg_0$. So, we translate the call into an indirect function call. The return value from the function is stored in `rax`, so it needs to be moved into the *lhs*.

$$lhs = (\texttt{Call } arg_0 \ arg_1 \ arg_2 \dots)$$
$$\Rightarrow$$
movq $arg_1$, %rdi
movq $arg_2$, %rsi
$$\vdots$$
callq *$arg_0$
movq %rax, *lhs*

The `IndirectCallq` AST node includes an integer for the arity of the function, that is, the number of parameters. That information is useful in the `uncover_live` pass for determining which argument-passing registers are potentially read during the call.

For tail calls, the parameter passing is the same as non-tail calls: generate instructions to move the arguments into the argument-passing registers. After that we need to pop the frame from the procedure call stack. However, we do not yet know how big the frame is; that gets determined during register allocation. So, instead of generating those instructions here, we invent a new instruction that means "pop the frame and then do an indirect jump," which we name `TailJmp`. The abstract syntax for this instruction includes an argument that specifies where to jump and an integer that represents the arity of the function being called.

## 7.9  Register Allocation

The addition of functions requires some changes to all three aspects of register allocation, which we discuss in the following subsections.

### 7.9.1 Liveness Analysis

The `IndirectCallq` instruction should be treated like `Callq` regarding its written locations $W$, in that they should include all the caller-saved registers. Recall that the reason for that is to force variables that are live across a function call to be assigned to callee-saved registers or to be spilled to the stack.

Regarding the set of read locations $R$, the arity fields of `TailJmp` and `IndirectCallq` determine how many of the argument-passing registers should be considered as read by those instructions. Also, the target field of `TailJmp` and `IndirectCallq` should be included in the set of read locations $R$.

### 7.9.2 Build Interference Graph

With the addition of function definitions, we compute a separate interference graph for each function (not just one for the whole program).

Recall that in section 6.7 we discussed the need to spill tuple-typed variables that are live during a call to `collect`, the garbage collector. With the addition of functions to our language, we need to revisit this issue. Functions that perform allocation contain calls to the collector. Thus, we should not only spill a tuple-typed variable when it is live during a call to `collect`, but we should spill the variable if it is live during a call to any user-defined function. Thus, in the `build_interference` pass, we recommend adding interference edges between call-live tuple-typed variables and the callee-saved registers (in addition to creating edges between call-live variables and the caller-saved registers).

### 7.9.3 Allocate Registers

The primary change to the `allocate_registers` pass is adding an auxiliary function for handling definitions (the *def* nonterminal shown in figure 7.10) with one case for function definitions. The logic is the same as described in chapter 3 except that now register allocation is performed many times, once for each function definition, instead of just once for the whole program.

### 7.10 Patch Instructions

In `patch_instructions`, you should deal with the x86 idiosyncrasy that the destination argument of `leaq` must be a register. Additionally, you should ensure that the argument of `TailJmp` is *rax*, our reserved register—because we trample many other registers before the tail call, as explained in the next section.

### 7.11 Prelude and Conclusion

Now that register allocation is complete, we can translate the `TailJmp` into a sequence of instructions. A naive translation of `TailJmp` would simply be `jmp *arg`. However, before the jump we need to pop the current frame to achieve efficient tail calls. This sequence of instructions is the same as the code for the conclusion of a function, except that the `retq` is replaced with `jmp *arg`.

Regarding function definitions, we generate a prelude and conclusion for each one. This code is similar to the prelude and conclusion generated for the **main** function presented in chapter 6. To review, the prelude of every function should carry out the following steps:

1. Push **rbp** to the stack and set **rbp** to current stack pointer.
2. Push to the stack all the callee-saved registers that were used for register allocation.
3. Move the stack pointer **rsp** down to make room for the regular spills (aligned to 16 bytes).
4. Move the root stack pointer **r15** up by the size of the root-stack frame for this function, which depends on the number of spilled tuple-typed variables.
5. Initialize to zero all new entries in the root-stack frame.
6. Jump to the start block.

The prelude of the **main** function has an additional task: call the **initialize** function to set up the garbage collector, and then move the value of the global **rootstack_begin** in **r15**. This initialization should happen before step 4, which depends on **r15**.

The conclusion of every function should do the following:

1. Move the stack pointer back up past the regular spills.
2. Restore the callee-saved registers by popping them from the stack.
3. Move the root stack pointer back down by the size of the root-stack frame for this function.
4. Restore **rbp** by popping it from the stack.
5. Return to the caller with the **retq** instruction.

The output of this pass is $\text{x86}_{\text{callq*}}$, which differs from $\text{x86}^{\text{Def}}_{\text{callq*}}$ in that there is no longer an AST node for function definitions. Instead, a program is just an association list of basic blocks, as in $\text{x86}_{\text{Global}}$. So we have the following grammar rule:

$$\text{x86}_{\text{callq*}} ::= (\texttt{X86Program}\ \textit{info}\ ((\textit{label}\ .\ \textit{block})\ \dots))$$

Figure 7.11 gives an overview of the passes for compiling $\mathcal{L}_{\text{Fun}}$ to x86.

**Exercise 7.1** Expand your compiler to handle $\mathcal{L}_{\text{Fun}}$ as outlined in this chapter. Create eight new programs that use functions including examples that pass functions and return functions from other functions, recursive functions, functions that create vectors, and functions that make tail calls. Test your compiler on these new programs and all your previously created test programs.

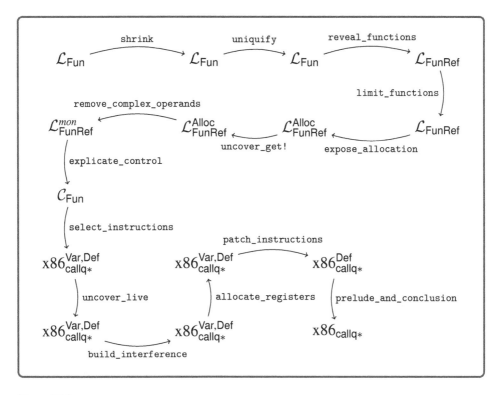

**Figure 7.11**
Diagram of the passes for $\mathcal{L}_{\mathsf{Fun}}$, a language with functions.

## 7.12 An Example Translation

Figure 7.12 shows an example translation of a simple function in $\mathcal{L}_{\mathsf{Fun}}$ to x86. The figure also includes the results of the `explicate_control` and `select_instructions` passes.

```
(define (add [x : Integer]
             [y : Integer])                  (define (add86) : Integer
         : Integer                            add86start:
  (+ x y))                                        movq %rdi, x87
                                                  movq %rsi, y88
(add 40 2)                                        movq x87, %rax
                                                  addq y88, %rax
⇓                                                 jmp inc1389conclusion
                                                )
(define (add86 [x87 : Integer]
               [y88 : Integer])  ⇒      (define (main) : Integer
         : Integer                          mainstart:
  add86start:                                  leaq (fun-ref add86 2), tmp89
    return (+ x87 y88);                        movq $40, %rdi
  )                                            movq $2, %rsi
                                               tail-jmp tmp89
(define (main) : Integer ()                   )
  mainstart:
    tmp89 = (fun-ref add86 2);
    (tail-call tmp89 40 2)         ⇓
  )


                                      .globl main
                                      .align 8
                              main:
      .globl add86              pushq  %rbp
      .align 8                  movq   %rsp, %rbp
add86:                          movq   $16384, %rdi
    pushq  %rbp                 movq   $16384, %rsi
    movq   %rsp, %rbp           callq  initialize
    jmp    add86start           movq   rootstack_begin(%rip), %r15
add86start:                     jmp    mainstart
    movq   %rdi, %rax     mainstart:
    addq   %rsi, %rax           leaq   add86(%rip), %rcx
    jmp add86conclusion         movq   $40, %rdi
add86conclusion:                movq   $2, %rsi
    popq   %rbp                 movq   %rcx, %rax
    retq                        popq   %rbp
                                jmp    *%rax
                          mainconclusion:
                                popq   %rbp
                                retq
```

**Figure 7.12**
Example compilation of a simple function to x86.

# 8 Lexically Scoped Functions

This chapter studies lexically scoped functions. Lexical scoping means that a function's body may refer to variables whose binding site is outside of the function, in an enclosing scope. Consider the example shown in figure 8.1 written in $\mathcal{L}_\lambda$, which extends $\mathcal{L}_{\mathsf{Fun}}$ with the `lambda` form for creating lexically scoped functions. The body of the `lambda` refers to three variables: x, y, and z. The binding sites for x and y are outside of the `lambda`. Variable y is bound by the enclosing `let`, and x is a parameter of function f. Note that function f returns the `lambda` as its result value. The main expression of the program includes two calls to f with different arguments for x: first 5 and then 3. The functions returned from f are bound to variables g and h. Even though these two functions were created by the same `lambda`, they are really different functions because they use different values for x. Applying g to 11 produces 20 whereas applying h to 15 produces 22, so the result of the program is 42.

The approach that we take for implementing lexically scoped functions is to compile them into top-level function definitions, translating from $\mathcal{L}_\lambda$ into $\mathcal{L}_{\mathsf{Fun}}$. However, the compiler must give special treatment to variable occurrences such as x and y in the body of the `lambda` shown in figure 8.1. After all, an $\mathcal{L}_{\mathsf{Fun}}$ function may not refer to variables defined outside of it. To identify such variable occurrences, we review the standard notion of free variable.

```
(define (f [x : Integer]) : (Integer -> Integer)
  (let ([y 4])
    (lambda: ([z : Integer]) : Integer
      (+ x (+ y z)))))

(let ([g (f 5)])
  (let ([h (f 3)])
    (+ (g 11) (h 15))))
```

**Figure 8.1**
Example of a lexically scoped function.

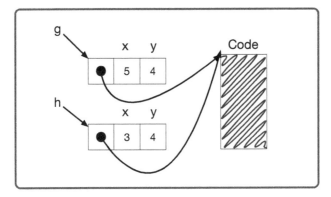

**Figure 8.2**
Flat closure representations for the two functions produced by the `lambda` in figure 8.1.

**Definition 8.1** A variable is *free in expression e* if the variable occurs inside *e* but does not have an enclosing definition that is also in *e*.

For example, in the expression `(+ x (+ y z))` the variables x, y, and z are all free. On the other hand, only x and y are free in the following expression, because z is defined by the `lambda`

```
(lambda: ([z : Integer]) : Integer
  (+ x (+ y z)))
```

Thus the free variables of a `lambda` are the ones that need special treatment. We need to transport at runtime the values of those variables from the point where the `lambda` was created to the point where the `lambda` is applied. An efficient solution to the problem, due to Cardelli (1983), is to bundle the values of the free variables together with a function pointer into a tuple, an arrangement called a *flat closure* (which we shorten to just *closure*). By design, we have all the ingredients to make closures: chapter 6 gave us tuples, and chapter 7 gave us function pointers. The function pointer resides at index 0, and the values for the free variables fill in the rest of the tuple.

Let us revisit the example shown in figure 8.1 to see how closures work. It is a three-step dance. The program calls function f, which creates a closure for the `lambda`. The closure is a tuple whose first element is a pointer to the top-level function that we will generate for the `lambda`; the second element is the value of x, which is 5; and the third element is 4, the value of y. The closure does not contain an element for z because z is not a free variable of the `lambda`. Creating the closure is step 1 of the dance. The closure is returned from f and bound to g, as shown in figure 8.2. The second call to f creates another closure, this time with 3 in the second slot (for x). This closure is also returned from f but bound to h, which is also shown in figure 8.2.

Continuing with the example, consider the application of g to 11 shown in figure 8.1. To apply a closure, we obtain the function pointer from the first element of the closure and call it, passing in the closure itself and then the regular

$$
\begin{array}{lll}
type & ::= & \texttt{Integer} \\
exp & ::= & int \mid \texttt{(read)} \mid \texttt{(-}\ exp\texttt{)} \mid \texttt{(+}\ exp\ exp\texttt{)} \mid \texttt{(-}\ exp\ exp\texttt{)} \\
\hline
exp & ::= & var \mid \texttt{(let (}[var\ exp]\texttt{)}\ exp\texttt{)} \\
\hline
type & ::= & \texttt{Boolean} \\
bool & ::= & \texttt{\#t} \mid \texttt{\#f} \\
cmp & ::= & \texttt{eq?} \mid \texttt{<} \mid \texttt{<=} \mid \texttt{>} \mid \texttt{>=} \\
exp & ::= & bool \mid \texttt{(and}\ exp\ exp\texttt{)} \mid \texttt{(or}\ exp\ exp\texttt{)} \mid \texttt{(not}\ exp\texttt{)} \\
 & \mid & \texttt{(}cmp\ exp\ exp\texttt{)} \mid \texttt{(if}\ exp\ exp\ exp\texttt{)} \\
\hline
type & ::= & \texttt{Void} \\
exp & ::= & \texttt{(set!}\ var\ exp\texttt{)} \mid \texttt{(begin}\ exp^*\ exp\texttt{)} \mid \texttt{(while}\ exp\ exp\texttt{)} \mid \texttt{(void)} \\
\hline
type & ::= & \texttt{(Vector}\ type^*\texttt{)} \\
exp & ::= & \texttt{(vector}\ exp^*\texttt{)} \mid \texttt{(vector-length}\ exp\texttt{)} \\
 & \mid & \texttt{(vector-ref}\ exp\ int\texttt{)} \mid \texttt{(vector-set!}\ exp\ int\ exp\texttt{)} \\
\hline
type & ::= & \texttt{(}type \ldots \texttt{->}\ type\texttt{)} \\
exp & ::= & \texttt{(}exp\ exp \ldots\texttt{)} \\
def & ::= & \texttt{(define (}var\ [var\!:\!type] \ldots\texttt{)} : type\ exp\texttt{)} \\
\hline
exp & ::= & \texttt{(lambda: (}[var\!:\!type] \ldots\texttt{)} : type\ exp\texttt{)} \\
 & \mid & \texttt{(procedure-arity}\ exp\texttt{)} \\
\mathcal{L}_\lambda & ::= & def \ldots exp
\end{array}
$$

**Figure 8.3**
The concrete syntax of $\mathcal{L}_\lambda$, extending $\mathcal{L}_{\mathsf{Fun}}$ (figure 7.1) with lambda.

arguments, in this case 11. This technique for applying a closure is step 2 of the dance. But doesn't this lambda take only one argument, for parameter z? The third and final step of the dance is generating a top-level function for a lambda. We add an additional parameter for the closure and insert an initialization at the beginning of the function for each free variable, to bind those variables to the appropriate elements from the closure parameter. This three-step dance is known as *closure conversion*. We discuss the details of closure conversion in section 8.4 and show the code generated from the example in section 8.5. First, we define the syntax and semantics of $\mathcal{L}_\lambda$ in section 8.1.

## 8.1  The $\mathcal{L}_\lambda$ Language

The definitions of the concrete syntax and abstract syntax for $\mathcal{L}_\lambda$, a language with anonymous functions and lexical scoping, are shown in figures 8.3 and 8.4. They add the lambda form to the grammar for $\mathcal{L}_{\mathsf{Fun}}$, which already has syntax for function application. The **procedure-arity** operation returns the number of parameters of a given function, an operation that we need for the translation of dynamic typing in chapter 9.

Figure 8.5 shows the definitional interpreter for $\mathcal{L}_\lambda$. The case for Lambda saves the current environment inside the returned function value. Recall that during function application, the environment stored in the function value, extended with

```
type  ::=  Integer
 op   ::=  read | + | -
exp   ::=  (Int int) | (Prim op (exp ...))
```
```
exp   ::=  (Var var) | (Let var exp exp)
```
```
type  ::=  Boolean
bool  ::=  #t | #f
cmp   ::=  eq? | < | <= | > | >=
 op   ::=  cmp | and | or | not
exp   ::=  (Bool bool) | (If exp exp exp)
```
```
type  ::=  Void
exp   ::=  (SetBang var exp) | (Begin exp* exp) | (WhileLoop exp exp) | (Void)
```
```
type  ::=  (Vector type*)
 op   ::=  vector | vector-length
exp   ::=  (Prim vector-ref (exp (Int int)))
      |    (Prim vector-set! (exp (Int int) exp))
```
```
type  ::=  (type ... -> type)
exp   ::=  (Apply exp exp ...)
def   ::=  (Def var ([var:type] ...) type '() exp)
```
```
exp   ::=  (Lambda ([var:type] ...) type exp)
 op   ::=  procedure-arity
 Lλ   ::=  (ProgramDefsExp '() (def ...) exp)
```

**Figure 8.4**
The abstract syntax of $\mathcal{L}_\lambda$, extending $\mathcal{L}_{\mathsf{Fun}}$ (figure 7.2).

the mapping of parameters to argument values, is used to interpret the body of the function.

Figure 8.6 shows how to type check the new `lambda` form. The body of the `lambda` is checked in an environment that includes the current environment (because it is lexically scoped) and also includes the `lambda`'s parameters. We require the body's type to match the declared return type.

```
(define interp-Llambda-class
  (class interp-Lfun-class
    (super-new)

    (define/override (interp-op op)
      (match op
        ['procedure-arity
         (lambda (v)
           (match v
             [`(function (,xs ...) ,body ,lam-env) (length xs)]
             [else (error 'interp-op "expected a function, not ~a" v)]))]
        [else (super interp-op op)]))

    (define/override ((interp-exp env) e)
      (define recur (interp-exp env))
      (match e
        [(Lambda (list `[,xs : ,Ts] ...) rT body)
         `(function ,xs ,body ,env)]
        [else ((super interp-exp env) e)]))
    ))

(define (interp-Llambda p)
  (send (new interp-Llambda-class) interp-program p))
```

**Figure 8.5**
Interpreter for $\mathcal{L}_\lambda$.

```
(define (type-check-Llambda env)
  (lambda (e)
    (match e
      [(Lambda (and params `([,xs : ,Ts] ...)) rT body)
       (define-values (new-body bodyT)
         ((type-check-exp (append (map cons xs Ts) env)) body))
       (define ty `(,@Ts -> ,rT))
       (cond
         [(equal? rT bodyT)
          (values (HasType (Lambda params rT new-body) ty) ty)]
         [else
          (error "mismatch in return type" bodyT rT)])]
      ...
      )))
```

**Figure 8.6**
Type checking $\mathcal{L}_\lambda$.

## 8.2   Assignment and Lexically Scoped Functions

The combination of lexically scoped functions and assignment to variables raises a challenge with the flat-closure approach to implementing lexically scoped functions. Consider the following example in which function f has a free variable x that is changed after f is created but before the call to f.

```
(let ([x 0])
  (let ([y 0])
    (let ([z 20])
      (let ([f (lambda: ([a : Integer]) : Integer (+ a (+ x z)))])
        (begin
          (set! x 10)
          (set! y 12)
          (f y))))))
```

The correct output for this example is 42 because the call to f is required to use the current value of x (which is 10). Unfortunately, the closure conversion pass (section 8.4) generates code for the lambda that copies the old value of x into a closure. Thus, if we naively applied closure conversion, the output of this program would be 32.

A first attempt at solving this problem would be to save a pointer to x in the closure and change the occurrences of x inside the lambda to dereference the pointer. Of course, this would require assigning x to the stack and not to a register. However, the problem goes a bit deeper. Consider the following example that returns a function that refers to a local variable of the enclosing function:

```
(define (f []) : Integer
  (let ([x 0])
    (let ([g (lambda: () : Integer x)])
      (begin
        (set! x 42)
        g))))
((f))
```

In this example, the lifetime of x extends beyond the lifetime of the call to f. Thus, if we were to store x on the stack frame for the call to f, it would be gone by the time we called g, leaving us with dangling pointers for x. This example demonstrates that when a variable occurs free inside a function, its lifetime becomes indefinite. Thus, the value of the variable needs to live on the heap. The verb *box* is often used for allocating a single value on the heap, producing a pointer, and *unbox* for dereferencing the pointer. We introduce a new pass named convert_assignments to address this challenge.

## 8.3   Assignment Conversion

The purpose of the convert_assignments pass is to address the challenge regarding the interaction between variable assignments and closure conversion. First we identify which variables need to be boxed, and then we transform the program to box those variables. In general, boxing introduces runtime overhead that we would like to avoid, so we should box as few variables as possible. We recommend boxing the variables in the intersection of the following two sets of variables:

1. The variables that are free in a `lambda`.
2. The variables that appear on the left-hand side of an assignment.

The first condition is a must but the second condition is conservative. It is possible to develop a more liberal condition using static program analysis.

Consider again the first example from section 8.2:

```
(let ([x 0])
  (let ([y 0])
    (let ([z 20])
      (let ([f (lambda: ([a : Integer]) : Integer (+ a (+ x z)))])
        (begin
          (set! x 10)
          (set! y 12)
          (f y))))))
```

The variables x and y appear on the left-hand side of assignments. The variables x and z occur free inside the `lambda`. Thus, variable x needs to be boxed but not y or z. The boxing of x consists of three transformations: initialize x with a tuple whose elements are uninitialized, replace reads from x with tuple reads, and replace each assignment to x with a tuple write. The output of `convert_assignments` for this example is as follows:

```
(define (main) : Integer
  (let ([x0 (vector 0)])
    (let ([y1 0])
      (let ([z2 20])
        (let ([f4 (lambda: ([a3 : Integer]) : Integer
                    (+ a3 (+ (vector-ref x0 0) z2)))])
          (begin
            (vector-set! x0 0 10)
            (set! y1 12)
            (f4 y1)))))))
```

To compute the free variables of all the `lambda` expressions, we recommend defining the following two auxiliary functions:

1. `free_variables` computes the free variables of an expression, and
2. `free_in_lambda` collects all the variables that are free in any of the `lambda` expressions, using `free_variables` in the case for each `lambda`.

To compute the variables that are assigned to, we recommend updating the `collect-set!` function that we introduced in section 5.4 to include the new AST forms such as `Lambda`.

Let *AF* be the intersection of the set of variables that are free in a `lambda` and that are assigned to in the enclosing function definition.

Next we discuss the `convert_assignments` pass. In the case for (Var $x$), if $x$ is in *AF*, then unbox it by translating (Var $x$) to a tuple read.

```
(Var x)
⇒
(Prim 'vector-ref (list (Var x) (Int 0)))
```

In the case for assignment, recursively process the right-hand side *rhs* to obtain *rhs'*. If the left-hand side $x$ is in *AF*, translate the assignment into a tuple write as follows:

```
(SetBang x rhs)
⇒
(Prim 'vector-set! (list (Var x) (Int 0) rhs'))
```

The case for `Lambda` is nontrivial, but it is similar to the case for function definitions, which we discuss next. To translate a function definition, we first compute *AF*, the intersection of the variables that are free in a `lambda` and that are assigned to. We then apply assignment conversion to the body of the function definition. Finally, we box the parameters of this function definition that are in *AF*. For example, the parameter x of the following function g needs to be boxed:

```
(define (g [x : Integer]) : Integer
  (let ([f (lambda: ([a : Integer]) : Integer (+ a x))])
    (begin
      (set! x 10)
      (f 32))))
```

We box parameter x by creating a local variable named x that is initialized to a tuple whose contents is the value of the parameter, which has been renamed to x_0.

```
(define (g [x_0 : Integer]) : Integer
  (let ([x (vector x_0)])
    (let ([f (lambda: ([a : Integer]) : Integer
                (+ a (vector-ref x 0)))])
      (begin
        (vector-set! x 0 10)
        (f 32)))))
```

## 8.4  Closure Conversion

The compiling of lexically scoped functions into top-level function definitions and flat closures is accomplished in the pass `convert_to_closures` that comes after `reveal_functions` and before `limit_functions`.

As usual, we implement the pass as a recursive function over the AST. The interesting cases are for `lambda` and function application. We transform a `lambda` expression into an expression that creates a closure, that is, a tuple for which the first element is a function pointer and the rest of the elements are the values of the free variables of the `lambda`. However, we use the `Closure` AST node instead of using a tuple so that we can record the arity. In the generated code that follows, *fvs* is the free variables of the lambda and *name* is a unique symbol generated to identify the lambda. The *arity* is the number of parameters (the length of *ps*).

```
(Lambda ps rt body)
⇒
(Closure arity (cons (FunRef name arity) fvs))
```

In addition to transforming each `Lambda` AST node into a tuple, we create a top-level function definition for each `Lambda`, as shown next.

```
(Def name ([clos : (Vector _ fvts ...)] ps' ...) rt'
  (Let fvs₁ (Prim 'vector-ref (list (Var clos) (Int 1))))
    ...
    (Let fvsₙ (Prim 'vector-ref (list (Var clos) (Int n))))
      body')...))
```

The `clos` parameter refers to the closure. Translate the type annotations in *ps* and the return type *rt*, as discussed in the next paragraph, to obtain *ps'* and *rt'*. The type *closTy* is a tuple type for which the first element type is _ (the dummy type) and the rest of the element types are the types of the free variables in the lambda. We use _ because it is nontrivial to give a type to the function in the closure's type.[1] The free variables become local variables that are initialized with their values in the closure.

Closure conversion turns every function into a tuple, so the type annotations in the program must also be translated. We recommend defining an auxiliary recursive function for this purpose. Function types should be translated as follows:

$$(T_1, \ldots, T_n \text{ -> } T_r)$$
⇒
$$(\text{Vector } ((\text{Vector}) \ T_1', \ldots, T_n' \text{ -> } T_r'))$$

This type indicates that the first thing in the tuple is a function. The first parameter of the function is a tuple (a closure) and the rest of the parameters are the ones from the original function, with types $T_1', \ldots, T_n'$. The type for the closure omits the types of the free variables because (1) those types are not available in this context, and (2) we do not need them in the code that is generated for function application. So this type describes only the first component of the closure tuple. At runtime the tuple may have more components, but we ignore them at this point.

We transform function application into code that retrieves the function from the closure and then calls the function, passing the closure as the first argument. We place *e'* in a temporary variable to avoid code duplication.

```
(Apply e es)
⇒
(Let tmp e'
  (Apply (Prim 'vector-ref (list (Var tmp) (Int 0))) (cons (Var tmp) es')))
```

---

1. To give an accurate type to a closure, we would need to add existential types to the type checker (Minamide, Morrisett, and Harper 1996).

```
(define (f6 [x7 : Integer]) : (Integer -> Integer)
   (let ([y8 4])
      (lambda: ([z9 : Integer]) : Integer
         (+ x7 (+ y8 z9)))))

(define (main) : Integer
   (let ([g0 ((fun-ref f6 1) 5)])
      (let ([h1 ((fun-ref f6 1) 3)])
         (+ (g0 11) (h1 15)))))

⇒

(define (f6 [fvs4 : _] [x7 : Integer]) : (Vector ((Vector _) Integer -> Integer))
   (let ([y8 4])
      (closure 1 (list (fun-ref lambda2 1) x7 y8))))

(define (lambda2 [fvs3 : (Vector _ Integer Integer)] [z9 : Integer]) : Integer
   (let ([x7 (vector-ref fvs3 1)])
      (let ([y8 (vector-ref fvs3 2)])
         (+ x7 (+ y8 z9)))))

(define (main) : Integer
   (let ([g0 (let ([clos5 (closure 1 (list (fun-ref f6 1)))])
                 ((vector-ref clos5 0) clos5 5))])
      (let ([h1 (let ([clos6 (closure 1 (list (fun-ref f6 1)))])
                    ((vector-ref clos6 0) clos6 3))])
         (+ ((vector-ref g0 0) g0 11) ((vector-ref h1 0) h1 15)))))
```

**Figure 8.7**
Example of closure conversion.

There is also the question of what to do with references to top-level function definitions. To maintain a uniform translation of function application, we turn function references into closures.

$$(\text{FunRef } f\ n) \quad\Rightarrow\quad (\text{Closure } n\ (\text{FunRef } f\ n)\ \text{'()})$$

We no longer need the annotated assignment statement AnnAssign to support the type checking of lambda expressions, so we translate it to a regular Assign statement.

The top-level function definitions need to be updated to take an extra closure parameter, but that parameter is ignored in the body of those functions.

## 8.5  An Example Translation

Figure 8.7 shows the result of reveal_functions and convert_to_closures for the example program demonstrating lexical scoping that we discussed at the beginning of this chapter.

**Exercise 8.1**  Expand your compiler to handle $\mathcal{L}_\lambda$ as outlined in this chapter. Create five new programs that use `lambda` functions and make use of lexical scoping. Test your compiler on these new programs and all your previously created test programs.

## 8.6  Expose Allocation

Compile the (`Closure` *arity exp**) form into code that allocates and initializes a tuple, similar to the translation of the tuple creation in section 6.3. The only difference is replacing the use of (`Allocate` *len type*) with (`AllocateClosure` *len type arity*).

## 8.7  Explicate Control and $\mathcal{C}_{\text{Clos}}$

The output language of `explicate_control` is $\mathcal{C}_{\text{Clos}}$; the definition of its abstract syntax is shown in figure 8.8. The only differences with respect to $\mathcal{C}_{\text{Fun}}$ are the addition of the `AllocateClosure` form to the grammar for *exp* and the `procedure-arity` operator. The handling of `AllocateClosure` in the `explicate_control` pass is similar to the handling of other expressions such as primitive operators.

## 8.8  Select Instructions

Compile (`AllocateClosure` *len type arity*) in almost the same way as the (`Allocate` *len type*) form (section 6.6). The only difference is that you should place the *arity* in the tag that is stored at position 0 of the vector. Recall that in section 6.6 a portion of the 64-bit tag was not used. We store the arity in the 5 bits starting at position 58.

Compile the `procedure-arity` operator into a sequence of instructions that access the tag from position 0 of the vector and extract the 5 bits starting at position 58 from the tag.

Figure 8.9 provides an overview of the passes needed for the compilation of $\mathcal{L}_\lambda$.

$$
\begin{array}{lll}
atm & ::= & (\text{Int } int) \mid (\text{Var } var) \\
exp & ::= & atm \mid (\text{Prim 'read ()}) \mid (\text{Prim '- } (atm)) \\
    & \mid & (\text{Prim '+ } (atm\ atm)) \mid (\text{Prim '- } (atm\ atm)) \\
stmt & ::= & (\text{Assign } (\text{Var } var)\ exp) \\
tail & ::= & (\text{Return } exp) \mid (\text{Seq } stmt\ tail)
\end{array}
$$

$$
\begin{array}{lll}
atm & ::= & (\text{Bool } bool) \\
cmp & ::= & \text{eq? } \mid < \mid <= \mid > \mid >= \\
exp & ::= & (\text{Prim 'not } (atm)) \mid (\text{Prim '}cmp\ (atm\ atm)) \\
tail & ::= & (\text{Goto } label) \\
     & \mid & (\text{IfStmt } (\text{Prim } cmp\ (atm\ atm))\ (\text{Goto } label)\ (\text{Goto } label))
\end{array}
$$

$$
\begin{array}{lll}
atm & ::= & (\text{Void}) \\
stmt & ::= & (\text{Prim 'read ()})
\end{array}
$$

$$
\begin{array}{lll}
exp & ::= & (\text{Allocate } int\ type) \\
    & \mid & (\text{Prim vector-ref } (atm\ (\text{Int } int))) \\
    & \mid & (\text{Prim vector-set! } (atm\ (\text{Int } int)\ atm)) \\
    & \mid & (\text{Prim vector-length } (atm)) \\
    & \mid & (\text{GlobalValue } var) \\
stmt & ::= & (\text{Prim vector-set! } (atm\ (\text{Int } int)\ atm)) \\
     & \mid & (\text{Collect } int)
\end{array}
$$

$$
\begin{array}{lll}
exp & ::= & (\text{FunRef } label\ int) \mid (\text{Call } atm\ (atm \ldots)) \\
tail & ::= & (\text{TailCall } atm\ atm \ldots) \\
def & ::= & (\text{Def } label\ ([var{:}type] \ldots)\ type\ info\ ((label\ .\ tail) \ldots))
\end{array}
$$

$$
\begin{array}{lll}
\mathbf{exp} & ::= & \mathbf{(AllocateClosure\ \mathit{int}\ \mathit{type}\ \mathit{int})} \\
\mathbf{op} & ::= & \mathbf{procedure\text{-}arity} \\
\mathcal{C}_{\text{Clos}} & ::= & \mathbf{(ProgramDefs\ \mathit{info}\ \mathit{def}^*)}
\end{array}
$$

**Figure 8.8**
The abstract syntax of $\mathcal{C}_{\text{Clos}}$, extending $\mathcal{C}_{\text{Fun}}$ (figure 7.8).

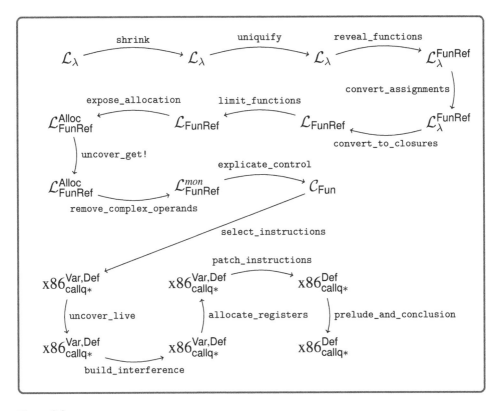

**Figure 8.9**
Diagram of the passes for $\mathcal{L}_\lambda$, a language with lexically scoped functions.

## 8.9   Challenge: Optimize Closures

In this chapter we compile lexically scoped functions into a relatively efficient representation: flat closures. However, even this representation comes with some overhead. For example, consider the following program with a function `tail_sum` that does not have any free variables and where all the uses of `tail_sum` are in applications in which we know that only `tail_sum` is being applied (and not any other functions):

```
(define (tail_sum [n : Integer] [s : Integer]) : Integer
  (if (eq? n 0)
      s
      (tail_sum (- n 1) (+ n s))))

(+ (tail_sum 3 0) 36)
```

As described in this chapter, we uniformly apply closure conversion to all functions, obtaining the following output for this program:

```
(define (tail_sum1 [fvs5 : _] [n2 : Integer] [s3 : Integer]) : Integer
  (if (eq? n2 0)
      s3
      (let ([clos4 (closure (list (fun-ref tail_sum1 2)))])
        ((vector-ref clos4 0) clos4 (+ n2 -1) (+ n2 s3)))))

(define (main) : Integer
  (+ (let ([clos6 (closure (list (fun-ref tail_sum1 2)))])
       ((vector-ref clos6 0) clos6 3 0)) 27))
```

If this program were compiled according to the previous chapter, there would be no allocation and the calls to `tail_sum` would be direct calls. In contrast, the program presented here allocates memory for each closure and the calls to `tail_sum` are indirect. These two differences incur considerable overhead in a program such as this, in which the allocations and indirect calls occur inside a tight loop.

One might think that this problem is trivial to solve: can't we just recognize calls of the form (Apply (FunRef *f n*) *args*) and compile them to direct calls instead of treating it like a call to a closure? We would also drop the new `fvs` parameter of `tail_sum`. However, this problem is not so trivial, because a global function may *escape* and become involved in applications that also involve closures. Consider the following example in which the application (`f 41`) needs to be compiled into a closure application because the `lambda` may flow into `f`, but the `inc` function might also flow into `f`:

```
(define (inc [x : Integer]) : Integer
  (+ x 1))

(let ([y (read)])
  (let ([f (if (eq? (read) 0)
              inc
              (lambda: ([x : Integer]) : Integer (- x y)))])
    (f 41)))
```

If a global function name is used in any way other than as the operator in a direct call, then we say that the function *escapes*. If a global function does not escape, then we do not need to perform closure conversion on the function.

**Exercise 8.2** Implement an auxiliary function for detecting which global functions escape. Using that function, implement an improved version of closure conversion that does not apply closure conversion to global functions that do not escape but instead compiles them as regular functions. Create several new test cases that check whether your compiler properly detects whether global functions escape or not.

So far we have reduced the overhead of calling global functions, but it would also be nice to reduce the overhead of calling a `lambda` when we can determine at compile time which `lambda` will be called. We refer to such calls as *known calls*. Consider the following example in which a `lambda` is bound to f and then applied.

```
(let ([y (read)])
  (let ([f (lambda: ([x : Integer]) : Integer
            (+ x y))])
    (f 21)))
```

Closure conversion compiles the application (f 21) into an indirect call, as follows:

```
(define (lambda5 [fvs6 : (Vector _ Integer)] [x3 : Integer]) : Integer
  (let ([y2 (vector-ref fvs6 1)])
    (+ x3 y2)))

(define (main) : Integer
  (let ([y2 (read)])
    (let ([f4 (Closure 1 (list (fun-ref lambda5 1) y2))])
      ((vector-ref f4 0) f4 21))))
```

However, we can instead compile the application (f 21) into a direct call, as follows:

```
(define (main) : Integer
  (let ([y2 (read)])
    (let ([f4 (Closure 1 (list (fun-ref lambda5 1) y2))])
      ((fun-ref lambda5 1) f4 21))))
```

The problem of determining which `lambda` will be called from a particular application is quite challenging in general and the topic of considerable research (Shivers 1988; Gilray et al. 2016). For the following exercise we recommend that you compile an application to a direct call when the operator is a variable and the variable is `let`-bound to a closure. This can be accomplished by maintaining an environment that maps variables to function names. Extend the environment whenever you encounter a closure on the right-hand side of a `let`, mapping the variable to the name of the global function for the closure. This pass should come after closure conversion.

**Exercise 8.3** Implement a compiler pass, named `optimize_known_calls`, that compiles known calls into direct calls. Verify that your compiler is successful in this regard on several example programs.

These exercises only scratch the surface of closure optimization. A good next step for the interested reader is to look at the work of Keep, Hearn, and Dybvig (2012).

### 8.10  Further Reading

The notion of lexically scoped functions predates modern computers by about a decade. They were invented by Church (1932), who proposed the lambda calculus as a foundation for logic. Anonymous functions were included in the LISP (McCarthy 1960) programming language but were initially dynamically scoped. The Scheme dialect of LISP adopted lexical scoping, and Steele (1978) demonstrated how to efficiently compile Scheme programs. However, environments were represented as linked lists, so variable look-up was linear in the size of the environment. Appel (1991) gives a detailed description of several closure representations. In this chapter we represent environments using flat closures, which were invented by Cardelli (1983, 1984) for the purpose of compiling the ML language (Gordon et al. 1978; Milner, Tofte, and Harper 1990). With flat closures, variable look-up is constant time but the time to create a closure is proportional to the number of its free variables. Flat closures were reinvented by Dybvig (1987b) in his PhD thesis and used in Chez Scheme version 1 (Dybvig 2006).

# 9 Dynamic Typing

In this chapter we learn how to compile $\mathcal{L}_{\text{Dyn}}$, a dynamically typed language that is a subset of Racket. The focus on dynamic typing is in contrast to the previous chapters, which have studied the compilation of statically typed languages. In dynamically typed languages such as $\mathcal{L}_{\text{Dyn}}$, a particular expression may produce a value of a different type each time it is executed. Consider the following example with a conditional `if` expression that may return a Boolean or an integer depending on the input to the program:

```
(not (if (eq? (read) 1) #f 0))
```

Languages that allow expressions to produce different kinds of values are called *polymorphic*, a word composed of the Greek roots *poly*, meaning *many*, and *morph*, meaning *form*. There are several kinds of polymorphism in programming languages, such as subtype polymorphism and parametric polymorphism (aka generics) (Cardelli and Wegner 1985). The kind of polymorphism that we study in this chapter does not have a special name; it is the kind that arises in dynamically typed languages.

Another characteristic of dynamically typed languages is that their primitive operations, such as `not`, are often defined to operate on many different types of values. In fact, in Racket, the `not` operator produces a result for any kind of value: given `#f` it returns `#t`, and given anything else it returns `#f`.

Furthermore, even when primitive operations restrict their inputs to values of a certain type, this restriction is enforced at runtime instead of during compilation. For example, the tuple read operation (`vector-ref #t 0`) results in a runtime error because the first argument must be a tuple, not a Boolean.

## 9.1 The $\mathcal{L}_{\text{Dyn}}$ Language

The definitions of the concrete and abstract syntax of $\mathcal{L}_{\text{Dyn}}$ are shown in figures 9.1 and 9.2. There is no type checker for $\mathcal{L}_{\text{Dyn}}$ because it checks types only at runtime.

The definitional interpreter for $\mathcal{L}_{\text{Dyn}}$ is presented in figure 9.3, and definitions of its auxiliary functions are shown in figure 9.4. Consider the match case for (`Int n`). Instead of simply returning the integer `n` (as in the interpreter for $\mathcal{L}_{\text{Var}}$ in figure 2.4), the interpreter for $\mathcal{L}_{\text{Dyn}}$ creates a *tagged value* that combines an underlying value

```
type  ::=  Integer
exp   ::=  int | (read) | (- exp) | (+ exp exp) | (- exp exp)
─────────────────────────────────────────────────────────────────
exp   ::=  var | (let ([var exp]) exp)
─────────────────────────────────────────────────────────────────
type  ::=  Boolean
bool  ::=  #t | #f
cmp   ::=  eq? | < | <= | > | >=
exp   ::=  bool | (and exp exp) | (or exp exp) | (not exp)
      |    (cmp exp exp) | (if exp exp exp)
─────────────────────────────────────────────────────────────────
type  ::=  Void
exp   ::=  (set! var exp) | (begin exp* exp) | (while exp exp) | (void)
─────────────────────────────────────────────────────────────────
type  ::=  (Vector type*)
exp   ::=  (vector exp*) | (vector-length exp)
      |    (vector-ref exp int) | (vector-set! exp int exp)
─────────────────────────────────────────────────────────────────
exp   ::=  (exp exp ... ) | (lambda (var ... ) exp)
      |    (boolean? exp) | (integer? exp)
      |    (vector? exp) | (procedure? exp) | (void? exp)
def   ::=  (define (var var ... ) exp)
L_Dyn ::=  def ... exp
```

**Figure 9.1**
Syntax of $\mathcal{L}_{\mathsf{Dyn}}$, an untyped language (a subset of Racket).

```
type  ::=  Integer
exp   ::=  (Int int) | (Prim 'read ())
      |    (Prim '- (exp)) | (Prim '+ (exp exp)) | (Prim '- (exp exp))
─────────────────────────────────────────────────────────────────
exp   ::=  (Var var) | (Let var exp exp)
─────────────────────────────────────────────────────────────────
type  ::=  Boolean
bool  ::=  #t | #f
cmp   ::=  eq? | < | <= | > | >=
op    ::=  cmp | and | or | not
exp   ::=  (Bool bool) | (If exp exp exp)
─────────────────────────────────────────────────────────────────
type  ::=  Void
exp   ::=  (SetBang var exp) | (Begin exp* exp) | (WhileLoop exp exp) | (Void)
─────────────────────────────────────────────────────────────────
type  ::=  (Vector type*)
op    ::=  vector | vector-length
exp   ::=  (Prim vector-ref (exp (Int int)))
      |    (Prim vector-set! (exp (Int int) exp))
─────────────────────────────────────────────────────────────────
exp   ::=  (Apply exp exp ... ) | (Lambda (var ... ) 'Any exp)
def   ::=  (Def var (var ... ) 'Any '() exp)
L_Dyn ::=  (ProgramDefsExp '() (def ... ) exp)
```

**Figure 9.2**
The abstract syntax of $\mathcal{L}_{\mathsf{Dyn}}$.

with a tag that identifies what kind of value it is. We define the following struct to represent tagged values:

```
(struct Tagged (value tag) #:transparent)
```

The tags are `Integer`, `Boolean`, `Void`, `Vector`, and `Procedure`. Tags are closely related to types but do not always capture all the information that a type does. For example, a vector of type `(Vector Any Any)` is tagged with `Vector`, and a procedure of type `(Any Any -> Any)` is tagged with `Procedure`.

Next consider the match case for accessing the element of a tuple. The `check-tag` auxiliary function (figure 9.4) is used to ensure that the first argument is a tuple and the second is an integer. If they are not, a `trapped-error` is raised. Recall from section 1.5 that when a definition interpreter raises a `trapped-error` error, the compiled code must also signal an error by exiting with return code 255. A `trapped-error` is also raised if the index is not less than the length of the vector.

```
(define ((interp-Ldyn-exp env) ast)
  (define recur (interp-Ldyn-exp env))
  (match ast
    [(Var x) (dict-ref env x)]
    [(Int n) (Tagged n 'Integer)]
    [(Bool b) (Tagged b 'Boolean)]
    [(Lambda xs rt body)
     (Tagged `(function ,xs ,body ,env) 'Procedure)]
    [(Prim 'vector es)
     (Tagged (apply vector (for/list ([e es]) (recur e))) 'Vector)]
    [(Prim 'vector-ref (list e1 e2))
     (define vec (recur e1)) (define i (recur e2))
     (check-tag vec 'Vector ast) (check-tag i 'Integer ast)
     (unless (< (Tagged-value i) (vector-length (Tagged-value vec)))
       (error 'trapped-error "index ~a too big\nin ~v" (Tagged-value i) ast))
     (vector-ref (Tagged-value vec) (Tagged-value i))]
    [(Prim 'vector-set! (list e1 e2 e3))
     (define vec (recur e1)) (define i (recur e2)) (define arg (recur e3))
     (check-tag vec 'Vector ast) (check-tag i 'Integer ast)
     (unless (< (Tagged-value i) (vector-length (Tagged-value vec)))
       (error 'trapped-error "index ~a too big\nin ~v" (Tagged-value i) ast))
     (vector-set! (Tagged-value vec) (Tagged-value i) arg)
     (Tagged (void) 'Void)]
    [(Let x e body) ((interp-Ldyn-exp (cons (cons x (recur e)) env)) body)]
    [(Prim 'and (list e1 e2)) (recur (If e1 e2 (Bool #f)))]
    [(Prim 'or (list e1 e2))
     (define v1 (recur e1))
     (match (Tagged-value v1) [#f (recur e2)] [else v1])]
    [(Prim 'eq? (list l r)) (Tagged (equal? (recur l) (recur r)) 'Boolean)]
    [(Prim op (list e1))
     #:when (set-member? type-predicates op)
     (tag-value ((interp-op op) (Tagged-value (recur e1))))]
    [(Prim op es)
     (define args (map recur es))
     (define tags (for/list ([arg args]) (Tagged-tag arg)))
     (unless (for/or ([expected-tags (op-tags op)])
               (equal? expected-tags tags))
       (error 'trapped-error "illegal argument tags ~a\nin ~v" tags ast))
     (tag-value
      (apply (interp-op op) (for/list ([a args]) (Tagged-value a))))]
    [(If q t f)
     (match (Tagged-value (recur q)) [#f (recur f)] [else (recur t)])]
    [(Apply f es)
     (define new-f (recur f)) (define args (map recur es))
     (check-tag new-f 'Procedure ast) (define f-val (Tagged-value new-f))
     (match f-val
       [`(function ,xs ,body ,lam-env)
        (unless (eq? (length xs) (length args))
          (error 'trapped-error "~a != ~a\nin ~v" (length args) (length xs) ast))
        (define new-env (append (map cons xs args) lam-env))
        ((interp-Ldyn-exp new-env) body)]
       [else (error "interp-Ldyn-exp, expected function, not" f-val)])]))
```

**Figure 9.3**
Interpreter for the $\mathcal{L}_{\text{Dyn}}$ language.

```
(define (interp-op op)
  (match op
    ['+ fx+]
    ['- fx-]
    ['read read-fixnum]
    ['not (lambda (v) (match v [#t #f] [#f #t]))]
    ['< (lambda (v1 v2)
          (cond [(and (fixnum? v1) (fixnum? v2)) (< v1 v2)]))]
    ['<= (lambda (v1 v2)
           (cond [(and (fixnum? v1) (fixnum? v2)) (<= v1 v2)]))]
    ['> (lambda (v1 v2)
          (cond [(and (fixnum? v1) (fixnum? v2)) (> v1 v2)]))]
    ['>= (lambda (v1 v2)
           (cond [(and (fixnum? v1) (fixnum? v2)) (>= v1 v2)]))]
    ['boolean? boolean?]
    ['integer? fixnum?]
    ['void? void?]
    ['vector? vector?]
    ['vector-length vector-length]
    ['procedure? (match-lambda
                   [`(functions ,xs ,body ,env) #t] [else #f])]
    [else (error 'interp-op "unknown operator" op)]))

(define (op-tags op)
  (match op
    ['+ '((Integer Integer))]
    ['- '((Integer Integer) (Integer))]
    ['read '(())]
    ['not '((Boolean))]
    ['< '((Integer Integer))]
    ['<= '((Integer Integer))]
    ['> '((Integer Integer))]
    ['>= '((Integer Integer))]
    ['vector-length '((Vector))]))

(define type-predicates
  (set 'boolean? 'integer? 'vector? 'procedure? 'void?))

(define (tag-value v)
  (cond [(boolean? v) (Tagged v 'Boolean)]
        [(fixnum? v) (Tagged v 'Integer)]
        [(procedure? v) (Tagged v 'Procedure)]
        [(vector? v) (Tagged v 'Vector)]
        [(void? v) (Tagged v 'Void)]
        [else (error 'tag-value "unidentified value ~a" v)]))

(define (check-tag val expected ast)
  (define tag (Tagged-tag val))
  (unless (eq? tag expected)
    (error 'trapped-error "expected ~a, not ~a\nin ~v" expected tag ast)))
```

**Figure 9.4**
Auxiliary functions for the $\mathcal{L}_{Dyn}$ interpreter.

## 9.2   Representation of Tagged Values

The interpreter for $\mathcal{L}_{\mathsf{Dyn}}$ introduced a new kind of value: the tagged value. To compile $\mathcal{L}_{\mathsf{Dyn}}$ to x86 we must decide how to represent tagged values at the bit level. Because almost every operation in $\mathcal{L}_{\mathsf{Dyn}}$ involves manipulating tagged values, the representation must be efficient. Recall that all our values are 64 bits. We shall steal the right-most 3 bits to encode the tag. We use 001 to identify integers, 100 for Booleans, 010 for tuples, 011 for procedures, and 101 for the void value. We define the following auxiliary function for mapping types to tag codes:

$$tagof(\mathtt{Integer}) = 001$$

$$tagof(\mathtt{Boolean}) = 100$$

$$tagof((\mathtt{Vector}\,...\,)) = 010$$

$$tagof((\,...\,{\texttt{->}}\,...\,)) = 011$$

$$tagof(\mathtt{Void}) = 101$$

This stealing of 3 bits comes at some price: integers are now restricted to the range $-2^{60}$ to $2^{60} - 1$. The stealing does not adversely affect tuples and procedures because those values are addresses, and our addresses are 8-byte aligned so the rightmost 3 bits are unused; they are always 000. Thus, we do not lose information by overwriting the rightmost 3 bits with the tag, and we can simply zero out the tag to recover the original address.

To make tagged values into first-class entities, we can give them a type called Any and define operations such as Inject and Project for creating and using them, yielding the statically typed $\mathcal{L}_{\mathsf{Any}}$ intermediate language. We describe how to compile $\mathcal{L}_{\mathsf{Dyn}}$ to $\mathcal{L}_{\mathsf{Any}}$ in section 9.4; in the next section we describe the $\mathcal{L}_{\mathsf{Any}}$ language in greater detail.

## 9.3   The $\mathcal{L}_{\mathsf{Any}}$ Language

The definition of the abstract syntax of $\mathcal{L}_{\mathsf{Any}}$ is given in figure 9.5. The (Inject $e$ $T$) form converts the value produced by expression $e$ of type $T$ into a tagged value. The (Project $e$ $T$) form either converts the tagged value produced by expression $e$ into a value of type $T$ or halts the program if the type tag does not match $T$. Note that in both Inject and Project, the type $T$ is restricted to be a flat type (the nonterminal *ftype*) which simplifies the implementation and complies with the needs for compiling $\mathcal{L}_{\mathsf{Dyn}}$.

The any-vector operators adapt the tuple operations so that they can be applied to a value of type Any. They also generalize the tuple operations in that the index is not restricted to a literal integer in the grammar but is allowed to be any expression.

The type predicates such as boolean? expect their argument to produce a tagged value; they return #t if the tag corresponds to the predicate and return #f otherwise.

| *type* | ::= | Integer |
| *op* | ::= | read \| + \| – |
| *exp* | ::= | (Int *int*) \| (Prim *op* (*exp* ... )) |
| *exp* | ::= | (Var *var*) \| (Let *var* *exp* *exp*) |
| *type* | ::= | Boolean |
| *bool* | ::= | #t \| #f |
| *cmp* | ::= | eq? \| < \| <= \| > \| >= |
| *op* | ::= | *cmp* \| and \| or \| not |
| *exp* | ::= | (Bool *bool*) \| (If *exp* *exp* *exp*) |
| *type* | ::= | Void |
| *exp* | ::= | (SetBang *var* *exp*) \| (Begin *exp** *exp*) \| (WhileLoop *exp* *exp*) \| (Void) |
| *type* | ::= | (Vector *type**) |
| *op* | ::= | vector \| vector-length |
| *exp* | ::= | (Prim vector-ref (*exp* (Int *int*))) |
| | \| | (Prim vector-set! (*exp* (Int *int*) *exp*)) |
| *type* | ::= | (*type* ... -> *type*) |
| *exp* | ::= | (Apply *exp* *exp* ... ) |
| *def* | ::= | (Def *var* ([*var*:*type*] ... ) *type* '() *exp*) |
| *exp* | ::= | (Lambda ([*var*:*type*] ... ) *type* *exp*) |
| *op* | ::= | procedure-arity |
| **type** | ::= | **Any** |
| **ftype** | ::= | **Integer \| Boolean \| Void \| (Vector Any ... ) \| (Any ... -> Any)** |
| **op** | ::= | **any-vector-length \| any-vector-ref \| any-vector-set!** |
| | **\|** | **boolean? \| integer? \| vector? \| procedure? \| void?** |
| **exp** | ::= | **(Inject *exp* *ftype*) \| (Project *exp* *ftype*)** |
| **$\mathcal{L}_{Any}$** | ::= | **(ProgramDefsExp '() (*def* ... ) *exp*)** |

**Figure 9.5**
The abstract syntax of $\mathcal{L}_{Any}$, extending $\mathcal{L}_\lambda$ (figure 8.4).

The type checker for $\mathcal{L}_{Any}$ is shown in figure 9.6 and uses the auxiliary functions presented in figure 9.7. The interpreter for $\mathcal{L}_{Any}$ is shown in figure 9.8 and its auxiliary functions are shown in figure 9.9.

```
(define type-check-Lany-class
  (class type-check-Llambda-class
    (super-new)
    (inherit check-type-equal?)

    (define/override (type-check-exp env)
      (lambda (e)
        (define recur (type-check-exp env))
        (match e
          [(Inject e1 ty)
           (unless (flat-ty? ty)
             (error 'type-check "may only inject from flat type, not ~a" ty))
           (define-values (new-e1 e-ty) (recur e1))
           (check-type-equal? e-ty ty e)
           (values (Inject new-e1 ty) 'Any)]
          [(Project e1 ty)
           (unless (flat-ty? ty)
             (error 'type-check "may only project to flat type, not ~a" ty))
           (define-values (new-e1 e-ty) (recur e1))
           (check-type-equal? e-ty 'Any e)
           (values (Project new-e1 ty) ty)]
          [(Prim 'any-vector-length (list e1))
           (define-values (e1^ t1) (recur e1))
           (check-type-equal? t1 'Any e)
           (values (Prim 'any-vector-length (list e1^)) 'Integer)]
          [(Prim 'any-vector-ref (list e1 e2))
           (define-values (e1^ t1) (recur e1))
           (define-values (e2^ t2) (recur e2))
           (check-type-equal? t1 'Any e)
           (check-type-equal? t2 'Integer e)
           (values (Prim 'any-vector-ref (list e1^ e2^)) 'Any)]
          [(Prim 'any-vector-set! (list e1 e2 e3))
           (define-values (e1^ t1) (recur e1))
           (define-values (e2^ t2) (recur e2))
           (define-values (e3^ t3) (recur e3))
           (check-type-equal? t1 'Any e)
           (check-type-equal? t2 'Integer e)
           (check-type-equal? t3 'Any e)
           (values (Prim 'any-vector-set! (list e1^ e2^ e3^)) 'Void)]
          [(Prim pred (list e1))
           #:when (set-member? (type-predicates) pred)
           (define-values (new-e1 e-ty) (recur e1))
           (check-type-equal? e-ty 'Any e)
           (values (Prim pred (list new-e1)) 'Boolean)]
          [(Prim 'eq? (list arg1 arg2))
           (define-values (e1 t1) (recur arg1))
           (define-values (e2 t2) (recur arg2))
           (match* (t1 t2)
             [(`(Vector ,ts1 ...) `(Vector ,ts2 ...)) (void)]
             [(other wise) (check-type-equal? t1 t2 e)])
           (values (Prim 'eq? (list e1 e2)) 'Boolean)]
          [else ((super type-check-exp env) e)]))))
  ))
```

**Figure 9.6**
Type checker for the $\mathcal{L}_{Any}$ language.

```
(define/override (operator-types)
  (append
   '((integer? . ((Any) . Boolean))
     (vector? . ((Any) . Boolean))
     (procedure? . ((Any) . Boolean))
     (void? . ((Any) . Boolean)))
   (super operator-types)))

(define/public (type-predicates)
  (set 'boolean? 'integer? 'vector? 'procedure? 'void?))

(define/public (flat-ty? ty)
  (match ty
    [(or `Integer `Boolean `Void) #t]
    [`(Vector ,ts ...) (for/and ([t ts]) (eq? t 'Any))]
    [`(,ts ... -> ,rt)
     (and (eq? rt 'Any) (for/and ([t ts]) (eq? t 'Any)))]
    [else #f]))
```

**Figure 9.7**

Auxiliary methods for type checking $\mathcal{L}_{\mathsf{Any}}$.

```
(define interp-Lany-class
  (class interp-Llambda-class
    (super-new)

    (define/override (interp-op op)
      (match op
        ['boolean? (match-lambda
                    [`(tagged ,v1 ,tg) (equal? tg (any-tag 'Boolean))]
                    [else #f])]
        ['integer? (match-lambda
                    [`(tagged ,v1 ,tg) (equal? tg (any-tag 'Integer))]
                    [else #f])]
        ['vector? (match-lambda
                    [`(tagged ,v1 ,tg) (equal? tg (any-tag `(Vector Any)))]
                    [else #f])]
        ['procedure? (match-lambda
                      [`(tagged ,v1 ,tg) (equal? tg (any-tag `(Any -> Any)))]
                      [else #f])]
        ['eq? (match-lambda*
               [`((tagged ,v1^ ,tg1) (tagged ,v2^ ,tg2))
                (and (eq? v1^ v2^) (equal? tg1 tg2))]
               [ls (apply (super interp-op op) ls)])]
        ['any-vector-ref (lambda (v i)
                          (match v [`(tagged ,v^ ,tg) (vector-ref v^ i)]))]
        ['any-vector-set! (lambda (v i a)
                           (match v [`(tagged ,v^ ,tg) (vector-set! v^ i a)]))]
        ['any-vector-length (lambda (v)
                             (match v [`(tagged ,v^ ,tg) (vector-length v^)]))]
        [else (super interp-op op)]))

    (define/override ((interp-exp env) e)
      (define recur (interp-exp env))
      (match e
        [(Inject e ty) `(tagged ,(recur e) ,(any-tag ty))]
        [(Project e ty2) (apply-project (recur e) ty2)]
        [else ((super interp-exp env) e)]))
    ))

(define (interp-Lany p)
  (send (new interp-Lany-class) interp-program p))
```

**Figure 9.8**
Interpreter for $\mathcal{L}_{\mathsf{Any}}$.

```
(define/public (apply-inject v tg) (Tagged v tg))

(define/public (apply-project v ty2)
  (define tag2 (any-tag ty2))
  (match v
    [(Tagged v1 tag1)
     (cond
       [(eq? tag1 tag2)
        (match ty2
          [`(Vector ,ts ...)
           (define l1 ((interp-op 'vector-length) v1))
           (cond
             [(eq? l1 (length ts)) v1]
             [else (error 'apply-project "vector length mismatch, ~a != ~a"
                          l1 (length ts))])]
          [`(,ts ... -> ,rt)
           (match v1
             [`(function ,xs ,body ,env)
              (cond [(eq? (length xs) (length ts)) v1]
                    [else
                     (error 'apply-project "arity mismatch ~a != ~a"
                            (length xs) (length ts))])]
             [else (error 'apply-project "expected function not ~a" v1)])]
          [else v1])]
       [else (error 'apply-project "tag mismatch ~a != ~a" tag1 tag2)])]
    [else (error 'apply-project "expected tagged value, not ~a" v)]))
```

**Figure 9.9**
Auxiliary functions for interpreting $\mathcal{L}_{\mathsf{Any}}$.

| | | |
|---|---|---|
| `#t` | $\Rightarrow$ | `(inject #t Boolean)` |
| `(+ `$e_1$` `$e_2$`)` | $\Rightarrow$ | `(inject`<br>`   (+ (project `$e_1'$` Integer)`<br>`      (project `$e_2'$` Integer))`<br>`   Integer)` |
| `(lambda (`$x_1$` ...) `$e$`)` | $\Rightarrow$ | `(inject`<br>`   (lambda: ([`$x_1$`:Any] ...):Any `$e'$`)`<br>`   (Any ... Any -> Any))` |
| `(`$e_0$` `$e_1$` ... `$e_n$`)` | $\Rightarrow$ | `((project `$e_0'$` (Any ... Any -> Any)) `$e_1'$` ... `$e_n'$`)` |
| `(vector-ref `$e_1$` `$e_2$`)` | $\Rightarrow$ | `(any-vector-ref `$e_1'$` (project `$e_2'$` Integer))` |
| `(if `$e_1$` `$e_2$` `$e_3$`)` | $\Rightarrow$ | `(if (eq? `$e_1'$` (inject #f Boolean)) `$e_3'$` `$e_2'$`)` |
| `(eq? `$e_1$` `$e_2$`)` | $\Rightarrow$ | `(inject (eq? `$e_1'$` `$e_2'$`) Boolean)` |
| `(not `$e_1$`)` | $\Rightarrow$ | `(if (eq? `$e_1'$` (inject #f Boolean))`<br>`    (inject #t Boolean) (inject #f Boolean))` |

**Figure 9.10**
Cast insertion.

## 9.4   Cast Insertion: Compiling $\mathcal{L}_{Dyn}$ to $\mathcal{L}_{Any}$

The `cast_insert` pass compiles from $\mathcal{L}_{Dyn}$ to $\mathcal{L}_{Any}$. Figure 9.10 shows the compilation of many of the $\mathcal{L}_{Dyn}$ forms into $\mathcal{L}_{Any}$. An important invariant of this pass is that given any subexpression $e$ in the $\mathcal{L}_{Dyn}$ program, the pass will produce an expression $e'$ in $\mathcal{L}_{Any}$ that has type Any. For example, the first row in figure 9.10 shows the compilation of the Boolean #t, which must be injected to produce an expression of type Any. The compilation of addition is shown in the second row of figure 9.10. The compilation of addition is representative of many primitive operations: the arguments have type Any and must be projected to Integer before the addition can be performed.

The compilation of lambda (third row of figure 9.10) shows what happens when we need to produce type annotations: we simply use Any. The compilation of if and eq? demonstrate how this pass has to account for some differences in behavior between $\mathcal{L}_{Dyn}$ and $\mathcal{L}_{Any}$. The $\mathcal{L}_{Dyn}$ language is more permissive than $\mathcal{L}_{Any}$ regarding what kind of values can be used in various places. For example, the condition of an if does not have to be a Boolean. For eq?, the arguments need not be of the same type (in that case the result is #f).

## 9.5  Reveal Casts

In the `reveal_casts` pass, we recommend compiling `Project` into a conditional expression that checks whether the value's tag matches the target type; if it does, the value is converted to a value of the target type by removing the tag; if it does not, the program exits. To perform these actions we need a new primitive operation, `tag-of-any`, and a new form, `ValueOf`. The `tag-of-any` operation retrieves the type tag from a tagged value of type `Any`. The `ValueOf` form retrieves the underlying value from a tagged value. The `ValueOf` form includes the type for the underlying value that is used by the type checker.

If the target type of the projection is `Boolean` or `Integer`, then `Project` can be translated as follows:

```
(Project e ftype)
⇒
(Let tmp e′
   (If (Prim 'eq? (list (Prim 'tag-of-any (list (Var tmp)))
                        (Int tagof(ftype))))
      (ValueOf tmp ftype)
      (Exit)))
```

If the target type of the projection is a tuple or function type, then there is a bit more work to do. For tuples, check that the length of the tuple type matches the length of the tuple. For functions, check that the number of parameters in the function type matches the function's arity.

Regarding `Inject`, we recommend compiling it to a slightly lower-level primitive operation named `make-any`. This operation takes a tag instead of a type.

```
(Inject e ftype)
⇒
(Prim 'make-any (list e′ (Int tagof(ftype))))
```

The type predicates (`boolean?`, etc.) can be translated into uses of `tag-of-any` and `eq?` in a similar way as in the translation of `Project`.

The `any-vector-ref` and `any-vector-set!` operations combine the projection action with the vector operation. Also, the read and write operations allow arbitrary expressions for the index, so the type checker for $\mathcal{L}_{\mathsf{Any}}$ (figure 9.6) cannot guarantee that the index is within bounds. Thus, we insert code to perform bounds checking at runtime. The translation for `any-vector-ref` is as follows, and the other two operations are translated in a similar way:

```
(Prim 'any-vector-ref (list e₁ e₂))
⇒
(Let v e₁'
  (Let i e₂'
    (If (Prim 'eq? (list (Prim 'tag-of-any (list (Var v))) (Int 2)))
      (If (Prim '< (list (Var i) (Prim 'any-vector-length (list (Var v)))))
        (Prim 'any-vector-ref (list (Var v) (Var i)))
        (Exit))
      (Exit))))
```

## 9.6  Remove Complex Operands

The `ValueOf` and `Exit` forms are both complex expressions. The subexpression of
`ValueOf` must be atomic.

## 9.7  Explicate Control and $\mathcal{C}_{\text{Any}}$

The output of `explicate_control` is the $\mathcal{C}_{\text{Any}}$ language, whose syntax definition is
shown in figure 9.11. The `ValueOf` form that we added to $\mathcal{L}_{\text{Any}}$ remains an expression
and the `Exit` expression becomes a *tail*. Also, note that the index argument of
`vector-ref` and `vector-set!` is an *atm*, instead of an integer as it was in $\mathcal{C}_{\text{Tup}}$
(figure 6.12).

## 9.8  Select Instructions

In the `select_instructions` pass, we translate the primitive operations on the
`Any` type to x86 instructions that manipulate the three tag bits of the tagged value.
In the following descriptions, given an atom $e$ we use a primed variable $e'$ to refer
to the result of translating $e$ into an x86 argument:

`make-any`  We recommend compiling the `make-any` operation as follows if the tag is
for `Integer` or `Boolean`. The `salq` instruction shifts the destination to the left by
the number of bits specified by its source argument (in this case three, the length
of the tag), and it preserves the sign of the integer. We use the `orq` instruction to
combine the tag and the value to form the tagged value.

```
(Assign lhs (Prim 'make-any (list e (Int tag))))
⇒
movq e', lhs'
salq $3, lhs'
orq $tag, lhs'
```

The instruction selection for tuples and procedures is different because there is
no need to shift them to the left. The rightmost 3 bits are already zeros, so we
simply combine the value and the tag using `orq`.

```
atm    ::=   (Int int) | (Var var)
exp    ::=   atm | (Prim 'read ()) | (Prim '- (atm))
       |     (Prim '+ (atm atm)) | (Prim '- (atm atm))
stmt   ::=   (Assign (Var var) exp)
tail   ::=   (Return exp) | (Seq stmt tail)
```
```
atm    ::=   (Bool bool)
cmp    ::=   eq? | < | <= | > | >=
exp    ::=   (Prim 'not (atm)) | (Prim 'cmp (atm atm))
tail   ::=   (Goto label)
       |     (IfStmt (Prim cmp (atm atm)) (Goto label) (Goto label))
```
```
atm    ::=   (Void)
stmt   ::=   (Prim 'read ())
```
```
exp    ::=   (Allocate int type)
       |     (Prim vector-ref (atm (Int int)))
       |     (Prim vector-set! (atm (Int int) atm))
       |     (Prim vector-length (atm))
       |     (GlobalValue var)
stmt   ::=   (Prim vector-set! (atm (Int int) atm))
       |     (Collect int)
```
```
exp    ::=   (FunRef label int) | (Call atm (atm ...))
tail   ::=   (TailCall atm atm ...)
def    ::=   (Def label ([var:type] ...) type info ((label . tail) ...))
```
```
exp    ::=   (AllocateClosure int type int)
op     ::=   procedure-arity
```
```
exp    ::=   (Prim 'any-vector-ref (atm atm))
       |     (Prim 'any-vector-set! (list atm atm atm))
       |     (ValueOf atm ftype)
tail   ::=   (Exit)
C_Any  ::=   (ProgramDefs info (def ...))
```

**Figure 9.11**
The abstract syntax of $C_{Any}$, extending $C_{Clos}$ (figure 8.8).

```
(Assign lhs (Prim 'make-any (list e (Int tag))))
⇒
movq e', lhs'
orq $tag, lhs'
```

**tag-of-any**   Recall that the **tag-of-any** operation extracts the type tag from a value of type **Any**. The type tag is the bottom 3 bits, so we obtain the tag by taking the bitwise-and of the value with 111 (7 decimal).

```
(Assign lhs (Prim 'tag-of-any (list e)))
⇒
movq e', lhs'
andq $7, lhs'
```

**ValueOf**   The instructions for **ValueOf** also differ, depending on whether the type $T$ is a pointer (tuple or function) or not (integer or Boolean). The following shows the instruction selection for integers and Booleans, in which we produce an untagged value by shifting it to the right by 3 bits:

(**Assign** *lhs* (**ValueOf** *e T*))
⇒
movq *e′*, *lhs′*
sarq $3, *lhs′*

In the case for tuples and procedures, we zero out the rightmost 3 bits. We accomplish this by creating the bit pattern ...0111 (7 decimal) and apply bitwise-not to obtain ...11111000 (-8 decimal), which we **movq** into the destination *lhs′*. Finally, we apply **andq** with the tagged value to get the desired result.

(**Assign** *lhs* (**ValueOf** *e T*))
⇒
movq $-8, *lhs′*
andq *e′*, *lhs′*

**any-vector-length**   The **any-vector-length** operation combines the effect of **ValueOf** with accessing the length of a tuple from the tag stored at the zero index of the tuple.

(**Assign** *lhs* (**Prim** 'any-vector-length (**list** $e_1$)))
⟹
movq $-8, %r11
andq $e_1′$, %r11
movq 0(%r11), %r11
andq $126, %r11
sarq $1, %r11
movq %r11, *lhs′*

**any-vector-ref**   This operation combines the effect of **ValueOf** with reading an element of the tuple (see section 6.6). However, the index may be an arbitrary atom, so instead of computing the offset at compile time, we must generate instructions to compute the offset at runtime as follows. Note the use of the new instruction imulq.

(**Assign** *lhs* (**Prim** 'any-vector-ref (**list** $e_1$ $e_2$)))
⟹
movq ¬111, %r11
andq $e_1′$, %r11
movq $e_2′$, %rax
addq $1, %rax
imulq $8, %rax
addq %rax, %r11
movq 0(%r11) *lhs′*

## 9.9  Register Allocation for $\mathcal{L}_{Any}$

There is an interesting interaction between tagged values and garbage collection that has an impact on register allocation. A variable of type **Any** might refer to a tuple, and therefore it might be a root that needs to be inspected and copied during garbage collection. Thus, we need to treat variables of type **Any** in a similar way to variables of tuple type for purposes of register allocation, with particular attention to the following:

- If a variable of type **Any** is live during a function call, then it must be spilled. This can be accomplished by changing `build_interference` to mark all variables of type **Any** that are live after a `callq` to be interfering with all the registers.
- If a variable of type **Any** is spilled, it must be spilled to the root stack instead of the normal procedure call stack.

Another concern regarding the root stack is that the garbage collector needs to differentiate among (1) plain old pointers to tuples, (2) a tagged value that points to a tuple, and (3) a tagged value that is not a tuple. We enable this differentiation by choosing not to use the tag 000 in the *tagof* function. Instead, that bit pattern is reserved for identifying plain old pointers to tuples. That way, if one of the first three bits is set, then we have a tagged value and inspecting the tag can differentiate between tuples (010) and the other kinds of values.

**Exercise 9.1** Expand your compiler to handle $\mathcal{L}_{Dyn}$ as outlined in this chapter. Create tests for $\mathcal{L}_{Dyn}$ by adapting ten of your previous test programs by removing type annotations. Add five more test programs that specifically rely on the language being dynamically typed. That is, they should not be legal programs in a statically typed language, but nevertheless they should be valid $\mathcal{L}_{Dyn}$ programs that run to completion without error.

Figure 9.12 provides an overview of the passes needed for the compilation of $\mathcal{L}_{Dyn}$.

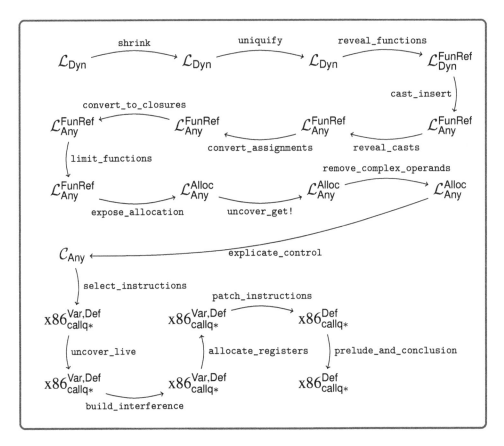

**Figure 9.12**
Diagram of the passes for $\mathcal{L}_{\mathsf{Dyn}}$, a dynamically typed language.

# 10 Gradual Typing

This chapter studies the language $\mathcal{L}_?$, in which the programmer can choose between static and dynamic type checking in different parts of a program, thereby mixing the statically typed $\mathcal{L}_\lambda$ language with the dynamically typed $\mathcal{L}_{\mathsf{Dyn}}$. There are several approaches to mixing static and dynamic typing, including multilanguage integration (Tobin-Hochstadt and Felleisen 2006; Matthews and Findler 2007) and hybrid type checking (Flanagan 2006; Gronski et al. 2006). In this chapter we focus on *gradual typing*, in which the programmer controls the amount of static versus dynamic checking by adding or removing type annotations on parameters and variables (Anderson and Drossopoulou 2003; Siek and Taha 2006).

The definition of the concrete syntax of $\mathcal{L}_?$ is shown in figure 10.1, and the definition of its abstract syntax is shown in figure 10.2. The main syntactic difference between $\mathcal{L}_\lambda$ and $\mathcal{L}_?$ is that type annotations are optional, which is specified in the grammar using the *prm* and *ret* nonterminals. In the abstract syntax, type annotations are not optional, but we use the **Any** type when a type annotation is absent. Both the type checker and the interpreter for $\mathcal{L}_?$ require some interesting changes to enable gradual typing, which we discuss in the next two sections.

## 10.1 Type Checking $\mathcal{L}_?$

We begin by discussing the type checking of a partially typed variant of the **map** example from chapter 7, shown in figure 10.3. The **map** function itself is statically typed, so there is nothing special happening there with respect to type checking. On the other hand, the **inc** function does not have type annotations, so the type checker assigns the type **Any** to parameter x and the return type. Now consider the + operator inside **inc**. It expects both arguments to have type **Integer**, but its first argument x has type **Any**. In a gradually typed language, such differences are allowed so long as the types are *consistent*; that is, they are equal except in places where there is an **Any** type. That is, the type **Any** is consistent with every other type. Figure 10.4 shows the definition of the **consistent?** method. So the type checker allows the + operator to be applied to x because **Any** is consistent with **Integer**. Next consider the call to the **map** function shown in figure 10.3 with the arguments **inc** and a tuple. The **inc** function has type (**Any** -> **Any**), but parameter f of **map** has type (**Integer** -> **Integer**). The type checker for $\mathcal{L}_?$ accepts this call because the two types are consistent.

| type | ::= | Integer |
|------|-----|---------|
| exp | ::= | *int* \| (read) \| (- *exp*) \| (+ *exp exp*) \| (- *exp exp*) |
| exp | ::= | *var* \| (let ([*var exp*]) *exp*) |
| type | ::= | Boolean |
| bool | ::= | #t \| #f |
| cmp | ::= | eq? \| < \| <= \| > \| >= |
| exp | ::= | *bool* \| (and *exp exp*) \| (or *exp exp*) \| (not *exp*) |
| | \| | (*cmp exp exp*) \| (if *exp exp exp*) |
| type | ::= | Void |
| exp | ::= | (set! *var exp*) \| (begin *exp** *exp*) \| (while *exp exp*) \| (void) |
| type | ::= | (Vector *type**) |
| exp | ::= | (vector *exp**) \| (vector-length *exp*) |
| | \| | (vector-ref *exp int*) \| (vector-set! *exp int exp*) |
| *type* | ::= | (*type* ... -> *type*) |
| *prm* | ::= | *var* \| [*var*:*type*] |
| *ret* | ::= | ϵ \| :*type* |
| *exp* | ::= | (*exp exp* ... ) \| (lambda: (*prm* ... ) *ret exp*) |
| | \| | (procedure-arity *exp*) |
| *def* | ::= | (define (*var prm* ... ) *ret exp*) |
| $\mathcal{L}_?$ | ::= | *def* ... *exp* |

**Figure 10.1**
The concrete syntax of $\mathcal{L}_?$, extending $\mathcal{L}_{\mathsf{Tup}}$ (figure 6.1).

It is also helpful to consider how gradual typing handles programs with an error, such as applying map to a function that sometimes returns a Boolean, as shown in figure 10.5. The type checker for $\mathcal{L}_?$ accepts this program because the type of maybe_inc is consistent with the type of parameter f of map; that is, (Any -> Any) is consistent with (Integer -> Integer). One might say that a gradual type checker is optimistic in that it accepts programs that might execute without a runtime type error. The definition of the type checker for $\mathcal{L}_?$ is shown in figures 10.7, 10.8, and 10.9.

Running this program with input 1 triggers an error when the maybe_inc function returns #t. The $\mathcal{L}_?$ language performs checking at runtime to ensure the integrity of the static types, such as the (Integer -> Integer) annotation on parameter f of map. Here we give a preview of how the runtime checking is accomplished; the following sections provide the details.

The runtime checking is carried out by a new Cast AST node that is generated in a new pass named cast_insert. The output of cast_insert is a program in the $\mathcal{L}_{\mathsf{Cast}}$ language, which simply adds Cast and Any to $\mathcal{L}_\lambda$. Figure 10.6 shows the output of cast_insert for map and maybe_inc. The idea is that Cast is inserted every time the type checker encounters two types that are consistent but not equal. In the inc function, x is cast to Integer and the result of the + is cast to Any. In the call to map, the inc argument is cast from (Any -> Any) to (Integer -> Integer). In the next section we see how to interpret the Cast node.

| | | |
|---|---|---|
| *type* | ::= | Integer |
| *op* | ::= | read \| + \| − |
| *exp* | ::= | (Int *int*) \| (Prim *op* (*exp* … )) |
| *exp* | ::= | (Var *var*) \| (Let *var* *exp* *exp*) |
| *type* | ::= | Boolean |
| *bool* | ::= | #t \| #f |
| *cmp* | ::= | eq? \| < \| <= \| > \| >= |
| *op* | ::= | *cmp* \| and \| or \| not |
| *exp* | ::= | (Bool *bool*) \| (If *exp* *exp* *exp*) |
| *type* | ::= | Void |
| *exp* | ::= | (SetBang *var* *exp*) \| (Begin *exp*\* *exp*) \| (WhileLoop *exp* *exp*) \| (Void) |
| *type* | ::= | (Vector *type*\*) |
| *op* | ::= | vector \| vector-length |
| *exp* | ::= | (Prim vector-ref (*exp* (Int *int*))) |
| | \| | (Prim vector-set! (*exp* (Int *int*) *exp*)) |
| *type* | ::= | (*type* … -> *type*) |
| *prm* | ::= | *var* \| [*var*:*type*] |
| *exp* | ::= | (Apply *exp* *exp* … ) \| (Lambda (*prm* … ) *type* *exp*) |
| *op* | ::= | procedure-arity |
| *def* | ::= | (Def *var* (*prm* … ) *type* '() *exp*) |
| $\mathcal{L}_?$ | ::= | (ProgramDefsExp '() (*def* … ) *exp*) |

**Figure 10.2**
The abstract syntax of $\mathcal{L}_?$, extending $\mathcal{L}_{\mathsf{Tup}}$ (figure 6.2).

```
(define (map [f : (Integer -> Integer)]
             [v : (Vector Integer Integer)])
           : (Vector Integer Integer)
  (vector (f (vector-ref v 0)) (f (vector-ref v 1)))))

(define (inc x) (+ x 1))

(vector-ref (map inc (vector 0 41)) 1)
```

**Figure 10.3**
A partially typed version of the map example.

```
(define/override (type-check-exp env)
  (lambda (e)
    (define recur (type-check-exp env))
    (match e
      [(Prim op es) #:when (not (set-member? explicit-prim-ops op))
       (define-values (new-es ts)
         (for/lists (exprs types) ([e es])
           (recur e)))
       (define t-ret (type-check-op op ts e))
       (values (Prim op new-es) t-ret)]
      [(Prim 'eq? (list e1 e2))
       (define-values (e1^ t1) (recur e1))
       (define-values (e2^ t2) (recur e2))
       (check-consistent? t1 t2 e)
       (define T (meet t1 t2))
       (values (Prim 'eq? (list e1^ e2^)) 'Boolean)]
      [(Prim 'and (list e1 e2))
       (recur (If e1 e2 (Bool #f)))]
      [(Prim 'or (list e1 e2))
       (define tmp (gensym 'tmp))
       (recur (Let tmp e1 (If (Var tmp) (Var tmp) e2)))]
      [(If e1 e2 e3)
       (define-values (e1^ T1) (recur e1))
       (define-values (e2^ T2) (recur e2))
       (define-values (e3^ T3) (recur e3))
       (check-consistent? T1 'Boolean e)
       (check-consistent? T2 T3 e)
       (define Tif (meet T2 T3))
       (values (If e1^ e2^ e3^) Tif)]
      [(SetBang x e1)
       (define-values (e1^ T1) (recur e1))
       (define varT (dict-ref env x))
       (check-consistent? T1 varT e)
       (values (SetBang x e1^) 'Void)]
      [(WhileLoop e1 e2)
       (define-values (e1^ T1) (recur e1))
       (check-consistent? T1 'Boolean e)
       (define-values (e2^ T2) ((type-check-exp env) e2))
       (values (WhileLoop e1^ e2^) 'Void)]
      [(Prim 'vector-length (list e1))
       (define-values (e1^ t) (recur e1))
       (match t
         [`(Vector ,ts ...)
          (values (Prim 'vector-length (list e1^)) 'Integer)]
         ['Any (values (Prim 'vector-length (list e1^)) 'Integer)])])
```

**Figure 10.7**
Type checker for the $\mathcal{L}_?$ language, part 1.

```
[(Prim 'vector-ref (list e1 e2))
 (define-values (e1^ t1) (recur e1))
 (define-values (e2^ t2) (recur e2))
 (check-consistent? t2 'Integer e)
 (match t1
   [`(Vector ,ts ...)
    (match e2^
      [(Int i)
       (unless (and (0 . <= . i) (i . < . (length ts)))
         (error 'type-check "invalid index ~a in ~a" i e))
       (values (Prim 'vector-ref (list e1^ (Int i))) (list-ref ts i))]
      [else (values (Prim 'vector-ref (list e1^ e2^)) 'Any)])]
   ['Any (values (Prim 'vector-ref (list e1^ e2^)) 'Any)]
   [else (error 'type-check "expected vector not ~a\nin ~v" t1 e)])]
[(Prim 'vector-set! (list e1 e2 e3) )
 (define-values (e1^ t1) (recur e1))
 (define-values (e2^ t2) (recur e2))
 (define-values (e3^ t3) (recur e3))
 (check-consistent? t2 'Integer e)
 (match t1
   [`(Vector ,ts ...)
    (match e2^
      [(Int i)
       (unless (and (0 . <= . i) (i . < . (length ts)))
         (error 'type-check "invalid index ~a in ~a" i e))
       (check-consistent? (list-ref ts i) t3 e)
       (values (Prim 'vector-set! (list e1^ (Int i) e3^)) 'Void)]
      [else (values (Prim 'vector-set! (list e1^ e2^ e3^)) 'Void)])]
   ['Any (values (Prim 'vector-set! (list e1^ e2^ e3^)) 'Void)]
   [else (error 'type-check "expected vector not ~a\nin ~v" t1 e)])]
[(Apply e1 e2s)
 (define-values (e1^ T1) (recur e1))
 (define-values (e2s^ T2s) (for/lists (e* ty*) ([e2 e2s]) (recur e2)))
 (match T1
   [`(,T1ps ... -> ,T1rt)
    (for ([T2 T2s] [Tp T1ps])
      (check-consistent? T2 Tp e))
    (values (Apply e1^ e2s^) T1rt)]
   [`Any (values (Apply e1^ e2s^) 'Any)]
   [else (error 'type-check "expected function not ~a\nin ~v" T1 e)])]
[(Lambda params Tr e1)
 (define-values (xs Ts) (for/lists (l1 l2) ([p params])
                          (match p
                            [`[,x : ,T] (values x T)]
                            [(? symbol? x) (values x 'Any)])))
 (define-values (e1^ T1)
   ((type-check-exp (append (map cons xs Ts) env)) e1))
 (check-consistent? Tr T1 e)
 (values (Lambda (for/list ([x xs] [T Ts]) `[,x : ,T]) Tr e1^)
         `(,@Ts -> ,Tr))]
[else ((super type-check-exp env) e)]
)))
```

**Figure 10.8**
Type checker for the $\mathcal{L}_?$ language, part 2.

```
(define/override (type-check-def env)
  (lambda (e)
    (match e
      [(Def f params rt info body)
       (define-values (xs ps) (for/lists (l1 l2) ([p params])
                                (match p
                                  [`[,x : ,T] (values x T)]
                                  [(? symbol? x) (values x 'Any)])))
       (define new-env (append (map cons xs ps) env))
       (define-values (body^ ty^) ((type-check-exp new-env) body))
       (check-consistent? ty^ rt e)
       (Def f (for/list ([x xs] [T ps]) `[,x : ,T]) rt info body^)]
      [else (error 'type-check "ill-formed function definition ~a" e)]
      )))

(define/override (type-check-program e)
  (match e
    [(Program info body)
     (define-values (body^ ty) ((type-check-exp '()) body))
     (check-consistent? ty 'Integer e)
     (ProgramDefsExp info '() body^)]
    [(ProgramDefsExp info ds body)
     (define new-env (for/list ([d ds])
                       (cons (Def-name d) (fun-def-type d))))
     (define ds^ (for/list ([d ds])
                   ((type-check-def new-env) d)))
     (define-values (body^ ty) ((type-check-exp new-env) body))
     (check-consistent? ty 'Integer e)
     (ProgramDefsExp info ds^ body^)]
    [else (super type-check-program e)]))
```

**Figure 10.9**
Type checker for the $\mathcal{L}_?$ language, part 3.

```
(define/public (join t1 t2)
  (match* (t1 t2)
    [('Integer 'Integer) 'Integer]
    [('Boolean 'Boolean) 'Boolean]
    [('Void 'Void) 'Void]
    [('Any t2) t2]
    [(t1 'Any) t1]
    [(`(Vector ,ts1 ...) `(Vector ,ts2 ...))
     `(Vector ,@(for/list ([t1 ts1] [t2 ts2]) (join t1 t2)))]
    [(`(,ts1 ... -> ,rt1) `(,ts2 ... -> ,rt2))
     `(,@(for/list ([t1 ts1] [t2 ts2]) (join t1 t2))
       -> ,(join rt1 rt2))]))

(define/public (meet t1 t2)
  (match* (t1 t2)
    [('Integer 'Integer) 'Integer]
    [('Boolean 'Boolean) 'Boolean]
    [('Void 'Void) 'Void]
    [('Any t2) 'Any]
    [(t1 'Any) 'Any]
    [(`(Vector ,ts1 ...) `(Vector ,ts2 ...))
     `(Vector ,@(for/list ([t1 ts1] [t2 ts2]) (meet t1 t2)))]
    [(`(,ts1 ... -> ,rt1) `(,ts2 ... -> ,rt2))
     `(,@(for/list ([t1 ts1] [t2 ts2]) (meet t1 t2))
       -> ,(meet rt1 rt2))]))

(define/public (check-consistent? t1 t2 e)
  (unless (consistent? t1 t2)
    (error 'type-check "~a is inconsistent with ~a\nin ~v" t1 t2 e)))

(define explicit-prim-ops
  (set-union
   (type-predicates)
   (set 'procedure-arity 'eq? 'not 'and 'or
        'vector 'vector-length 'vector-ref 'vector-set!
        'any-vector-length 'any-vector-ref 'any-vector-set!)))

(define/override (fun-def-type d)
  (match d
    [(Def f params rt info body)
     (define ps
       (for/list ([p params])
         (match p
           [`[,x : ,T] T]
           [(? symbol?) 'Any]
           [else (error 'fun-def-type "unmatched parameter ~a" p)])))
     `(,@ps -> ,rt)]
    [else (error 'fun-def-type "ill-formed definition in ~a" d)]))
```

**Figure 10.10**
Auxiliary functions for type checking $\mathcal{L}_?$.

```
(define (map_inplace [f : (Any -> Any)]
                     [v : (Vector Any Any)]) : Void
  (begin
    (vector-set! v 0 (f (vector-ref v 0)))
    (vector-set! v 1 (f (vector-ref v 1)))))

(define (inc x) (+ x 1))

(let ([v (vector 0 41)])
  (begin (map_inplace inc v) (vector-ref v 1)))
```

**Figure 10.11**
An example involving casts on arrays.

## 10.2  Interpreting $\mathcal{L}_{Cast}$

The runtime behavior of casts involving simple types such as Integer and Boolean is straightforward. For example, a cast from Integer to Any can be accomplished with the Inject operator of $\mathcal{L}_{Any}$, which puts the integer into a tagged value (figure 9.8). Similarly, a cast from Any to Integer is accomplished with the Project operator, by checking the value's tag and either retrieving the underlying integer or signaling an error if the tag is not the one for integers (figure 9.9). Things get more interesting with casts involving function and tuple types.

Consider the cast of the function maybe_inc from (Any -> Any) to (Integer -> Integer) shown in figure 10.5. When the maybe_inc function flows through this cast at runtime, we don't know whether it will return an integer, because that depends on the input from the user. The $\mathcal{L}_{Cast}$ interpreter therefore delays the checking of the cast until the function is applied. To do so it wraps maybe_inc in a new function that casts its parameter from Integer to Any, applies maybe_inc, and then casts the return value from Any to Integer.

Consider the example presented in figure 10.11 that defines a partially typed version of map whose parameter v has type (Vector Any Any) and that updates v in place instead of returning a new tuple. We name this function map_inplace. We apply map_inplace to a tuple of integers, so the type checker inserts a cast from (Vector Integer Integer) to (Vector Any Any). A naive way for the $\mathcal{L}_{Cast}$ interpreter to cast between tuple types would be to build a new tuple whose elements are the result of casting each of the original elements to the appropriate target type. However, this approach is not valid for mutable data structures. In the example of figure 10.11, if the cast created a new tuple, then the updates inside map_inplace would happen to the new tuple and not the original one.

Instead the interpreter needs to create a new kind of value, a *proxy*, that intercepts every tuple operation. On a read, the proxy reads from the underlying tuple and then applies a cast to the resulting value. On a write, the proxy casts the argument value and then performs the write to the underlying tuple. For the first

```
(define (map_inplace [f : (Any -> Any)] v) : Void
  (begin
    (vector-set! v 0 (f (vector-ref v 0)))
    (vector-set! v 1 (f (vector-ref v 1)))))

(define (inc x) (+ x 1))

(let ([v (vector 0 41)])
  (begin (map_inplace inc v) (vector-ref v 1)))
```

**Figure 10.12**
Casting a tuple to Any.

(vector-ref v 0) in map_inplace, the proxy casts 0 from Integer to Any. For
the first vector-set!, the proxy casts a tagged 1 from Any to Integer.

Finally we consider casts between the Any type and higher-order types such as
functions and tuples. Figure 10.12 shows a variant of map_inplace in which parameter v does not have a type annotation, so it is given type Any. In the call to
map_inplace, the tuple has type (Vector Integer Integer), so the type checker
inserts a cast to Any. A first thought is to use Inject, but that doesn't work
because (Vector Integer Integer) is not a flat type. Instead, we must first cast
to (Vector Any Any), which is flat, and then inject to Any.

The $\mathcal{L}_{Cast}$ interpreter uses an auxiliary function named apply_cast to cast a
value from a source type to a target type, shown in figure 10.13. You'll find that it
handles all the kinds of casts that we've discussed in this section. The definition of
the interpreter for $\mathcal{L}_{Cast}$ is shown in figure 10.14, with the case for Cast dispatching to apply_cast. To handle the addition of tuple proxies, we update the tuple
primitives in interp-op using the functions given in figure 10.15. Next we turn to
the individual passes needed for compiling $\mathcal{L}_?$.

## 10.3   Cast Insertion

In our discussion of type checking of $\mathcal{L}_?$, we mentioned how the runtime aspect of
type checking is carried out by the Cast AST node, which is added to the program
by a new pass named cast_insert. The target of this pass is the $\mathcal{L}_{Cast}$ language.
We now discuss the details of this pass.

The cast_insert pass is closely related to the type checker for $\mathcal{L}_?$ (starting in
figure 10.7). In particular, the type checker allows implicit casts between consistent
types. The job of the cast_insert pass is to make those casts explicit. It does so
by inserting Cast nodes into the AST. For the most part, the implicit casts occur
in places where the type checker checks two types for consistency. Consider the
case for binary operators in figure 10.7. The type checker requires that the type of
the left operand is consistent with Integer. Thus, the cast_insert pass should
insert a Cast around the left operand, converting from its type to Integer. The

```
(define/public (apply_cast v s t)
  (match* (s t)
    [(t1 t2) #:when (equal? t1 t2) v]
    [('Any t2)
     (match t2
       [`(,ts ... -> ,rt)
        (define any->any `(,@(for/list ([t ts]) 'Any) -> Any))
        (define v^ (apply-project v any->any))
        (apply_cast v^ any->any `(,@ts -> ,rt))]
       [`(Vector ,ts ...)
        (define vec-any `(Vector ,@(for/list ([t ts]) 'Any)))
        (define v^ (apply-project v vec-any))
        (apply_cast v^ vec-any `(Vector ,@ts))]
       [else (apply-project v t2)])]
    [(t1 'Any)
     (match t1
       [`(,ts ... -> ,rt)
        (define any->any `(,@(for/list ([t ts]) 'Any) -> Any))
        (define v^ (apply_cast v `(,@ts -> ,rt) any->any))
        (apply-inject v^ (any-tag any->any))]
       [`(Vector ,ts ...)
        (define vec-any `(Vector ,@(for/list ([t ts]) 'Any)))
        (define v^ (apply_cast v `(Vector ,@ts) vec-any))
        (apply-inject v^ (any-tag vec-any))]
       [else (apply-inject v (any-tag t1))])]
    [(`(Vector ,ts1 ...) `(Vector ,ts2 ...))
     (define x (gensym 'x))
     (define cast-reads (for/list ([t1 ts1] [t2 ts2])
                          `(function (,x) ,(Cast (Var x) t1 t2) ())))
     (define cast-writes
       (for/list ([t1 ts1] [t2 ts2])
         `(function (,x) ,(Cast (Var x) t2 t1) ())))
     `(vector-proxy ,(vector v (apply vector cast-reads)
                            (apply vector cast-writes)))]
    [(`(,ts1 ... -> ,rt1) `(,ts2 ... -> ,rt2))
     (define xs (for/list ([t2 ts2]) (gensym 'x)))
     `(function ,xs ,(Cast
                      (Apply (Value v)
                             (for/list ([x xs][t1 ts1][t2 ts2])
                               (Cast (Var x) t2 t1)))
                      rt1 rt2) ())]
    ))
```

**Figure 10.13**
The `apply_cast` auxiliary method.

story is similar for the right operand. It is not always necessary to insert a cast, for example, if the left operand already has type `Integer` then there is no need for a `Cast`.

Some of the implicit casts are not as straightforward. One such case arises with the conditional expression. In figure 10.7 we see that the type checker requires that the two branches have consistent types and that type of the conditional expression is the meet of the branches' types. In the target language $\mathcal{L}_{\text{Cast}}$, both branches will need to have the same type, and that type will be the type of the conditional

```
(define interp-Lcast-class
  (class interp-Llambda-class
    (super-new)
    (inherit apply-fun apply-inject apply-project)

    (define/override (interp-op op)
      (match op
        ['vector-length guarded-vector-length]
        ['vector-ref guarded-vector-ref]
        ['vector-set! guarded-vector-set!]
        ['any-vector-ref (lambda (v i)
                           (match v [`(tagged ,v^ ,tg)
                                      (guarded-vector-ref v^ i)])))]
        ['any-vector-set! (lambda (v i a)
                            (match v [`(tagged ,v^ ,tg)
                                       (guarded-vector-set! v^ i a)])))]
        ['any-vector-length (lambda (v)
                              (match v [`(tagged ,v^ ,tg)
                                         (guarded-vector-length v^)])))]
        [else (super interp-op op)]
        ))

    (define/override ((interp-exp env) e)
      (define (recur e) ((interp-exp env) e))
      (match e
        [(Value v) v]
        [(Cast e src tgt) (apply_cast (recur e) src tgt)]
        [else ((super interp-exp env) e)]))
      ))

(define (interp-Lcast p)
  (send (new interp-Lcast-class) interp-program p))
```

**Figure 10.14**
The interpreter for $\mathcal{L}_{\text{Cast}}$.

expression. Thus, each branch requires a Cast to convert from its type to the meet of the branches' types.

The case for the function call exhibits another interesting situation. If the function expression is of type Any, then it needs to be cast to a function type so that it can be used in a function call in $\mathcal{L}_{\text{Cast}}$. Which function type should it be cast to? The parameter and return types are unknown, so we can simply use Any for all of them. Furthermore, in $\mathcal{L}_{\text{Cast}}$ the argument types will need to exactly match the parameter types, so we must cast all the arguments to type Any (if they are not already of that type).

Likewise, the cases for the tuple operators vector-length, vector-ref, and vector-set! need to handle the situation where the tuple expression is of type Any. Instead of handling these situations with casts, we recommend translating the special-purpose variants of the tuple operators that handle tuples of type Any: any-vector-length, any-vector-ref, and any-vector-set!.

```
(define (guarded-vector-ref vec i)
  (match vec
    [`(vector-proxy ,proxy)
     (define val (guarded-vector-ref (vector-ref proxy 0) i))
     (define rd (vector-ref (vector-ref proxy 1) i))
     (apply-fun rd (list val) 'guarded-vector-ref)]
    [else (vector-ref vec i)]))

(define (guarded-vector-set! vec i arg)
  (match vec
    [`(vector-proxy ,proxy)
     (define wr (vector-ref (vector-ref proxy 2) i))
     (define arg^ (apply-fun wr (list arg) 'guarded-vector-set!))
     (guarded-vector-set! (vector-ref proxy 0) i arg^)]
    [else (vector-set! vec i arg)]))

(define (guarded-vector-length vec)
  (match vec
    [`(vector-proxy ,proxy)
     (guarded-vector-length (vector-ref proxy 0))]
    [else (vector-length vec)]))
```

**Figure 10.15**
The `guarded-vector` auxiliary functions.

## 10.4  Lower Casts

The next step in the journey toward x86 is the `lower_casts` pass that translates the casts in $\mathcal{L}_{\text{Cast}}$ to the lower-level `Inject` and `Project` operators and new operators for proxies, extending the $\mathcal{L}_\lambda$ language to $\mathcal{L}_{\text{Proxy}}$. The $\mathcal{L}_{\text{Proxy}}$ language can also be described as an extension of $\mathcal{L}_{\text{Any}}$, with the addition of proxies. We recommend creating an auxiliary function named `lower_cast` that takes an expression (in $\mathcal{L}_{\text{Cast}}$), a source type, and a target type and translates it to an expression in $\mathcal{L}_{\text{Proxy}}$.

The `lower_cast` function can follow a code structure similar to the `apply_cast` function (figure 10.13) used in the interpreter for $\mathcal{L}_{\text{Cast}}$, because it must handle the same cases as `apply_cast` and it needs to mimic the behavior of `apply_cast`. The most interesting cases concern the casts involving tuple and function types.

As mentioned in section 10.2, a cast from one tuple type to another tuple type is accomplished by creating a proxy that intercepts the operations on the underlying tuple. Here we make the creation of the proxy explicit with the `vector-proxy` AST node. It takes three arguments: the first is an expression for the tuple, the second is a tuple of functions for casting an element that is being read from the tuple, and the third is a tuple of functions for casting an element that is being written to the array. You can create the functions for reading and writing using lambda expressions. Also, as we show in the next section, we need to differentiate these tuples of functions from the user-created ones, so we recommend using a new AST node named `raw-vector` instead of `vector`. Figure 10.16 shows the output of

```
(define (map_inplace [f : (Any -> Any)] [v : (Vector Any Any)]) : Void
  (begin
    (vector-set! v 0 (f (vector-ref v 0)))
    (vector-set! v 1 (f (vector-ref v 1)))))

(define (inc [x : Any]) : Any
  (inject (+ (project x Integer) 1) Integer))

(let ([v (vector 0 41)])
  (begin
    (map_inplace inc (vector-proxy v
                       (raw-vector (lambda: ([x9 : Integer]) : Any
                                     (inject x9 Integer))
                                   (lambda: ([x9 : Integer]) : Any
                                     (inject x9 Integer)))
                       (raw-vector (lambda: ([x9 : Any]) : Integer
                                     (project x9 Integer))
                                   (lambda: ([x9 : Any]) : Integer
                                     (project x9 Integer)))))
    (vector-ref v 1)))
```

**Figure 10.16**
Output of `lower_casts` on the example shown in figure 10.11.

`lower_casts` on the example given in figure 10.11 that involved casting a tuple of integers to a tuple of `Any`.

A cast from one function type to another function type is accomplished by generating a `lambda` whose parameter and return types match the target function type. The body of the `lambda` should cast the parameters from the target type to the source type. (Yes, backward! Functions are contravariant in the parameters.) Afterward, call the underlying function and then cast the result from the source return type to the target return type. Figure 10.17 shows the output of the `lower_casts` pass on the `map` example give in figure 10.3. Note that the `inc` argument in the call to `map` is wrapped in a `lambda`.

## 10.5 Differentiate Proxies

So far, the responsibility of differentiating tuples and tuple proxies has been the job of the interpreter. For example, the interpreter for $\mathcal{L}_{\mathsf{Cast}}$ implements `vector-ref` using the `guarded-vector-ref` function shown in figure 10.15. In the `differentiate_proxies` pass we shift this responsibility to the generated code.

We begin by designing the output language $\mathcal{L}_{\mathsf{POr}}$. In $\mathcal{L}_?$ we used the type `Vector` for both real tuples and tuple proxies. In $\mathcal{L}_{\mathsf{POr}}$ we return the `Vector` type to its original meaning, as the type of just tuples, and we introduce a new type, `PVector`, whose values can be either real tuples or tuple proxies.

```
(define (map [f : (Integer -> Integer)]
             [v : (Vector Integer Integer)])
           : (Vector Integer Integer)
  (vector (f (vector-ref v 0)) (f (vector-ref v 1)))))

(define (inc [x : Any]) : Any
  (inject (+ (project x Integer) 1) Integer))

(vector-ref (map (lambda: ([x9 : Integer]) : Integer
                   (project (inc (inject x9 Integer)) Integer))
                 (vector 0 41)) 1)
```

**Figure 10.17**
Output of `lower_casts` on the example shown in figure 10.3.

A tuple proxy is represented by a tuple containing three things: (1) the underlying tuple, (2) a tuple of functions for casting elements that are read from the tuple, and (3) a tuple of functions for casting values to be written to the tuple. So, we define the following abbreviation for the type of a tuple proxy:

$$TupleProxy(T \ldots \Rightarrow T' \ldots) = (\text{Vector } (\text{PVector } T \ldots) \ R \ W) \rightarrow (\text{PVector } T' \ldots))$$

where $R = (\text{Vector } (T \rightarrow T') \ldots)$ and $W = (\text{Vector } (T' \rightarrow T) \ldots)$. Next we describe each of the new primitive operations.

**inject-vector : (Vector $T \ldots$) $\rightarrow$ (PVector $T \ldots$)**
This operation brands a vector as a value of the `PVector` type.

**inject-proxy : $TupleProxy(T \ldots \Rightarrow T' \ldots)$ $\rightarrow$ (PVector $T' \ldots$)**
This operation brands a vector proxy as value of the `PVector` type.

**proxy? : (PVector $T \ldots$) $\rightarrow$ Boolean**
This returns true if the value is a tuple proxy and false if it is a real tuple.

**project-vector : (PVector $T \ldots$) $\rightarrow$ (Vector $T \ldots$)**
Assuming that the input is a tuple, this operation returns the tuple.

**proxy-vector-length : (PVector $T \ldots$) $\rightarrow$ Boolean**
Given a tuple proxy, this operation returns the length of the tuple.

**proxy-vector-ref : (PVector $T \ldots$) $\rightarrow$ ($i$ : Integer) $\rightarrow$ $T_i$**
Given a tuple proxy, this operation returns the $i$th element of the tuple.

**proxy-vector-set! : (PVector $T \ldots$) $\rightarrow$ ($i$ : Integer) $\rightarrow$ $T_i$ $\rightarrow$ Void**
Given a tuple proxy, this operation writes a value to the $i$th element of the tuple.

Now we discuss the translation that differentiates tuples and arrays from proxies. First, every type annotation in the program is translated (recursively) to replace

Vector with PVector. Next, we insert uses of PVector operations in the appropriate places. For example, we wrap every tuple creation with an inject-vector.

(vector $e_1 \ldots e_n$)
⇒
(inject-vector (vector $e_1' \ldots e_n'$))

The raw-vector AST node that we introduced in the previous section does not get injected.

(raw-vector $e_1 \ldots e_n$)
⇒
(vector $e_1' \ldots e_n'$)

The vector-proxy AST translates as follows:

(vector-proxy $e_1$ $e_2$ $e_3$)
⇒
(inject-proxy (vector $e_1'$ $e_2'$ $e_3'$))

We translate the element access operations into conditional expressions that check whether the value is a proxy and then dispatch to either the appropriate proxy tuple operation or the regular tuple operation.

(vector-ref $e_1$ $i$)
⇒
(let ([$v$ $e_1$])
  (if (proxy? $v$)
    (proxy-vector-ref $v$ $i$)
    (vector-ref (project-vector $v$) $i$)))

Note that in the branch for a tuple, we must apply project-vector before reading from the tuple.

The translation of array operations is similar to the ones for tuples.

## 10.6  Reveal Casts

Recall that the reveal_casts pass (section 9.5) is responsible for lowering Inject and Project into lower-level operations. In particular, Project turns into a conditional expression that inspects the tag and retrieves the underlying value. Here we need to augment the translation of Project to handle the situation in which the target type is PVector. Instead of using vector-length we need to use proxy-vector-length.

(project $e$ (PVector $Any_1$ ... $Any_n$))
⇒
(let $tmp$ $e'$
  (if (eq? (tag-of-any $tmp$ 2))
    (let $tup$ (value-of $tmp$ (PVector Any ... Any))
      (if (eq? (proxy-vector-length $tup$) $n$) $tup$ (exit)))
    (exit)))

Otherwise, the only other changes are adding cases that copy the new AST nodes.

## 10.7 Closure Conversion

The auxiliary function that translates type annotations needs to be updated to handle the `PVector` type. Otherwise, the only other changes are adding cases that copy the new AST nodes.

## 10.8 Select Instructions

Recall that the `select_instructions` pass is responsible for lowering the primitive operations into x86 instructions. So, we need to translate the new operations on `PVector` to x86. To do so, the first question we need to answer is how to differentiate between tuple and tuple proxies. We need just one bit to accomplish this; we use the bit in position 63 of the 64-bit tag at the front of every tuple (see figure 6.8). So far, this bit has been set to 0, so for `inject-vector` we leave it that way.

```
(Assign lhs (Prim 'inject-vector (list e₁)))
⇒
movq e′₁, lhs′
```

On the other hand, `inject-proxy` sets bit 63 to 1.

```
(Assign lhs (Prim 'inject-proxy (list e₁)))
⇒
movq e′₁, %r11
movq (1 << 63), %rax
orq 0(%r11), %rax
movq %rax, 0(%r11)
movq %r11, lhs′
```

The `proxy?` operation consumes the information so carefully stashed away by the injections. It isolates bit 63 to tell whether the value is a proxy.

```
(Assign lhs (Prim 'proxy? (list e₁)))
⇒
movq e′₁, %r11
movq 0(%r11), %rax
sarq $63, %rax
andq $1, %rax
movq %rax, lhs′
```

The `project-vector` operation is straightforward to translate, so we leave that to the reader.

Regarding the element access operations for tuples, the runtime provides procedures that implement them (they are recursive functions!), so here we simply need to translate these tuple operations into the appropriate function call. For example, here is the translation for `proxy-vector-ref`.

```
(Assign lhs (Prim 'proxy-vector-ref (list e₁ e₂)))
⇒
movq e₁', %rdi
movq e₂', %rsi
callq proxy_vector_ref
movq %rax, lhs'
```

We have another batch of operations to deal with: those for the **Any** type. Recall that we generate an **any-vector-ref** when there is a element access on something of type **Any**, and similarly for **any-vector-set!** and **any-vector-length**. In section 9.8 we selected instructions for these operations on the basis of the idea that the underlying value was a tuple or array. But in the current setting, the underlying value is of type **PVector**. We have added three runtime functions to deal with this: **proxy_vector_ref**, **proxy_vector_set**, and **proxy_vector_length** that inspect bit 62 of the tag to determine whether the value is a proxy, and then dispatches to the the appropriate code. So **any-vector-ref** can be translated as follows. We begin by projecting the underlying value out of the tagged value and then call the **proxy_vector_ref** procedure in the runtime.

```
(Assign lhs (Prim 'any-vec-ref (list e₁ e₂)))
⇒
movq ¬111, %rdi
andq e₁', %rdi
movq e₂', %rsi
callq proxy_vector_ref
movq %rax, lhs'
```

The **any-vector-set!** and **any-vector-length** operators are translated in a similar way. Alternatively, you could generate instructions to open-code the **proxy_vector_ref**, **proxy_vector_set**, and **proxy_vector_length** functions.

**Exercise 10.1** Implement a compiler for the gradually typed $\mathcal{L}_?$ language by extending and adapting your compiler for $\mathcal{L}_\lambda$. Create ten new partially typed test programs. In addition to testing with these new programs, test your compiler on all the tests for $\mathcal{L}_\lambda$ and for $\mathcal{L}_{\mathsf{Dyn}}$. Sometimes you may get a type checking error on the $\mathcal{L}_{\mathsf{Dyn}}$ programs, but you can adapt them by inserting a cast to the **Any** type around each subexpression that has caused a type error. Although $\mathcal{L}_{\mathsf{Dyn}}$ does not have explicit casts, you can induce one by wrapping the subexpression e with a call to an unannotated identity function, as follows: ((lambda (x) x) e).

Figure 10.18 provides an overview of the passes needed for the compilation of $\mathcal{L}_?$.

## 10.9 Further Reading

This chapter just scratches the surface of gradual typing. The basic approach described here is missing two key ingredients that one would want in a implementation of gradual typing: blame tracking (Tobin-Hochstadt and Felleisen 2006;

Wadler and Findler 2009) and space-efficient casts (Herman, Tomb, and Flanagan 2007, 2010). The problem addressed by blame tracking is that when a cast on a higher-order value fails, it often does so at a point in the program that is far removed from the original cast. Blame tracking is a technique for propagating extra information through casts and proxies so that when a cast fails, the error message can point back to the original location of the cast in the source program.

The problem addressed by space-efficient casts also relates to higher-order casts. It turns out that in partially typed programs, a function or tuple can flow through a great many casts at runtime. With the approach described in this chapter, each cast adds another `lambda` wrapper or a tuple proxy. Not only does this take up considerable space, but it also makes the function calls and tuple operations slow. For example, a partially typed version of quicksort could, in the worst case, build a chain of proxies of length $O(n)$ around the tuple, changing the overall time complexity of the algorithm from $O(n^2)$ to $O(n^3)$! Herman, Tomb, and Flanagan (2007) suggested a solution to this problem by representing casts using the coercion calculus of Henglein (1994), which prevents the creation of long chains of proxies by compressing them into a concise normal form. Siek, Thiemann, and Wadler (2015) give an algorithm for compressing coercions, and Kuhlenschmidt, Almahallawi, and Siek (2019) show how to implement these ideas in the Grift compiler:

https://github.com/Gradual-Typing/Grift

There are also interesting interactions between gradual typing and other language features, such as generics, information-flow types, and type inference, to name a few. We recommend to the reader the online gradual typing bibliography for more material:

http://samth.github.io/gradual-typing-bib/

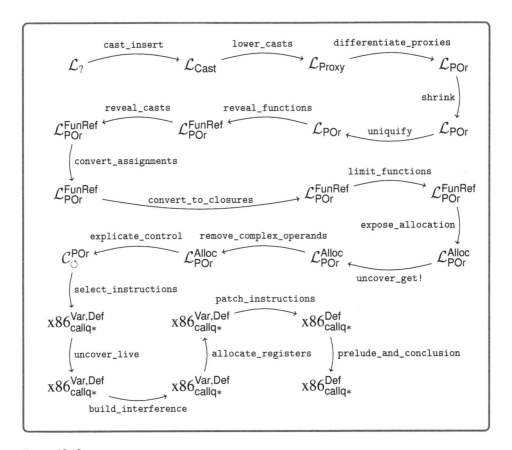

**Figure 10.18**
Diagram of the passes for $\mathcal{L}_?$ (gradual typing).

# 11 Generics

This chapter studies the compilation of generics (aka parametric polymorphism), compiling the $\mathcal{L}_{\mathsf{Gen}}$ subset of Typed Racket. Generics enable programmers to make code more reusable by parameterizing functions and data structures with respect to the types on which they operate. For example, figure 11.1 revisits the map example and this time gives it a more fitting type. This map function is parameterized with respect to the element type of the tuple. The type of map is the following generic type specified by the All type with parameter T:

```
(All (T) ((T -> T) (Vector T T) -> (Vector T T)))
```

The idea is that map can be used at *all* choices of a type for parameter T. In the example shown in figure 11.1 we apply map to a tuple of integers, implicitly choosing Integer for T, but we could have just as well applied map to a tuple of Booleans. A *monomorphic* function is simply one that is not generic. We use the term *instantiation* for the process (within the language implementation) of turning a generic function into a monomorphic one, where the type parameters have been replaced by types.

Figure 11.2 presents the definition of the concrete syntax of $\mathcal{L}_{\mathsf{Gen}}$, and figure 11.3 shows the definition of the abstract syntax. We add a second form for function definitions in which a type declaration comes before the define. In the abstract syntax, the return type in the Def is Any, but that should be ignored in favor of the return type in the type declaration. (The Any comes from using the same parser

```
(: map (All (T) ((T -> T) (Vector T T) -> (Vector T T))))
(define (map f v)
  (vector (f (vector-ref v 0)) (f (vector-ref v 1))))

(define (inc [x : Integer]) : Integer (+ x 1))

(vector-ref (map inc (vector 0 41)) 1)
```

**Figure 11.1**
A generic version of the map function.

$$
\begin{array}{lll}
type & ::= & \text{Integer} \\
exp & ::= & int \mid (\text{read}) \mid (\text{-} \ exp) \mid (\text{+} \ exp \ exp) \mid (\text{-} \ exp \ exp) \\
\hline
exp & ::= & var \mid (\text{let} \ ([var \ exp]) \ exp) \\
\hline
type & ::= & \text{Boolean} \\
bool & ::= & \text{\#t} \mid \text{\#f} \\
cmp & ::= & \text{eq?} \mid \text{<} \mid \text{<=} \mid \text{>} \mid \text{>=} \\
exp & ::= & bool \mid (\text{and} \ exp \ exp) \mid (\text{or} \ exp \ exp) \mid (\text{not} \ exp) \\
 & \mid & (cmp \ exp \ exp) \mid (\text{if} \ exp \ exp \ exp) \\
\hline
type & ::= & \text{Void} \\
exp & ::= & (\text{set!} \ var \ exp) \mid (\text{begin} \ exp^* \ exp) \mid (\text{while} \ exp \ exp) \mid (\text{void}) \\
\hline
type & ::= & (\text{Vector} \ type^*) \\
exp & ::= & (\text{vector} \ exp^*) \mid (\text{vector-length} \ exp) \\
 & \mid & (\text{vector-ref} \ exp \ int) \mid (\text{vector-set!} \ exp \ int \ exp) \\
\hline
type & ::= & (type \ \dots \ \text{->} \ type) \\
exp & ::= & (exp \ exp \ \dots) \\
def & ::= & (\text{define} \ (var \ [var\text{:}type] \ \dots) \ \text{:} \ type \ exp) \\
\hline
exp & ::= & (\text{lambda:} \ ([var\text{:}type] \ \dots) \ \text{:} \ type \ exp) \\
 & \mid & (\text{procedure-arity} \ exp) \\
\hline
type & ::= & (\text{All} \ (var \ \dots) \ type) \mid var \\
def & ::= & (\text{:} \ var \ type) \\
 & & (\text{define} \ (var \ var \ \dots) \ exp) \\
\mathcal{L}_{\text{Gen}} & ::= & def \ \dots \ exp \\
\end{array}
$$

**Figure 11.2**
The concrete syntax of $\mathcal{L}_{\text{Gen}}$, extending $\mathcal{L}_\lambda$ (figure 8.3).

as discussed in chapter 9.) The presence of a type declaration enables the use of an **All** type for a function, thereby making it generic. The grammar for types is extended to include the type of a generic (**All**) and type variables.

By including the **All** type in the *type* nonterminal of the grammar we choose to make generics first class, which has interesting repercussions on the compiler.[1] Many languages with generics, such as C++ (Stroustrup 1988) and Standard ML (Milner, Tofte, and Harper 1990), support only second-class generics, so it may be helpful to see an example of first-class generics in action. In figure 11.4 we define a function **apply_twice** whose parameter is a generic function. Indeed, because the grammar for *type* includes the **All** type, a generic function may also be returned from a function or stored inside a tuple. The body of **apply_twice** applies the generic function **f** to a Boolean and also to an integer, which would not be possible if **f** were not generic.

The type checker for $\mathcal{L}_{\text{Gen}}$ shown in figure 11.5 has several new responsibilities (compared to $\mathcal{L}_\lambda$) which we discuss in the following paragraphs.

The type checking of a function application is extended to handle the case in which the operator expression is a generic function. In that case the type arguments are deduced by matching the types of the parameters with the types of the arguments. The **match_types** auxiliary function (figure 11.6) carries out this deduction by recursively descending through a parameter type **param_ty** and the

---

1. The Python **typing** library does not include syntax for the **All** type. It is inferred for functions whose type annotations contain type variables.

```
type  ::= Integer
op    ::= read | + | -
exp   ::= (Int int) | (Prim op (exp ...))
-----------------------------------------------------------------
exp   ::= (Var var) | (Let var exp exp)
-----------------------------------------------------------------
type  ::= Boolean
bool  ::= #t | #f
cmp   ::= eq? | < | <= | > | >=
op    ::= cmp | and | or | not
exp   ::= (Bool bool) | (If exp exp exp)
-----------------------------------------------------------------
type  ::= Void
exp   ::= (SetBang var exp) | (Begin exp* exp) | (WhileLoop exp exp) | (Void)
-----------------------------------------------------------------
type  ::= (Vector type*)
op    ::= vector | vector-length
exp   ::= (Prim vector-ref (exp (Int int)))
       |  (Prim vector-set! (exp (Int int) exp))
-----------------------------------------------------------------
type  ::= (type ... -> type)
exp   ::= (Apply exp exp ...)
def   ::= (Def var ([var:type] ...) type '() exp)
-----------------------------------------------------------------
exp   ::= (Lambda ([var:type] ...) type exp)
op    ::= procedure-arity
-----------------------------------------------------------------
type  ::= (All (var ...) type) | var
def   ::= (Decl var type)
          (Def var (var ...) 'Any '() exp)
L_Gen ::= (ProgramDefsExp '() (def ...) exp)
```

**Figure 11.3**
The abstract syntax of $\mathcal{L}_{\mathsf{Gen}}$, extending $\mathcal{L}_{\lambda}$ (figure 8.4).

```
(: apply_twice ((All (U) (U -> U)) -> Integer))
(define (apply_twice f)
  (if (f #t) (f 42) (f 777)))

(: id (All (T) (T -> T)))
(define (id x) x)

(apply_twice id)
```

**Figure 11.4**
An example illustrating first-class generics.

corresponding argument type `arg_ty`, making sure that they are equal except when there is a type parameter in the parameter type. Upon encountering a type parameter for the first time, the algorithm deduces an association of the type parameter to the corresponding part of the argument type. If it is not the first time that the type parameter has been encountered, the algorithm looks up its deduced type and makes sure that it is equal to the corresponding part of the argument type. The return type of the application is the return type of the generic function with the type parameters replaced by the deduced type arguments, using the `substitute_type` auxiliary function, which is also listed in figure 11.6.

The type checker extends type equality to handle the `All` type. This is not quite as simple as for other types, such as function and tuple types, because two `All` types can be syntactically different even though they are equivalent. For example,

$$(\text{All (T) (T -> T))}$$

is equivalent to

$$(\text{All (U) (U -> U)}).$$

Two generic types are equal if they differ only in the choice of the names of the type parameters. The definition of type equality shown in figure 11.6 renames the type parameters in one type to match the type parameters of the other type.

The type checker also ensures that only defined type variables appear in type annotations. The `check_well_formed` function for which the definition is shown in figure 11.7 recursively inspects a type, making sure that each type variable has been defined.

```
(define type-check-poly-class
  (class type-check-Llambda-class
    (super-new)
    (inherit check-type-equal?)

    (define/override (type-check-apply env e1 es)
      (define-values (e^ ty) ((type-check-exp env) e1))
      (define-values (es^ ty*) (for/lists (es^ ty*) ([e (in-list es)])
                                 ((type-check-exp env) e)))
      (match ty
        [`(,ty^* ... -> ,rt)
         (for ([arg-ty ty*] [param-ty ty^*])
           (check-type-equal? arg-ty param-ty (Apply e1 es)))
         (values e^ es^ rt)]
        [`(All ,xs (,tys ... -> ,rt))
         (define env^ (append (for/list ([x xs]) (cons x 'Type)) env))
         (define env^^ (for/fold ([env^^ env^]) ([arg-ty ty*] [param-ty tys])
                         (match_types env^^ param-ty arg-ty)))
         (define targs
           (for/list ([x xs])
             (match (dict-ref env^^ x (lambda () #f))
               [#f (error 'type-check "type variable ~a not deduced\nin ~v"
                          x (Apply e1 es))]
               [ty ty])))
         (values (Inst e^ ty targs) es^ (substitute_type env^^ rt))]
        [else (error 'type-check "expected a function, not ~a" ty)]))

    (define/override ((type-check-exp env) e)
      (match e
        [(Lambda `([,xs : ,Ts] ...) rT body)
         (for ([T Ts]) ((check_well_formed env) T))
         ((check_well_formed env) rT)
         ((super type-check-exp env) e)]
        [(HasType e1 ty)
         ((check_well_formed env) ty)
         ((super type-check-exp env) e)]
        [else ((super type-check-exp env) e)]))

    (define/override ((type-check-def env) d)
      (verbose 'type-check "poly/def" d)
      (match d
        [(Generic ts (Def f (and p:t* (list `[,xs : ,ps] ...)) rt info body))
         (define ts-env (for/list ([t ts]) (cons t 'Type)))
         (for ([p ps]) ((check_well_formed ts-env) p))
         ((check_well_formed ts-env) rt)
         (define new-env (append ts-env (map cons xs ps) env))
         (define-values (body^ ty^) ((type-check-exp new-env) body))
         (check-type-equal? ty^ rt body)
         (Generic ts (Def f p:t* rt info body^))]
        [else ((super type-check-def env) d)]))

    (define/override (type-check-program p)
      (match p
        [(Program info body)
         (type-check-program (ProgramDefsExp info '() body))]
        [(ProgramDefsExp info ds body)
         (define ds^ (combine-decls-defs ds))
         (define new-env (for/list ([d ds^])
                           (cons (def-name d) (fun-def-type d))))
         (define ds^^ (for/list ([d ds^]) ((type-check-def new-env) d)))
         (define-values (body^ ty) ((type-check-exp new-env) body))
         (check-type-equal? ty 'Integer body)
         (ProgramDefsExp info ds^^ body^)]))
    ))
```

**Figure 11.5**

Type checker for the $\mathcal{L}_{\mathsf{Gen}}$ language.

```
(define/override (type-equal? t1 t2)
  (match* (t1 t2)
    [(`(All ,xs ,T1) `(All ,ys ,T2))
     (define env (map cons xs ys))
     (type-equal? (substitute_type env T1) T2)]
    [(other wise)
     (super type-equal? t1 t2)]))

(define/public (match_types env pt at)
  (match* (pt at)
    [('Integer 'Integer) env] [('Boolean 'Boolean) env]
    [('Void 'Void) env] [('Any 'Any) env]
    [(`(Vector ,pts ...) `(Vector ,ats ...))
     (for/fold ([env^ env]) ([pt1 pts] [at1 ats])
       (match_types env^ pt1 at1))]
    [(`(,pts ... -> ,prt) `(,ats ... -> ,art))
     (define env^ (match_types env prt art))
     (for/fold ([env^^ env^]) ([pt1 pts] [at1 ats])
       (match_types env^^ pt1 at1))]
    [(`(All ,pxs ,pt1) `(All ,axs ,at1))
     (define env^ (append (map cons pxs axs) env))
     (match_types env^ pt1 at1)]
    [((? symbol? x) at)
     (match (dict-ref env x (lambda () #f))
       [#f (error 'type-check "undefined type variable ~a" x)]
       ['Type (cons (cons x at) env)]
       [t^ (check-type-equal? at t^ 'matching) env])]
    [(other wise) (error 'type-check "mismatch ~a != a" pt at)]))

(define/public (substitute_type env pt)
  (match pt
    ['Integer 'Integer] ['Boolean 'Boolean]
    ['Void 'Void] ['Any 'Any]
    [`(Vector ,ts ...)
     `(Vector ,@(for/list ([t ts]) (substitute_type env t)))]
    [`(,ts ... -> ,rt)
     `(,@(for/list ([t ts]) (substitute_type env t)) -> ,(substitute_type env rt))]
    [`(All ,xs ,t)
     `(All ,xs ,(substitute_type (append (map cons xs xs) env) t))]
    [(? symbol? x) (dict-ref env x)]
    [else (error 'type-check "expected a type not ~a" pt)]))

(define/public (combine-decls-defs ds)
  (match ds
    ['() '()]
    [`(,(Decl name type) . ,(Def f params _ info body) . ,ds^))
     (unless (equal? name f)
       (error 'type-check "name mismatch, ~a != ~a" name f))
     (match type
       [`(All ,xs (,ps ... -> ,rt))
        (define params^ (for/list ([x params] [T ps]) `[,x : ,T]))
        (cons (Generic xs (Def name params^ rt info body))
              (combine-decls-defs ds^))]
       [`(,ps ... -> ,rt)
        (define params^ (for/list ([x params] [T ps]) `[,x : ,T]))
        (cons (Def name params^ rt info body) (combine-decls-defs ds^))]
       [else (error 'type-check "expected a function type, not ~a" type) ])]
    [`(,(Def f params rt info body) . ,ds^)
     (cons (Def f params rt info body) (combine-decls-defs ds^))]))
```

**Figure 11.6**
Auxiliary functions for type checking $\mathcal{L}_{\mathsf{Gen}}$.

```
(define/public ((check_well_formed env) ty)
  (match ty
    ['Integer (void)]
    ['Boolean (void)]
    ['Void (void)]
    [(? symbol? a)
     (match (dict-ref env a (lambda () #f))
       ['Type (void)]
       [else (error 'type-check "undefined type variable ~a" a)])]
    [`(Vector ,ts ...)
     (for ([t ts]) ((check_well_formed env) t))]
    [`(,ts ... -> ,t)
     (for ([t ts]) ((check_well_formed env) t))
     ((check_well_formed env) t)]
    [`(All ,xs ,t)
     (define env^ (append (for/list ([x xs]) (cons x 'Type)) env))
     ((check_well_formed env^) t)]
    [else (error 'type-check "unrecognized type ~a" ty)]))
```

**Figure 11.7**
Well-formed types.

## 11.1 Compiling Generics

Broadly speaking, there are four approaches to compiling generics, as follows:

**Monomorphization** generates a different version of a generic function for each
set of type arguments with which it is used, producing type-specialized code.
This approach results in the most efficient code but requires whole-program
compilation (no separate compilation) and may increase code size. Unfortunately, monomorphization is incompatible with first-class generics because it is
not always possible to determine which generic functions are used with which
type arguments during compilation. (It can be done at runtime with just-in-time
compilation.) Monomorphization is used to compile C++ templates (Stroustrup
1988) and generic functions in NESL (Blelloch et al. 1993) and ML (Weeks 2006).

**Uniform representation** generates one version of each generic function and requires
all values to have a common *boxed* format, such as the tagged values of type Any
in $\mathcal{L}_{\mathsf{Any}}$. Both generic and monomorphic code is compiled similarly to code in
a dynamically typed language (like $\mathcal{L}_{\mathsf{Dyn}}$), in which primitive operators require
their arguments to be projected from Any and their results to be injected into Any.
(In object-oriented languages, the projection is accomplished via virtual method
dispatch.) The uniform representation approach is compatible with separate compilation and with first-class generics. However, it produces the least efficient code
because it introduces overhead in the entire program. This approach is used in
Java (Bracha et al. 1998), CLU (Liskov et al. 1979; Liskov 1993), and some
implementations of ML (Cardelli 1984; Appel and MacQueen 1987).

**Mixed representation** generates one version of each generic function, using a boxed
representation for type variables. However, monomorphic code is compiled as
usual (as in $\mathcal{L}_{\lambda}$), and conversions are performed at the boundaries between
monomorphic code and polymorphic code (for example, when a generic function
is instantiated and called). This approach is compatible with separate compilation and first-class generics and maintains efficiency in monomorphic code.
The trade-off is increased overhead at the boundary between monomorphic and
generic code. This approach is used in implementations of ML (Leroy 1992) and
Java, starting in Java 5 with the addition of autoboxing.

**Type passing** uses the unboxed representation in both monomorphic and generic
code. Each generic function is compiled to a single function with extra parameters
that describe the type arguments. The type information is used by the generated
code to determine how to access the unboxed values at runtime. This approach
is used in implementation of Napier88 (Morrison et al. 1991) and ML (Harper
and Morrisett 1995). Type passing is compatible with separate compilation and
first-class generics and maintains the efficiency for monomorphic code. There is
runtime overhead in polymorphic code from dispatching on type information.

In this chapter we use the mixed representation approach, partly because of its
favorable attributes and partly because it is straightforward to implement using the
tools that we have already built to support gradual typing. The work of compiling

generic functions is performed in two passes, `resolve` and `erase_types`, that we discuss next. The output of `erase_types` is $\mathcal{L}_{Cast}$ (section 10.3), so the rest of the compilation is handled by the compiler of chapter 10.

## 11.2   Resolve Instantiation

Recall that the type checker for $\mathcal{L}_{Gen}$ deduces the type arguments at call sites to a generic function. The purpose of the `resolve` pass is to turn this implicit instantiation into an explicit one, by adding `inst` nodes to the syntax of the intermediate language. An `inst` node records the mapping of type parameters to type arguments. The semantics of the `inst` node is to instantiate the result of its first argument, a generic function, to produce a monomorphic function. However, because the interpreter never analyzes type annotations, instantiation can be a no-op and simply return the generic function. The output language of the `resolve` pass is $\mathcal{L}_{Inst}$, for which the definition is shown in figure 11.8.

The `resolve` pass combines the type declaration and polymorphic function into a single definition, using the `Poly` form, to make polymorphic functions more convenient to process in the next pass of the compiler.

The output of the `resolve` pass on the generic `map` example is listed in figure 11.9. Note that the use of `map` is wrapped in an `inst` node, with the parameter T chosen to be `Integer`.

## 11.3   Erase Generic Types

We use the `Any` type presented in chapter 9 to represent type variables. For example, figure 11.10 shows the output of the `erase_types` pass on the generic `map` (figure 11.1). The occurrences of type parameter `a` are replaced by `Any`, and the generic `All` types are removed from the type of `map`.

This process of type erasure creates a challenge at points of instantiation. For example, consider the instantiation of `map` shown in figure 11.9. The type of `map` is

```
(All (T) ((T -> T) (Vector T T) -> (Vector T T)))
```

and it is instantiated to

```
((Integer -> Integer) (Vector Integer Integer)
  -> (Vector Integer Integer))
```

After erasure, the type of `map` is

```
((Any -> Any) (Vector Any Any) -> (Vector Any Any))
```

but we need to convert it to the instantiated type. This is easy to do in the language $\mathcal{L}_{Cast}$ with a single `cast`. In the example shown in figure 11.10, the instantiation of `map` has been compiled to a `cast` from the type of `map` to the instantiated type. The source and the target type of a cast must be consistent (figure 10.4), which indeed is the case because both the source and target are obtained from the same generic type of `map`, replacing the type parameters with `Any` in the former

```
type    ::=   Integer
  op    ::=   read | + | -
 exp    ::=   (Int int) | (Prim op (exp ... ))
 exp    ::=   (Var var) | (Let var exp exp)
type    ::=   Boolean
bool    ::=   #t | #f
 cmp    ::=   eq? | < | <= | > | >=
  op    ::=   cmp | and | or | not
 exp    ::=   (Bool bool) | (If exp exp exp)
type    ::=   Void
 exp    ::=   (SetBang var exp) | (Begin exp* exp) | (WhileLoop exp exp) | (Void)
type    ::=   (Vector type*)
  op    ::=   vector | vector-length
 exp    ::=   (Prim vector-ref (exp (Int int)))
        |    (Prim vector-set! (exp (Int int) exp))
type    ::=   (type ... -> type)
 exp    ::=   (Apply exp exp ... )
 def    ::=   (Def var ([var:type] ... ) type '() exp)
 exp    ::=   (Lambda ([var:type] ... ) type exp)
  op    ::=   procedure-arity
type    ::=   (All (var ... ) type) | var
 exp    ::=   (Inst exp type (type ... ))
 def    ::=   (Def var ([var:type] ... ) type '() exp)
        |    (Poly (var ... ) (Def var ([var:type] ... ) type '() exp))
L_Inst  ::=   (ProgramDefsExp '() (def ... ) exp)
```

**Figure 11.8**
The abstract syntax of $\mathcal{L}_{\text{Inst}}$, extending $\mathcal{L}_\lambda$ (figure 8.4).

```
(poly (T) (define (map [f : (T -> T)] [v : (Vector T T)]) : (Vector T T)
  (vector (f (vector-ref v 0)) (f (vector-ref v 1)))))

(define (inc [x : Integer]) : Integer (+ x 1))

(vector-ref ((inst map (All (T) ((T -> T) (Vector T T) -> (Vector T T)))
                    (Integer))
          inc (vector 0 41)) 1)
```

**Figure 11.9**
Output of the resolve pass on the map example.

and with the deduced type arguments in the latter. (Recall that the Any type is consistent with any type.)

```
(define (map [f : (Any -> Any)] [v : (Vector Any Any)])
             : (Vector Any Any)
   (vector (f (vector-ref v 0)) (f (vector-ref v 1))))

(define (inc [x : Integer]) : Integer (+ x 1))

(vector-ref ((cast map
                   ((Any -> Any) (Vector Any Any) -> (Vector Any Any))
                   ((Integer -> Integer) (Vector Integer Integer)
                              -> (Vector Integer Integer)))
             inc (vector 0 41)) 1)
```

**Figure 11.10**
The generic map example after type erasure.

To implement the **erase_types** pass, we first recommend defining a recursive function that translates types, named **erase_type**. It replaces type variables with **Any** as follows.

$T$
$\Rightarrow$
**Any**

The **erase_type** function also removes the generic **All** types.

(All $xs$ $T_1$)
$\Rightarrow$
$T_1'$

where $T_1'$ is the result of applying **erase_type** to $T_1$. In this compiler pass, apply the **erase_type** function to all the type annotations in the program.

Regarding the translation of expressions, the case for **Inst** is the interesting one. We translate it into a **Cast**, as shown next. The type of the subexpression $e$ is a generic type of the form (All $xs$ $T$). The source type of the cast is the erasure of $T$, the type $T_s$. The target type $T_t$ is the result of substituting the argument types $ts$ for the type parameters $xs$ in $T$ followed by doing type erasure.

(Inst $e$ (All $xs$ $T$) $ts$)
$\Rightarrow$
(Cast $e'$ $T_s$ $T_t$)

where $T_t =$ (erase_type (substitute_type $s$ $T$)), and $s =$ (map cons $xs$ $ts$).

Finally, each generic function is translated to a regular function in which type erasure has been applied to all the type annotations and the body.

**Exercise 11.1** Implement a compiler for the polymorphic language $\mathcal{L}_{\mathsf{Gen}}$ by extending and adapting your compiler for $\mathcal{L}_?$. Create six new test programs that use polymorphic functions. Some of them should make use of first-class generics.

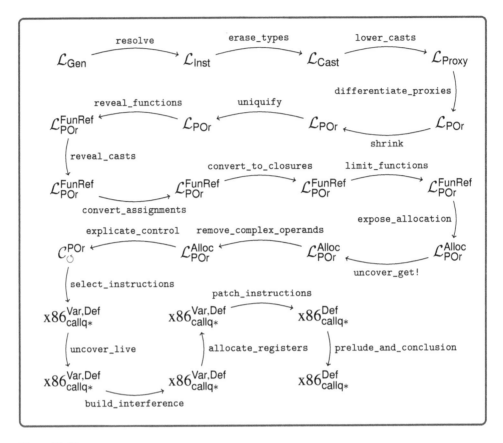

**Figure 11.11**
Diagram of the passes for $\mathcal{L}_{\text{Gen}}$ (generics).

Figure 11.11 provides an overview of the passes needed to compile $\mathcal{L}_{\text{Gen}}$.

# A  Appendix

## A.1  Interpreters

We provide interpreters for each of the source languages $\mathcal{L}_{\mathsf{Int}}$, $\mathcal{L}_{\mathsf{Var}}$, ... in the files `interp-Lint.rkt`, `interp-Lvar.rkt`, and so on. The interpreters for the intermediate languages $\mathcal{C}_{\mathsf{Var}}$ and $\mathcal{C}_{\mathsf{If}}$ are in `interp-Cvar.rkt` and `interp-C1.rkt`. The interpreters for $\mathcal{C}_{\mathsf{Tup}}$, $\mathcal{C}_{\mathsf{Fun}}$, pseudo-x86, and x86 are in the `interp.rkt` file.

## A.2  Utility Functions

The utility functions described in this section are in the `utilities.rkt` file of the support code.

`interp-tests`  This function runs the compiler passes and the interpreters on each of the specified tests to check whether each pass is correct. The `interp-tests` function has the following parameters:

**name (a string)** A name to identify the compiler.

**typechecker** A function of exactly one argument that either raises an error using the `error` function when it encounters a type error, or returns `#f` when it encounters a type error. If there is no type error, the type checker returns the program.

**passes** A list with one entry per pass. An entry is a list consisting of four things:

1. a string giving the name of the pass;
2. the function that implements the pass (a translator from AST to AST);
3. a function that implements the interpreter (a function from AST to result value) for the output language; and,
4. a type checker for the output language. Type checkers for all the $\mathcal{L}$ and $\mathcal{C}$ languages are provided in the support code. For example, the type checkers for $\mathcal{L}_{\mathsf{Var}}$ and $\mathcal{C}_{\mathsf{Var}}$ are in `type-check-Lvar.rkt` and `type-check-Cvar.rkt`. The type checker entry is optional. The support code does not provide type checkers for the x86 languages.

**source-interp** An interpreter for the source language. The interpreters from appendix A.1 make a good choice.

**test-family (a string)** For example, `"var"` or `"cond"`.

**tests** A list of test numbers that specifies which tests to run (explained next).

The `interp-tests` function assumes that the subdirectory `tests` has a collection of Racket programs whose names all start with the family name, followed by an underscore and then the test number, and ending with the file extension `.rkt`. Also, for each test program that calls `read` one or more times, there is a file with the same name except that the file extension is `.in`, which provides the input for the Racket program. If the test program is expected to fail type checking, then there should be an empty file of the same name with extension `.tyerr`.

**compiler-tests** This function runs the compiler passes to generate x86 (a `.s` file) and then runs the GNU C compiler (gcc) to generate machine code. It runs the machine code and checks that the output is 42. The parameters to the `compiler-tests` function are similar to those of the `interp-tests` function, and they consist of

- a compiler name (a string),
- a type checker,
- description of the passes,
- name of a test-family, and
- a list of test numbers.

**compile-file** This function takes a description of the compiler passes (see the comment for `interp-tests`) and returns a function that, given a program file name (a string ending in `.rkt`), applies all the passes and writes the output to a file whose name is the same as the program file name with extension `.rkt` replaced by `.s`.

**read-program** This function takes a file path and parses that file (it must be a Racket program) into an abstract syntax tree.

**parse-program** This function takes an S-expression representation of an abstract syntax tree and converts it into the struct-based representation.

**assert** This function takes two parameters, a string (`msg`) and Boolean (`bool`), and displays the message `msg` if the Boolean `bool` is false.

**lookup** This function takes a key and an alist and returns the first value that is associated with the given key, if there is one. If not, an error is triggered. The alist may contain both immutable pairs (built with `cons`) and mutable pairs (built with `mcons`).

## A.3   x86 Instruction Set Quick Reference

Table A.1 lists some x86 instructions and what they do. We write $A \rightarrow B$ to mean that the value of $A$ is written into location $B$. Address offsets are given in bytes. The instruction arguments $A, B, C$ can be immediate constants (such as $4), registers

| Instruction | Operation |
|---|---|
| addq $A$, $B$ | $A + B \rightarrow B$ |
| negq $A$ | $-A \rightarrow A$ |
| subq $A$, $B$ | $B - A \rightarrow B$ |
| imulq $A$, $B$ | $A \times B \rightarrow B$ |
| callq $L$ | Pushes the return address and jumps to label $L$ |
| callq *$A$ | Calls the function at the address $A$ |
| retq | Pops the return address and jumps to it |
| popq $A$ | $*\mathrm{rsp} \rightarrow A; \mathrm{rsp} + 8 \rightarrow \mathrm{rsp}$ |
| pushq $A$ | $\mathrm{rsp} - 8 \rightarrow \mathrm{rsp}; A \rightarrow *\mathrm{rsp}$ |
| leaq $A,B$ | $A \rightarrow B$ ($B$ must be a register) |
| cmpq $A$, $B$ | Compare $A$ and $B$ and set the flag register ($B$ must not be an immediate) |
| je $L$<br>jl $L$<br>jle $L$<br>jg $L$<br>jge $L$ | Jump to label $L$ if the flag register matches the condition code of the instruction; otherwise go to the next instructions. The condition codes are e for *equal*, l for *less*, le for *less or equal*, g for *greater*, and ge for *greater or equal*. |
| jmp $L$ | Jump to label $L$ |
| movq $A$, $B$ | $A \rightarrow B$ |
| movzbq $A$, $B$ | $A \rightarrow B$, where $A$ is a single-byte register (e.g., al or cl), $B$ is an 8-byte register, and the extra bytes of $B$ are set to zero. |
| notq $A$ | $\sim A \rightarrow A$    (bitwise complement) |
| orq $A$, $B$ | $A|B \rightarrow B$    (bitwise-or) |
| andq $A$, $B$ | $A\&B \rightarrow B$     (bitwise-and) |
| salq $A$, $B$ | $B \ll A \rightarrow B$ (arithmetic shift left, where $A$ is a constant) |
| sarq $A$, $B$ | $B \gg A \rightarrow B$ (arithmetic shift right, where $A$ is a constant) |
| sete $A$<br>setl $A$<br>setle $A$<br>setg $A$<br>setge $A$ | If the flag matches the condition code, then $1 \rightarrow A$; else $0 \rightarrow A$. Refer to je for the description of the condition codes. $A$ must be a single byte register (e.g., al or cl). |

**Table A.1**
Quick reference for the x86 instructions used in this book.

(such as %rax), or memory references (such as -4(%ebp)). Most x86 instructions allow at most one memory reference per instruction. Other operands must be immediates or registers.

# References

Abelson, Harold, and Gerald J. Sussman. 1996. *Structure and Interpretation of Computer Programs.* 2nd edition. MIT Press.

Aho, Alfred V., Monica S. Lam, Ravi Sethi, and Jeffrey D. Ullman. 2006. *Compilers: Principles, Techniques, and Tools.* 2nd edition. Addison-Wesley Longman.

Allen, Frances E. 1970. "Control Flow Analysis." In *Proceedings of a Symposium on Compiler Optimization,* 1–19. Association for Computing Machinery.

Anderson, Christopher, and Sophia Drossopoulou. 2003. "BabyJ: From Object Based to Class Based Programming via Types." *Electron. Notes Theor. Comput. Sci.* 82 (8): 53–81.

Appel, Andrew W. 1989. "Runtime Tags Aren't Necessary." *LISP and Symbolic Computation* 2 (2): 153–162.

Appel, Andrew W. 1990. "A Runtime System." *LISP and Symbolic Computation* 3 (4): 343–380.

Appel, Andrew W. 1991. *Compiling with Continuations.* Cambridge University Press.

Appel, Andrew W., and David B. MacQueen. 1987. "A Standard ML Compiler." In *Functional Programming Languages and Computer Architecture,* 301–324. Springer.

Appel, Andrew W., and Jens Palsberg. 2003. *Modern Compiler Implementation in Java.* Cambridge University Press.

Backus, J. W., F. L. Bauer, J. Green, C. Katz, J. McCarthy, A. J. Perlis, H. Rutishauser, et al. 1960. "Report on the Algorithmic Language ALGOL 60." Edited by Peter Naur. *Commun. ACM* 3 (5): 299–314.

Backus, John. 1978. "The History of Fortran I, II, and III." In *History of Programming Languages,* 25–74. Association for Computing Machinery.

Baker, J., A. Cunei, T. Kalibera, F. Pizlo, and J. Vitek. 2009. "Accurate Garbage Collection in Uncooperative Environments Revisited." *Concurr. Comput.: Pract. Exper.* 21 (12): 1572–1606.

Balakrishnan, V. K. 1996. *Introductory Discrete Mathematics.* Dover.

Blackburn, Stephen M., Perry Cheng, and Kathryn S. McKinley. 2004. "Myths and Realities: The Performance Impact of Garbage Collection." In *Proceedings of the Joint International Conference on Measurement and Modeling of Computer Systems, SIGMETRICS '04/Performance '04,* 25–36. Association for Computing Machinery.

Blelloch, Guy E., Jonathan C. Hardwick, Siddhartha Chatterjee, Jay Sipelstein, and Marco Zagha. 1993. "Implementation of a Portable Nested Data-Parallel Language." In *Proceedings of the Fourth ACM SIGPLAN Symposium on Principles and Practice of Parallel Programming, PPOPP '93,* 102–111. Association for Computing Machinery.

Bracha, Gilad, Martin Odersky, David Stoutamire, and Philip Wadler. 1998. "Making the Future Safe for the Past: Adding Genericity to the Java Programming Language." In *Proceedings of the 13th ACM SIGPLAN Conference on Object-Oriented Programming, Systems, Languages, and Applications, OOPSLA '98,* 183–200. Association for Computing Machinery.

Brélaz, Daniel. 1979. "New Methods to Color the Vertices of a Graph." *Commun. ACM* 22 (4): 251–256.

Briggs, Preston, Keith D. Cooper, and Linda Torczon. 1994. "Improvements to Graph Coloring Register Allocation." *ACM Trans. Program. Lang. Syst.* 16 (3): 428–455.

Bryant, Randal, and David O'Hallaron. 2005. *x86-64 Machine-Level Programming.* Carnegie Mellon University.

Bryant, Randal, and David O'Hallaron. 2010. *Computer Systems: A Programmer's Perspective.* 2nd edition. Addison-Wesley.

Cardelli, Luca. 1983. *The Functional Abstract Machine.* Technical report TR-107. AT&T Bell Laboratories.

Cardelli, Luca. 1984. "Compiling a Functional Language." In *ACM Symposium on LISP and Functional Programming, LFP '84,* 208–221. Association for Computing Machinery.

Cardelli, Luca, and Peter Wegner. 1985. "On Understanding Types, Data Abstraction, and Polymorphism." *ACM Comput. Surv.* 17 (4): 471–523.

Chaitin, G. J. 1982. "Register Allocation & Spilling via Graph Coloring." In *SIGPLAN '82: Proceedings of the 1982 SIGPLAN Symposium on Compiler Construction,* 98–105. Association for Computing Machinery.

Chaitin, Gregory J., Marc A. Auslander, Ashok K. Chandra, John Cocke, Martin E. Hopkins, and Peter W. Markstein. 1981. "Register Allocation via Coloring." *Computer Languages* 6:47–57.

Cheney, C. J. 1970. "A Nonrecursive List Compacting Algorithm." *Commun. of the ACM* 13 (11).

Chow, Frederick, and John Hennessy. 1984. "Register Allocation by Priority-Based Coloring." In *Proceedings of the 1984 SIGPLAN Symposium on Compiler Construction,* 222–232. Association for Computing Machinery.

Church, Alonzo. 1932. "A Set of Postulates for the Foundation of Logic." *Annals of Mathematics,* Second Series, 33 (2): 346–366.

Clarke, Keith. 1989. "One-Pass Code Generation Using Continuations." *Softw. Pract. Exper.* 19 (12): 1175–1192.

Collins, George E. 1960. "A Method for Overlapping and Erasure of Lists." *Commun. ACM* 3 (12): 655–657.

Cooper, Keith, and Linda Torczon. 2011. *Engineering a Compiler.* 2nd edition. Morgan Kaufmann.

Cooper, Keith D., and L. Taylor Simpson. 1998. "Live Range Splitting in a Graph Coloring Register Allocator." In *Compiler Construction: Proceedings of the 7th International Conference, CC '98, Held as Part of the Joint European Conferences on Theory and Practice of Software, ETAPS '98.* Lecture Notes in Computer Science 1383. Springer.

Cormen, Thomas H., Clifford Stein, Ronald L. Rivest, and Charles E. Leiserson. 2001. *Introduction to Algorithms.* McGraw-Hill Higher Education.

Cutler, Cody, and Robert Morris. 2015. "Reducing Pause Times with Clustered Collection." In *Proceedings of the 2015 International Symposium on Memory Management, ISMM '15,* 131–142. Association for Computing Machinery.

Danvy, Olivier. 1991. *Three Steps for the CPS Transformation.* Technical report CIS-92-02. Kansas State University.

Danvy, Olivier. 2003. "A New One-Pass Transformation into Monadic Normal Form." In *Compiler Construction: Proceedings of the 12th International Conference, CC '03, Held as Part of the Joint European Conferences on Theory and Practice of Software, ETAPS '03.* Lecture Notes in Computer Science 2622, 77–89. Springer.

Detlefs, David, Christine Flood, Steve Heller, and Tony Printezis. 2004. "Garbage-First Garbage Collection." In *Proceedings of the 4th International Symposium on Memory Management, ISMM '04,* 37–48. Association for Computing Machinery.

Dijkstra, E. W. 1982. *Why Numbering Should Start at Zero.* Technical report EWD831. University of Texas at Austin.

Diwan, Amer, Eliot Moss, and Richard Hudson. 1992. "Compiler Support for Garbage Collection in a Statically Typed Language." In *Proceedings of the ACM SIGPLAN 1992 Conference on Programming Language Design and Implementation, PLDI '92,* 273–282. Association for Computing Machinery.

Dybvig, R. Kent. 1987a. *The Scheme Programming Language.* Prentice Hall.

Dybvig, R. Kent. 1987b. "Three Implementation Models for Scheme." PhD diss., University of North Carolina at Chapel Hill.

Dybvig, R. Kent. 2006. "The Development of Chez Scheme." In *Proceedings of the Eleventh ACM SIGPLAN International Conference on Functional Programming, ICFP '06*, 1–12. Association for Computing Machinery.

Dybvig, R. Kent, and Andrew Keep. 2010. *P523 Compiler Assignments*. Technical report. Indiana University.

Felleisen, Matthias, M.D. Barski Conrad, David Van Horn, and Eight Students of Northeastern University. 2013. *Realm of Racket: Learn to Program, One Game at a Time!* No Starch Press.

Felleisen, Matthias, Robert Bruce Findler, Matthew Flatt, and Shriram Krishnamurthi. 2001. *How to Design Programs: An Introduction to Programming and Computing*. MIT Press.

Fischer, Michael J. 1972. "Lambda Calculus Schemata." In *Proceedings of ACM Conference on Proving Assertions about Programs*, 104–109. Association for Computing Machinery.

Flanagan, Cormac. 2006. "Hybrid Type Checking." In *Proceedings of the 33rd ACM SIGPLAN-SIGACT Symposium on Principles of Programming Languages, POPL '06*, 245–256. Association for Computing Machinery.

Flanagan, Cormac, Amr Sabry, Bruce F. Duba, and Matthias Felleisen. 1993. "The Essence of Compiling with Continuations." In *Proceedings of the ACM SIGPLAN 1993 Conference on Programming Language Design and Implementation, PLDI '93*, 502–514. Association for Computing Machinery.

Flatt, Matthew, Caner Derici, R. Kent Dybvig, Andrew W. Keep, Gustavo E. Massaccesi, Sarah Spall, Sam Tobin-Hochstadt, and Jon Zeppieri. 2019. "Rebuilding Racket on Chez Scheme (Experience Report)." *Proc. ACM Program. Lang., ICFP (August)* 3:1–15.

Flatt, Matthew, Robert Bruce Findler, and PLT. 2014. *The Racket Guide*. Technical report 6.0. PLT.

Flatt, Matthew, and PLT. 2014. *The Racket Reference 6.0*. Technical report. PLT. https://docs .racket-lang.org/reference/index.html.

Friedman, Daniel P., and Matthias Felleisen. 1996. *The Little Schemer*. 4th edition. MIT Press.

Friedman, Daniel P., Mitchell Wand, and Christopher T. Haynes. 2001. *Essentials of Programming Languages*. 2nd edition. MIT Press.

Friedman, Daniel P., and David S. Wise. 1976. *Cons Should Not Evaluate Its Arguments*. Technical report TR44. Indiana University.

Gamari, Ben, and Laura Dietz. 2020. "Alligator Collector: A Latency-Optimized Garbage Collector for Functional Programming Languages." In *Proceedings of the 2020 ACM SIGPLAN International Symposium on Memory Management, ISMM '20*, 87–99. Association for Computing Machinery.

George, Lal, and Andrew W. Appel. 1996. "Iterated Register Coalescing." *ACM Trans. Program. Lang. Syst.* 18 (3): 300–324.

Ghuloum, Abdulaziz. 2006. "An Incremental Approach to Compiler Construction." In *Scheme '06: Proceedings of the Workshop on Scheme and Functional Programming*. http://www.schemework shop.org/2006/.

Gilray, Thomas, Steven Lyde, Michael D. Adams, Matthew Might, and David Van Horn. 2016. "Pushdown Control-Flow Analysis for Free." In *Proceedings of the 43rd Annual ACM SIGPLAN-SIGACT Symposium on Principles of Programming Languages, POPL '16*, 691–704. Association for Computing Machinery.

Goldberg, Benjamin. 1991. "Tag-free Garbage Collection for Strongly Typed Programming Languages." In *Proceedings of the ACM SIGPLAN 1991 Conference on Programming Language Design and Implementation, PLDI '91*, 165–176. Association for Computing Machinery.

Gordon, M., R. Milner, L. Morris, M. Newey, and C. Wadsworth. 1978. "A Metalanguage for Interactive Proof in LCF." In *Proceedings of the 5th ACM SIGACT-SIGPLAN Symposium on Principles of Programming Languages, POPL '78*, 119–130. Association for Computing Machinery.

Gronski, Jessica, Kenneth Knowles, Aaron Tomb, Stephen N. Freund, and Cormac Flanagan. 2006. "Sage: Hybrid Checking for Flexible Specifications." In *Scheme '06: Proceedings of the Workshop on Scheme and Functional Programming*, 93–104. http://www.schemeworkshop.org/2006/.

Harper, Robert. 2016. *Practical Foundations for Programming Languages.* 2nd edition. Cambridge University Press.

Harper, Robert, and Greg Morrisett. 1995. "Compiling Polymorphism Using Intensional Type Analysis." In *Proceedings of the 22nd ACM SIGPLAN-SIGACT Symposium on Principles of Programming Languages, POPL '95,* 130–141. Association for Computing Machinery.

Hatcliff, John, and Olivier Danvy. 1994. "A Generic Account of Continuation-Passing Styles." In *Proceedings of the 21st ACM SIGPLAN-SIGACT Symposium on Principles of Programming Languages, POPL '94,* 458–471. Association for Computing Machinery.

Henderson, Fergus. 2002. "Accurate Garbage Collection in an Uncooperative Environment." In *Proceedings of the 3rd International Symposium on Memory Management, ISMM '02,* 150–156. Association for Computing Machinery.

Henglein, Fritz. 1994. "Dynamic Typing: Syntax and Proof Theory." *Science of Computer Programming* 22 (3): 197–230.

Herman, David, Aaron Tomb, and Cormac Flanagan. 2007. "Space-Efficient Gradual Typing." In *Trends in Functional Programming, TFP '07.*

Herman, David, Aaron Tomb, and Cormac Flanagan. 2010. "Space-Efficient Gradual Typing." *Higher-Order and Symbolic Computation* 23 (2): 167–189.

Horwitz, L. P., R. M. Karp, R. E. Miller, and S. Winograd. 1966. "Index Register Allocation." *J. ACM* 13 (1): 43–61.

Intel. 2015. *Intel 64 and IA-32 Architectures Software Developer's Manual Combined Volumes: 1, 2A, 2B, 2C, 3A, 3B, 3C and 3D.*

Jacek, Nicholas, and J. Eliot B. Moss. 2019. "Learning When to Garbage Collect with Random Forests." In *Proceedings of the 2019 ACM SIGPLAN International Symposium on Memory Management, ISMM '19,* 53–63. Association for Computing Machinery.

Jones, Neil D., Carsten K. Gomard, and Peter Sestoft. 1993. *Partial Evaluation and Automatic Program Generation.* Prentice Hall.

Jones, Richard, Antony Hosking, and Eliot Moss. 2011. *The Garbage Collection Handbook: The Art of Automatic Memory Management.* Chapman & Hall/CRC.

Jones, Richard, and Rafael Lins. 1996. *Garbage Collection: Algorithms for Automatic Dynamic Memory Management.* John Wiley & Sons.

Keep, Andrew W. 2012. "A Nanopass Framework for Commercial Compiler Development." PhD diss., Indiana University.

Keep, Andrew W., Alex Hearn, and R. Kent Dybvig. 2012. "Optimizing Closures in O(0)-time." In *Scheme '12: Proceedings of the Workshop on Scheme and Functional Programming.* Association for Computing Machinery.

Kelsey, R., W. Clinger, and J. Rees, eds. 1998. "Revised[5] Report on the Algorithmic Language Scheme." *Higher-Order and Symbolic Computation* 11 (1).

Kempe, A. B. 1879. "On the Geographical Problem of the Four Colours." *American Journal of Mathematics* 2 (3): 193–200.

Kernighan, Brian W., and Dennis M. Ritchie. 1988. *The C Programming Language.* Prentice Hall.

Kildall, Gary A. 1973. "A Unified Approach to Global Program Optimization." In *Proceedings of the 1st Annual ACM SIGACT-SIGPLAN Symposium on Principles of Programming Languages, POPL '73,* 194–206. Association for Computing Machinery.

Kleene, S. 1952. *Introduction to Metamathematics.* Van Nostrand.

Knuth, Donald E. 1964. "Backus Normal Form vs. Backus Naur Form." *Commun. ACM* 7 (12): 735–736.

Kuhlenschmidt, Andre, Deyaaeldeen Almahallawi, and Jeremy G. Siek. 2019. "Toward Efficient Gradual Typing for Structural Types via Coercions." In *Proceedings of the ACM SIGPLAN 2019 Conference on Programming Language Design and Implementation, PLDI '19.* Association for Computing Machinery.

Lawall, Julia L., and Olivier Danvy. 1993. "Separating Stages in the Continuation-Passing Style Transformation." In *Proceedings of the 20th ACM SIGPLAN-SIGACT Symposium on Principles of Programming Languages, POPL '93,* 124–136. Association for Computing Machinery.

Leroy, Xavier. 1992. "Unboxed Objects and Polymorphic Typing." In *Proceedings of the 19th ACM SIGPLAN-SIGACT Symposium on Principles of Programming Languages, POPL '92,* 177–188. Association for Computing Machinery.

Lieberman, Henry, and Carl Hewitt. 1983. "A Real-Time Garbage Collector Based on the Lifetimes of Objects." *Commun. ACM* 26 (6): 419–429.

Liskov, Barbara. 1993. "A History of CLU." In *The Second ACM SIGPLAN Conference on History of Programming Languages, HOPL-II,* 133–147. Association for Computing Machinery.

Liskov, Barbara, Russ Atkinson, Toby Bloom, Eliot Moss, Craig Schaffert, Bob Scheifler, and Alan Snyder. 1979. *CLU Reference Manual.* Technical report LCS-TR-225. MIT.

Logothetis, George, and Prateek Mishra. 1981. "Compiling Short-Circuit Boolean Expressions in One Pass." *Software: Practice and Experience* 11 (11): 1197–1214.

Matthews, Jacob, and Robert Bruce Findler. 2007. "Operational Semantics for Multi-Language Programs." In *Proceedings of the 34th ACM SIGPLAN-SIGACT Symposium on Principles of Programming Languages, POPL '07.* Association for Computing Machinery.

Matula, David W., George Marble, and Joel D. Isaacson. 1972. "Graph Coloring Algorithms." In *Graph Theory and Computing,* 109–122. Academic Press.

Matz, Michael, Jan Hubicka, Andreas Jaeger, and Mark Mitchell. 2013. *System V Application Binary Interface, AMD64 Architecture Processor Supplement.* Linux Foundation.

McCarthy, John. 1960. "Recursive Functions of Symbolic Expressions and their Computation by Machine, Part I." *Commun. ACM* 3 (4): 184–195.

Microsoft. 2018. *x64 Architecture.* https://docs.microsoft.com/en-us/windows-hardware/drivers/debugger/x64-architecture.

Microsoft. 2020. *x64 Calling Convention.* https://docs.microsoft.com/en-us/cpp/build/x64-calling-convention.

Milner, Robin, Mads Tofte, and Robert Harper. 1990. *The Definition of Standard ML.* MIT Press.

Minamide, Yasuhiko, Greg Morrisett, and Robert Harper. 1996. "Typed Closure Conversion." In *Proceedings of the 23rd ACM SIGPLAN-SIGACT Symposium on Principles of Programming Languages, POPL '96,* 271–283. Association for Computing Machinery.

Moggi, Eugenio. 1991. "Notions of Computation and Monads." *Inf. Comput.* 93 (1): 55–92.

Moore, E.F. 1959. "The Shortest Path Through a Maze." In *Proceedings of an International Symposium on the Theory of Switching.* Harvard University Press.

Morrison, R., A. Dearle, R. C. H. Connor, and A. L. Brown. 1991. "An Ad Hoc Approach to the Implementation of Polymorphism." *ACM Trans. Program. Lang. Syst.* 13 (3): 342–371.

Österlund, Erik, and Welf Löwe. 2016. "Block-Free Concurrent GC: Stack Scanning and Copying." In *Proceedings of the 2016 ACM SIGPLAN International Symposium on Memory Management, ISMM '16,* 1–12. Association for Computing Machinery.

Palsberg, Jens. 2007. "Register Allocation via Coloring of Chordal Graphs." In *Proceedings of the Thirteenth Australasian Symposium on Theory of Computing,* 3–3. Australian Computer Society.

Peyton Jones, Simon L., and André L. M. Santos. 1998. "A Transformation-Based Optimiser for Haskell." *Science of Computer Programming* 32 (1): 3–47.

Pierce, Benjamin C. 2002. *Types and Programming Languages.* MIT Press.

Pierce, Benjamin C., ed. 2004. *Advanced Topics in Types and Programming Languages.* MIT Press.

Pierce, Benjamin C., Arthur Azevedo de Amorim, Chris Casinghino, Marco Gaboardi, Michael Greenberg, Cătălin Hrițcu, Vilhelm Sjöberg, Andrew Tolmach, and Brent Yorgey. 2018. *Programming Language Foundations.* Vol. 2. Software Foundations. Electronic textbook. https://softwarefoundations.cis.upenn.edu/plf-current/index.html.

Plotkin, G. D. 1975. "Call-by-Name, Call-by-Value and the Lambda-Calculus." *Theoretical Computer Science* 1 (2): 125–159.

Poletto, Massimiliano, and Vivek Sarkar. 1999. "Linear Scan Register Allocation." *ACM Trans. Program. Lang. Syst.* 21 (5): 895–913.

Reynolds, John C. 1972. "Definitional Interpreters for Higher-Order Programming Languages." In *ACM '72: Proceedings of the ACM Annual Conference*, 717–740. Association for Computing Machinery.

Rosen, Kenneth H. 2002. *Discrete Mathematics and Its Applications*. McGraw-Hill Higher Education.

Russell, Stuart J., and Peter Norvig. 2003. *Artificial Intelligence: A Modern Approach*. 2nd ed. Pearson Education.

Sarkar, Dipanwita, Oscar Waddell, and R. Kent Dybvig. 2004. "A Nanopass Infrastructure for Compiler Education." In *Proceedings of the Ninth ACM SIGPLAN International Conference on Functional Programming, ICFP '04*, 201–212. Association for Computing Machinery.

Shahriyar, Rifat, Stephen M. Blackburn, Xi Yang, and Kathryn M. McKinley. 2013. "Taking Off the Gloves with Reference Counting Immix." In *Proceedings of the 24th ACM SIGPLAN Conference on Object Oriented Programming Systems Languages and Applications, OOPSLA '13*. Association for Computing Machinery.

Shidal, Jonathan, Ari J. Spilo, Paul T. Scheid, Ron K. Cytron, and Krishna M. Kavi. 2015. "Recycling Trash in Cache." In *Proceedings of the 2015 International Symposium on Memory Management, ISMM '15*, 118–130. Association for Computing Machinery.

Shivers, O. 1988. "Control Flow Analysis in Scheme." In *Proceedings of the ACM SIGPLAN 1988 Conference on Programming Language Design and Implementation, PLDI '88*, 164–174. Association for Computing Machinery.

Siebert, Fridtjof. 2001. "Constant-Time Root Scanning for Deterministic Garbage Collection." In *Proceedings of Compiler Construction: 10th International Conference, CC 2001, Held as Part of the Joint European Conferences on Theory and Practice of Software, ETAPS '01*, edited by Reinhard Wilhelm, 304–318. Springer.

Siek, Jeremy G., and Walid Taha. 2006. "Gradual Typing for Functional Languages." In *Scheme '06: Proceedings of the Workshop on Scheme and Functional Programming*, 81–92. http://www.schemeworkshop.org/2006/.

Siek, Jeremy G., Peter Thiemann, and Philip Wadler. 2015. "Blame and Coercion: Together Again for the First Time." In *Proceedings of the ACM SIGPLAN 2015 Conference on Programming Language Design and Implementation, PLDI '15*. Association for Computing Machinery.

Sperber, Michael, R. Kent Dybvig, Matthew Flatt, Anton van Straaten, Robby Findler, and Jacob Matthews. 2009. "Revised[6] Report on the Algorithmic Language Scheme." *Journal of Functional Programming* 19:1–301.

Steele, Guy L. 1977. *Data Representations in PDP-10 MacLISP*. AI Memo 420. MIT Artificial Intelligence Lab.

Steele, Guy L. 1978. *Rabbit: A Compiler for Scheme*. Technical report. MIT.

Stroustrup, Bjarne. 1988. "Parameterized Types for C++." In *Proceedings of the USENIX C++ Conference*. USENIX.

Tene, Gil, Balaji Iyengar, and Michael Wolf. 2011. "C4: The Continuously Concurrent Compacting Collector." In *Proceedings of the International Symposium on Memory Management, ISMM '11*, 79–88. Association for Computing Machinery.

Tobin-Hochstadt, Sam, and Matthias Felleisen. 2006. "Interlanguage Migration: From Scripts to Programs." In *Companion to the 21st ACM SIGPLAN Conference on Object Oriented Programming Systems Languages and Applications (Dynamic Languages Symposium), DLS '06*. Association for Computing Machinery.

Ungar, David. 1984. "Generation Scavenging: A Non-Disruptive High Performance Storage Reclamation Algorithm." In *Proceedings of the First ACM SIGSOFT/SIGPLAN Software Engineering Symposium on Practical Software Development Environments, SDE 1*, 157–167. Association for Computing Machinery.

van Wijngaarden, Adriaan. 1966. "Recursive Definition of Syntax and Semantics." In *Formal Language Description Languages for Computer Programming*, edited by T. B. Steel Jr., 13–24. North-Holland.

Wadler, Philip, and Robert Bruce Findler. 2009. "Well-Typed Programs Can't Be Blamed." In *Proceedings of Programming Languages and Systems, 31st European Symposium on Programming, ESOP '09, Held as Part of the Joint European Conferences on Theory and Practice of Software, ETAPS '09*, edited by Giuseppe Castagna, 1–16. Springer.

Weeks, Stephen. 2006. "Whole-Program Compilation in MLton." In *Proceedings of the 2006 Workshop on ML '06*, 1. Association for Computing Machinery.

Wilson, Paul. 1992. "Uniprocessor Garbage Collection Techniques. Lecture Notes in Computer Science 637." In *Memory Management*, edited by Yves Bekkers and Jacques Cohen, 1–42. Springer.

# Index